SUCCULENTS

THE ILLUSTRATED DICTIONARY

SUCCULENTS

THE ILLUSTRATED DICTIONARY

Maurizio Sajeva

and

Mariangela Costanzo

Timber Press
Portland, Oregon

First published in the UK 1994
by Cassell, London

First published in North America in 1994
by Timber Press, Inc.
The Haseltine Building
133 S.W. Second Ave., Suite 450
Portland, Oregon 97204-3527, U.S.A.

ISBN 0-88192-289-7

Typeset by Associated Print Production Ltd
Printed and bound in Singapore by Kyodo Printing Co Ltd

CONTENTS

ACKNOWLEDGEMENTS

We would like to thank Luca Magagnoli for his encouragement and for his help in locating interesting plants; Andrea Cattabriga for many useful suggestions; Annarosa Nicola and Pasquale Ruocco for supplying transparencies; Sara Oldfield for permission to reprint extracts from the IOS Code of Conduct; Rosemary Anderson of Cassell and Lydia Darbyshire for their assistance in preparing the manuscript; and all the nurserymen, private collectors and keepers of public collections who gave permission for plants in their collections to be photographed. We would also like to thank Dr Ger van Vliet, Plant Officer, CITES Secretariat, for the chapter on CITES, which unfortunately had to be shortened for reasons of space.

The plants illustrated are shown in habitat and in the authors' collections. They have also been photographed in the public collections of the Botanical Garden of the University of Bologna, the Botanical Garden of the University of Palermo, the Garden of the National Herbarium of Namibia, Windhoek, and the Succulent Collection of the City of Zurich; the private collections of Andrea Cattabriga, Viviana Didoni, Annarosa Nicola and Pasquale Ruocco; and the nurseries of Luciano Crevenna, Bergamo, Cactus Centre, Florence, Lalla Pelliconi, Ravenna, and Anna Peyron, Turin.

All the photographs were taken by Pierfranco and Daniele Costanzo unless otherwise stated on page 240, and without their help the publication of this dictionary would not have been possible. Thanks also to Pierfranco Costanzo for drawing the line illustrations.

Special thanks are due to Marina Di Stefano Sajeva for her patience and support during the preparation of this book.

FOREWORD

The decision to write this dictionary was prompted by *Cacti: The Illustrated Dictionary* by Rod and Ken Preston-Mafham, which so successfully met a need among cactus enthusiasts. Succulents other than cacti are described and illustrated in several monographic studies dealing with a single genus or a specific geographical region, but there is no single book with a large number of colour illustrations covering a wide range of genera. It is hoped that this dictionary will go some way towards filling this gap, helping collectors to identify their plants and encouraging newcomers to select interesting species to study and grow.

We would like to emphasize that we do not pretend to have found a solution to the chaos afflicting the classification of succulent plants – rather, we are completely involved in that chaos. The classification of both succulents and cacti is affected by several factors that lead to frequent changes and to the creation of very small genera and new species. The main problem is probably the horticultural value of new species. Nurserymen often offer unidentified specimens as *sp. nova* to stimulate the potential collector's interest. If a plant is described and published as a new species in accordance with the rules of the International Code of Botanical Nomenclature but without the plant's variability in habitat having been verified, a new species could be established, which, although valid in formal terms, has no biological meaning.

It is essential that a group of experts attempt to define a system that will bring some stability to the naming of succulent plants and will cut the plethora of generic and specific names that afflicts this group of plants. The International Organization for Succulent Plants Study (IOS) is aiming to complete a project that will find a consensus among cactus experts on the naming of the Cactaceae. It is to be hoped that the IOS will be able to carry out a similar project for succulents.

In this dictionary we have used the names currently found in private and public collections. Including available revisions would have resulted in a partial work with no coherent criteria that would confuse the average collector. Some revisions are noted in the descriptions of the succulent species and for those readers who are interested in pursuing the subject further there are books listed in Further Reading.

INTRODUCTION

Succulents are defined as plants that are able to withstand drought because of the water stored in some of their organs. They constitute a widespread group, being represented in several families of flowering plants and, to some extent, in the Gymnosperms as well. The definition is somewhat problematic because several plants, although not true succulents, are included among their number for aesthetic reasons. The most precise scientific definition is given in *Life Strategies of Succulents in Deserts* by D.J. von Willert, B.M. Eller, M.J.A. Werger, E. Brinckmann and H.D. Ihlenfeldt:

> A succulent (or succophyte) is a plant possessing at least one succulent tissue. A succulent tissue is a living tissue that, besides possible other tasks, serves and guarantees an at least temporary storage of utilizable water, which makes the plant temporarily independent of an external water supply when soil water conditions have so deteriorated that the root is no longer able to provide the necessary water from soil.

This definition implies that succulence may be present in one or more plant organs. The specialization of an organ is determined by the particular selective pressure in the species' habitat.

Leaf succulence occurs in several families, and it is usually associated with environments that do not have a long dry season. When the dry season is very long the succulent leaves are highly specialized. *Lithops* is, perhaps, the best example: the stem is absent and the leaves grow hidden in the soil, thus reducing water loss.

Stem succulence, which is seen in the cactus family, is also familiar to succulent enthusiasts. Succulent stems have leaves that are reduced in size or are caducous when well developed, and photosynthesis is performed by the green stems. Stem succulents may inhabit more arid environments, but the critical point is their size: gigantic species need regular water to support growth, and in very dry environments stems are reduced in size.

In root succulence the organ of reserve is subterranean, which is thus protected from the stresses of wind and predation. Root succulence is often associated with annual stems, which desiccate during the dry season.

In addition to these visible characteristics, succulents have several less evident features that give them strong selective advantages in arid habitats. The number and size of the stomata (the holes that allow air to enter leaves and leaves to capture carbon dioxide) are usually reduced. Not only does this reduce water loss but it also reduces the amount of carbon dioxide taken in. Moreover, the opening of stomata during the day, in the presence of strong sunlight and dry air, would lead to the evaporation of water without a compensatory intake of water in the form of rain. A particular type of photosynthesis, Crassulacean Acid Metabolism (CAM), has evolved in several families. In CAM the stomata of plants open at night, when the temperature is lower and the humidity of the air is higher. These plants store carbon dioxide, using organic acids – namely malic acid – during the night when the stomata are open. Carbon dioxide is released during the day when the stomata are closed but light is available for photosynthesis to transform the carbon dioxide into sugars. CAM is not only efficient in the economic use of water but is also highly effective in capturing carbon dioxide from the air. CAM photosynthesis evolved independently in several families, and it is also present in some aquatic plants, when the selective advantage arises from the efficiency of capturing carbon dioxide that is not abundant in water.

In arid habitats succulent plants may be the only source of food for wild animals. Several features have been evolved to cope with this predation, the most common being the presence of spines, which make the plants less appetizing, and mimicry, which makes them difficult to see against the soil. Another defence against predators is the presence of toxic or repellent chemicals – once the predator has tasted the plant it will not try to eat a similar specimen.

The different adaptive characteristics are present in various groups of plants. Often species that are distant in geographic or phylogenic terms may look similar. The most striking example of this is probably the columnar or globular euphorbia and cacti. The volume to surface ratio is critical from the point of view of storing water, and it is possible to identify a trend in stem shape, from the cylindrical to the almost spherical, that is the ideal for the volume to surface ratio. These plants may have very similar shapes even though they are native to different continents and have different ancestors. The resemblance is caused by the same selective pressure that causes convergent evolution.

CONSERVATION

The problems of nature conservation are widely appreciated. Those who are considering growing, collecting and studying succulent plants must be aware of the impact that they can have on the wild populations of the plants they wish to study. Most succulents grow in habitats that have a fragile ecological equilibrium, and the environmental conditions often lead to slow rates of growth and low reproductive rates. For example, only 0.1 per cent of the seeds produced by *Welwitschia mirabilis* will raise a new specimen, even in favourable conditions. In the plant's habitat, the Namib Desert, favourable conditions may not occur for several years, as rain is very rare. If mature plants were to be removed, the reproduction rate of the species would fall below a sustainable level. Similar conditions apply to several other species.

In some instances the demand from collectors has meant that the limit in sustainable collecting of wild species has been reached. In response to this, in 1973 more than one hundred nations signed the Convention on International Trade in Endangered Species of Wild Fauna and Flora (CITES). Some collectors regard the CITES convention as a disaster. It must be borne in mind, however, that CITES does not prohibit the trade in plants and animals; it merely regulates and monitors international trade in endangered species with the aim of preserving them in their habitats.

There are three Appendices in which species endangered by trade are listed:

- Appendix I includes species that are threatened with extinction. The trade in any wild plant or animal contained in this Appendix is forbidden.
- Appendix II includes species that are not necessarily threatened with extinction but that may become so unless trade is strictly regulated, and the trade in wild plants and animals is, therefore, subject to the issue of an export licence.
- Appendix III includes those species in which the regulation in trade is within the jurisdiction of the nation concerned.

Several succulents are currently included in Appendices I and II; none is at present included in Appendix III. All artificially propagated plants may be legally traded, even if they are listed in the Convention. It is necessary, however, to check with local regulations to avoid any problems. A useful reference is *The Evolution of CITES* by W. Wijnstekers.

It is important to remember that even species that are not listed in CITES may be protected by local legislation. If you are going to collect any wild plant, first check the local regulations and ask for an official permit.

Collectors can play an important role in conservation. The management of well-documented collections can help in conserving the genetic diversity of endangered species, and propagation helps to relieve the pressure on wild plants. Collectors should, however, always be aware of the damage caused by illegal collecting, and they should never buy wild-collected plants of endangered species, even with the aim of saving the specimen. The aim must always be to save the species not the individual.

USING THIS DICTIONARY

The succulents included in this book are organized in alphabetical order, by genus and by species within each genus. Each description is laid out as follows:

The author who published the present name; where applicable the name of the author who originally described this species in a different genus or rank is given in brackets

Authors' reference number

The family to which the taxon belongs

Name of the species

0350

Aloe humilis var. echinata (Willd.) Baker
LILIACEAE

A smaller variety with fleshy spines on upper surface of leaves.

Brief description of the species

Aloe echinata Willd.; *A. tuberculata* Haw.

South Africa (Cape Province)   CITES App. II

Other names in use to denote the same species

Range of distribution of the species

Status of the species under the CITES (up-dated as at March 1992):
App. I = species listed in Appendix I
App. II = species listed in Appendix II

The colour photographs were taken in a number of public and private collections and commercial nurseries or in the habitat. The colour and shape of individual plants depend on their geographical position and the type of greenhouse or glasshouse in which they are grown and on the attention they receive from the grower. Plants also vary according to the time of year. During resting periods they may shrink, have fewer leaves or acquire a reddish tinge. Plants grown in sunny positions and plants that receive little water may also have a reddish tinge, while those grown in shade and that receive plenty of water are greener. For these reasons the colour and form of the plants illustrated may vary slightly from the descriptions of the type species.

———

SUCCULENT FAMILIES AND GENERA

The families and the genera illustrated in this dictionary are described briefly in this chapter. Some reference books, most of which are monographic studies, that may be of use to interested readers are included in Further Reading. The most complete work on succulent plants is undoubtedly the three-volume *A Handbook of Succulents Plants* by H. Jacobsen, which covers most succulents in cultivation, although it does not include the most recent discoveries. Several periodicals specialize in succulent plants, and they are the best source of up-to-date information.

AGAVACEAE Endl. (MONOCOTYLEDONS)

The Agavaceae family includes several plants of horticultural interest. It consists of about 18 genera, of which seven are illustrated in this book. The stems of the plants in this family are short or even absent. The leaves are usually arranged in rosettes, and they are long-lived, rigid and often have dentate margins. The roots are fibrous and stoloniferous. The flowers are arranged on tall inflorescences. The fruit is a capsule or a berry.

Genera Illustrated

Agave L.
This genus includes several species of use to humans. The leaves of *Agave sisalana*, for example, are a source of sisal, which is used for making ropes, sacking, insulation and so on. *A. sisalana* used to be cultivated in Sicily until 1940, but it was not economically viable, and now the remains of abandoned sisal orchards may be seen. Other species are used in Mexico to produce alcoholic beverages by fermenting the central part of the stem.

The leaves of agaves, which are very variable in size, are arranged in rosettes. The inflorescence is a tall spike – to 10 m or more – and usually has thick, modified leaves (bracts). The tubular flowers, which are borne in clusters, have six sepals. The fruit is a capsule with black seeds.

All agaves are monocarpic – i.e., the plant dies after flowering and seeding – but it takes several years for an inflorescence to be produced.
DISTRIBUTION: America; a few species are naturalized in Mediterranean countries and tropical regions.

Calibanus Rose
A monotypic genus.
DISTRIBUTION: Mexico.

Dasylirion Zucc.
There are approximately 18 species of simple-stemmed plants with long, lanceolate leaves with spiny margins. The inflorescence is branched, and the flowers are campanulate.
DISTRIBUTION: Mexico and southern USA.

Furcraea Vente
The 20 or so species are similar to agaves but have taller stems and longer leaves. The tall inflorescence is branched, and the flowers are campanulate. The fruits contain many black seeds. The plant dies after flowering.
DISTRIBUTION: Mexico.

Nolina Michx.
There are about 20 species of small trees. Each plant has a succulent, swollen caudex covered with thick bark. The fibrous leaves are long and narrow. The tall inflorescence is branched and bears numerous small flowers.
DISTRIBUTION: Mexico to Guatemala.

Sansevieria Thunb.
There are approximately 70 species of rhizomatous or stoloniferous plants with fibrous, succulent leaves. The elongated inflorescence is unbranched and is seldom produced in cultivation; the flowers are white or greenish. Several species are tolerant of shade and may be grown as house-plants.
DISTRIBUTION: tropical Africa, India and Madagascar.

Yucca L.
Between 40 and 50 species of small trees bear simple or branched stems. The leaves, which are arranged in rosettes, are flexible to rigid. The branched inflorescence bears nocturnal flowers. During the day the flowers do not close fully, giving refuge to the moths that pollinate them. The fruit is a dry or fleshy capsule with black seeds. Some species are hardy and can be cultivated outside the greenhouse if the cold season is not too long.
DISTRIBUTION: North America and West Indies.

AMARYLLIDACEAE J.St.Hil. (MONOCOTYLEDONS)

There are about 70 genera of bulbous plants, with corms or rhizomes. Only the genus *Ammocharis* Herb. is included here.

ANACARDIACEAE Lindl. (DICOTYLEDONS)

About 70 genera of trees or shrubs with resinous bark are found in tropical and temperate regions of the northern hemisphere. The family contains several species of economic interest, including *Mangifera indica* (mango), *Anacardium occidentale* (cashew nut) and *Pistacia lentiscus* (pistachio nut).

Only the genera *Pachycormus* Coville and *Operculycaria* H. Perrier are considered succulent and are included in this dictionary.

APOCYNACEAE Juss. (DICOTYLEDONS)

The family contains about 215 genera of lactiferous herbs, lianas, shrubs and trees. The simple leaves have parallel veins. The flowers, which may be solitary or borne in clusters, have five petals and five sepals; the buds are contorted. The fruit is divided into two follicles. Several species are sources of pharmacological substances – alkaloids, glucosides and so on. The plants belonging to the three genera illustrated in this dictionary are very tender and need a warm position, and they require plenty of water during the growing season.

DISTRIBUTION: widespread.

Genera Illustrated

Adenium Roem. & Schult.
Succulent shrubs or trees with swollen caudices and lanceolate leaves, crowded at the stem apices.
DISTRIBUTION: tropical Africa, Arabian Peninsula and South Yemen (Socotra).

Pachypodium Lindl.
Spiny trees or subterranean, caudiciform stems with caducous leaves.
DISTRIBUTION: Angola, Madgascar, Namibia and South Africa.

Plumeria L.
Shrub or trees with cylindrical stems and branches, lanceolate, dark reddish-green leaves and showy, fragrant flowers in various colours.
DISTRIBUTION: Mexico and tropical South America.

ASCLEPIADACEAE R. Br. (DICOTYLEDONS)

The family contains over 2,800 species of lianas or low shrubs, some of which are succulent. The leaves are simple and caducous in most succulent species. The flowers have five sepals and five petals and are often malodorous. In the Stapeliae group pollen grains adhere together to form waxy pollinia (Fig. 1). The fruit is a follicle containing several seeds with a terminal tuft of hairs. The genera containing succulent plants have a complex and confusing taxonomy. The species with succulent stems are prone to rot if over-watered.

DISTRIBUTION: tropical and temperate regions.

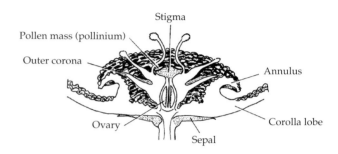

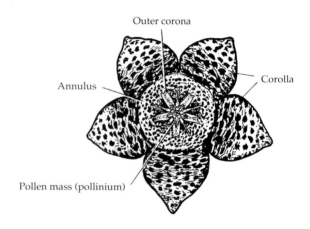

Fig. 1 *A diagram of the flower of a plant in the Stapeliae group, based on* Orbea. *Pollen grains adhere together to form waxy pollinia.*

Genera Illustrated

Brachystelma R. Br.
Plants have tuberous or fusiform roots with thin, caducous stems. Leaves are variable in shape. The flowers, which may be solitary or borne in clusters, have a round corolla and five lobes; the lobes may be free or united at the tips.
DISTRIBUTION: southern and tropical Africa.

Caralluma R. Br.
Stoloniferous, clump-forming plants, with four- or five-angled stems bearing reduced, caducous leaves. The flowers are very variable in size and may be campanulate or have an open corolla; the corona has two whorls; the five outer lobes may be free or fused, and the five inner lobes are fused to the outer whorl.
DISTRIBUTION: Arabian Peninsula, north and eastern Africa, India, Mediterranean countries and South Yemen (Socotra).

Ceropegia L.

These climbing or erect plants often have swollen tubers or fusiform roots. The calyx has five sepals, and the five petals of the corolla are united to form a tube, which is almost spherical at the base; the tips of the lobes are united to form a lantern-like structure (Fig. 2).

DISTRIBUTION: central and southern Africa, Canary Islands, India and Madeira.

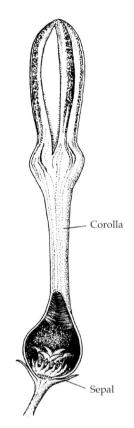

Corolla

Sepal

Fig. 2 *A side view of the schematic flower of* Ceropegia. *The corolla has five petals, which are united to form an almost spherical tube at the base while the tips of the lobes are united into a lantern-like structure. This type of flower can be pollinated only by specific pollinators, which are able to reach the pollinia down the long tube.*

Cynanchum L.

Climbing shrubs with fleshy branches. The corolla lobes of the small flowers form a pentagon.

DISTRIBUTION: central and southern Africa and Madagascar.

Dischidia R. Br.

These are epiphytic plants with small, waxy leaves, some of which are modified into large, inflated pitchers inhabited by ants (see also *Myrmecodia* under Rubiaceae). The flowers are small.

DISTRIBUTION: Australia and India.

Duvalia Haw.

The four- to six-angled stems have spreading teeth. The leaves are small. The flowers, which appear on younger stems, are solitary or borne in clusters on stalks 1–3 cm long.

DISTRIBUTION: eastern and western Africa.

Echidnopsis Hook.f.

The stems have between 6 and 20 angles, the ribs being divided into hexagonal tubercles. Flowers are borne in clusters of two to four; they have no tube, triangular lobes and an inner whorl with five reflexed lobes.

DISTRIBUTION: tropical Africa, Arabian Peninsula and South Yemen (Socotra).

Edithcolea N.E. Br.

The few species have five-angled stems to 30 cm high. Large, hemispherical flowers are borne at the stem apices.

DISTRIBUTION: Kenya, Somalia, South Yemen (Socotra) and Tanzania.

Fockea Endl.

These caudiciform plants have tuberous roots and thin, twining branches. The flowers, which may be solitary or borne in clusters, are starfish-like.

DISTRIBUTION: Angola, Namibia, South Africa and Zimbabwe.

Frerea Dalzell

A monotypic genus very similar to *Caralluma* but with persistent leaves to 6 cm long.

DISTRIBUTION: India.

Hoodia Sweet

The many-angled stems, to 1 m tall, are covered with conical tubercles and hard teeth. Flowers, which are borne near the apex of stems, have a flat corolla, very small lobes and a five-lobed corona in two whorls.

DISTRIBUTION: Angola, Namibia and South Africa.

Hoya R. Br.

These epiphytic plants have climbing stems and branches. The leaves are variable in shape and size, and in some species are thick and succulent. Inflorescences are borne in pendent clusters with several waxy, star-like and fragrant flowers.

DISTRIBUTION: Asia, Australia and Polynesia.

Huernia R. Br.

The short stems, which branch from the base, are four- to six-angled and have large teeth. Flowers are produced from the base of young stems and have a campanulate corolla.

DISTRIBUTION: southern and eastern Africa, Arabian Peninsula and Ethiopia.

Notechidnopsis Lavranos & Bleck
Similar to Echidnopsis but leafless at all stages of growth.
DISTRIBUTION: southern Africa.

Orbea Haw.
The plants are similar to *Stapelia* and are often included in that genus.
DISTRIBUTION: southern Africa.

Orbeanthus L.C. Leach
The stems spread horizontally. The flowers are very showy and have a hairy corona.
DISTRIBUTION: southern Africa.

Orbeopsis L.C. Leach
Flowers are borne in clusters from the base of stems; the corolla is flat and there is no annulus.
DISTRIBUTION: southern Africa.

Pachycymbium L.C. Leach
Rhizomatous stems. The corolla may be campanulate or flat.
DISTRIBUTION: southern Africa.

Piaranthus R. Br.
The flowers are small; the corolla is flat, and the tube is absent or campanulate; the lobes are lanceolate.
DISTRIBUTION: southern Africa.

Pseudolithos P.R.O. Bally
The unbranched stems are stone-like. The inflorescence has many small flowers.
DISTRIBUTION: Somalia.

Quaqua (N.E. Br.) Bruyns
This genus is related to *Caralluma*.
DISTRIBUTION: southern Africa.

Raphionacme Harv.
A genus distinguished by its tuberous roots, climbing stems and loose pollinia.
DISTRIBUTION: eastern Africa.

Rhytidocaulon P.R.O. Bally
The unbranched stems are papillose. Solitary flowers are borne on short stalks; the corolla has spreading lobes.
DISTRIBUTION: eastern Africa.

Sarcostemma R. Br.
Thin-stemmed shrubs with clusters of flowers, with small, projecting corolla lobes.
DISTRIBUTION: tropical Africa.

Stapelia L.
There are about 100 species. The flowers, which are borne on long stalks, have a five-lobed, usually flat, corolla; the

deep lobes are triangular. The corona has two, five-lobed whorls, an inner and outer whorl.
DISTRIBUTION: tropical and southern Africa.

Stapelianthus Choux
This genus is closely related to *Huernia*.
DISTRIBUTION: Madagascar.

Tavaresia Welw.
Flowers with a long corolla are produced from the base of the stems.
DISTRIBUTION: central and southern Africa.

Trichocaulon N.E. Br.
Cylindrical stems are simple or branching from the base. The small flowers are borne between the tubercles towards the stem apices. The flat corolla has acute lobes.
DISTRIBUTION: southern Africa, Madagascar and Somalia.

Tromotriche Haw.
A genus that is very similar to *Stapelia* and that was, in fact, formerly included in it.
DISTRIBUTION: southern Africa.

BASELLACEAE Moq. (DICOTYLEDONS)

A family of about six genera of rhizomatous, climbing plants with simple, often succulent leaves. The branched inflorescence bears small flowers. Only one genus, *Boussingaultia* H.B. & K., is illustrated here.
DISTRIBUTION: tropical and subtropical America.

BOMBACACEAE Kunth (DICOTYLEDONS)

There are 30 genera of very large trees with soft wood. The leaves, which may be simple or compound, are covered with hairs or hairy scales. The flowers are large. The two genera illustrated have woolly fruits with numerous seeds
DISTRIBUTION: tropical Africa and America.

Genera Illustrated

Bombax L.
These large trees often have spiny trunks and palmate leaves. The very large flowers appear before the leaves.
DISTRIBUTION: tropical regions.

Chorisia H.B. & K.
The trees have swollen trunks that are usually spiny. The large flowers appear before the palmate leaves.
DISTRIBUTION: tropical America.

BROMELIACEAE Juss. (MONOCOTYLEDONS)

The family contains about 50 genera of terrestrial or epiphytic plants. The basal leaves, which may have spiny margins, are often arranged in rosettes. Flowers are borne in spikes with coloured bracts. The epiphytic genera grow on the trunks and stems of trees.
Distribution: tropical America.

Genera Illustrated

Abromeitiella Mez
Small, terrestrial rosettes form large clumps. The greenish flowers are usually solitary, and the petals are much longer than the sepals.
DISTRIBUTION: Argentina and Bolivia.

Deuterochnia Mez
These short-stemmed plants have rosettes of leaves with spinose margins.
DISTRIBUTION: South America.

Dyckia Schult.f.
The stemless rosettes have thick rhizomes. The leaves are rigid and have spinose margins.
DISTRIBUTION: South America.

Hechtia Klotzsch
Stemless or short-stemmed rosettes are formed from grey or red-brown leaves with spiny margins.
DISTRIBUTION: Mexico and southern USA.

Puya Molina
The toothed and spinose leaves are arranged in rosettes, which may be stemless or long-stemmed, to 10 m tall when in flower.
DISTRIBUTION: Argentina, Bolivia and Chile.

BURSERACEAE Kunth (DICOTYLEDONS)

A family of about 20 genera of shrubs or large trees. The trunks, bark and wood are resinous. The leaves are compound.

Genera Illustrated

Bursera Jacq.
These shrubs have caudiciform trunks and compound leaves.
DISTRIBUTION: Mexico and southern USA.

Commiphora Jacq.
Shrubs with a very thick, tuberous caudex; similar to *Bursera*.
DISTRIBUTION: Namibia.

COMMELINACEAE R. Br. (MONOCOTYLEDONS)

These tropical plants have jointed stems. The flowers are usually blue, a colour that is seldom seen among succulent plants.

Genera Illustrated

Callisia L.
These plants, which have succulent leaves, are similar to *Tradescantia*.
DISTRIBUTION: Mexico, tropical South America and southeastern USA.

Cyanotis D. Don
A genus of plants with tuberous roots and succulent leaves.
DISTRIBUTION: tropical Africa and Asia.

Tradescantia L.
These plants have fibrous or tuberous roots, jointed stems and leaves that are often covered with hairs.
DISTRIBUTION: North and South America.

COMPOSITAE Giseke (DICOTYLEDONS)

A very large family containing both annual and perennial plants, ranging from herbaceous plants to trees and including epiphytic and aquatic species. The inflorescence may bear from one to many heads of clustered, stalkless flowers, and the calyx has many bristles and scales (pappus), which remain attached to the seeds and facilitate their dispersal by the wind.
DISTRIBUTION: widespread.

Genera Illustrated

Othonna L.
These small shrubs have either entire or lobed leaves. They are winter growing and should be kept dry in summer.
DISTRIBUTION: Namibia and South Africa.

Senecio L.
This very large genus contains several succulent species. The genus *Kleinia* has been included in this genus for the purposes of this dictionary.
DISTRIBUTION: widespread.

CONVOLVULACEAE Juss. (DICOTYLEDONS)

This family contains plants of very diverse habit, including some parasitic species. The showy, campanulate flowers are usually white or pink.

DISTRIBUTION: widespread.

Genera Illustrated

Ipomoea L.

A large and variable genus of trees, shrubs and herbaceous plants. The species cultivated by succulent enthusiasts have tuberous roots and slender stems. Several 'new species' are being imported.

DISTRIBUTION: tropical and subtropical regions.

Merremia Dennst.

These small, climbing plants have lobed or compound leaves. They are very similar to *Ipomoea*, from which they may be distinguished by differences in the pollen structure.

DISTRIBUTION: tropical regions.

CRASSULACEAE DC. (DICOTYLEDONS)

The family of Crassulaceae contains a large number of widely found annual, biennial and perennial species, with more or less succulent leaves, which grow in a wide range of climatic conditions (from wetlands to deserts). The inflorescence usually bears small flowers (Fig. 3). The seeds are dust-like, but plants are easily propagated from stem and leaf cuttings.

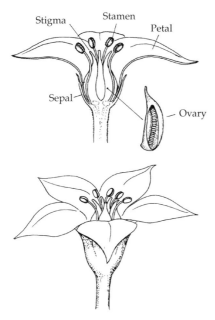

Fig. 3 *The flowers of members of the Crassulaceae family are very simple and are arranged in inflorescences. The number of stamens is equal to the number of petals or is a multiple of them.*

Genera Illustrated

Adromischus Lem.

Succulent herbaceous or shrubby plants with fleshy, persistent leaves. The inflorescences have flowers at right angles to the peduncles.

DISTRIBUTION: Namibia and South Africa (Cape Province).

Aeonium Webb & Berthel.

Shrubs with simple or branched stems and leaves arranged in rosettes at the tips of the branches. The characteristic rosettes die after flowering.

DISTRIBUTION: north Africa, Canary Islands, Madeira and Mediterranean regions.

Aichryson Webb & Berthel.

Very close to *Aeonium*.

DISTRIBUTION: Azores, Canary Islands and Madeira.

Cotyledon L.

Branching shrubs with opposite waxy leaves. The campanulate flowers, which may be red, yellow or orange, are pollinated by birds.

DISTRIBUTION: Arabian Peninsula, Namibia and South Africa.

Crassula L.

Herbaceous plants or shrubs with succulent leaves of various shapes. There are 250-300 species, which are found in habitats ranging from wetland to desert. The southern African species are widely cultivated.

DISTRIBUTION: southern and tropical Africa; a few species are widespread.

Dudleya Br. & R.

Low-growing plants with leaves arranged in rosettes. The branched inflorescences bear star-shaped flowers.

DISTRIBUTION: Mexico and USA (Arizona, California, Nevada).

Echeveria DC.

Low-growing rosettes bear erect stems of lateral inflorescences with numerous bracts.

DISTRIBUTION: Central America and Mexico.

Graptopetalum Rose

A genus that is closely related to *Echeveria*, from which it is distinguished by its star-like flowers and the red spots on the petals.

DISTRIBUTION: Mexico.

Greenovia Webb & Berthel.

The rosettes are very similar to those of *Sempervivum*. The flowers are golden yellow, and the rosette dies after flowering.

DISTRIBUTION: Canary Islands.

Jovibarba Opiz

A very small genus, closely allied to *Sempervivum*. The flowers are campanulate.

DISTRIBUTION: east Europe (Balkans and eastern Alps).

Kalanchoe Adans.

A very variable genus containing herbaceous plants, shrubs and climbers. The leaves in some species produce plantlets. The terminal inflorescence bears showy flowers.

DISTRIBUTION: southern and tropical Africa, Asia and Madagascar.

Monanthes Haw.

A genus of small plants with fleshy leaves and hairy inflorescences.

DISTRIBUTION: Canary Islands and Madeira.

Orostachys (DC.) Fisch.

The small rosettes die after producing a tall inflorescence.

DISTRIBUTION: Asia.

Pachyphytum Link, Klotzsch & Otto

The fleshy-leaved rosettes may be distinguished from *Echeveria* by the presence of a pair of scales inside each petal.

DISTRIBUTION: Mexico.

Rosularia (DC.) Stapf

The plants in this genus are similar to *Sedum* and *Sempervivum*, but the rosettes have lateral inflorescences.

DISTRIBUTION: east Europe and Asia (Caucasus and Himalayas).

Sedum L.

There are approximately 600 species of herbaceous or shrubby plants, with erect or decumbent stems. The star-shaped flowers are various colours. European and Asiatic species are hardy and suitable for the rock garden.

DISTRIBUTION: Asia, Europe, north Africa and North America.

Sempervivella Stapf

These small plants have leaves arranged in rosettes and white or pink flowers.

DISTRIBUTION: Asia (Himalayas).

Sempervivum L.

The leaves of these stoloniferous plants are arranged in rosettes, and the flowers are star-shaped. There are about 40 species and more than 250 cultivars, all of which are hardy.

DISTRIBUTION: north Africa, Asia and Europe.

Sinocrassula A. Berger

A small genus, similar to *Sedum*.

DISTRIBUTION: Asia (Himalayas to China).

Tacitus Moran & J. Meyrán

See *Graptopetalum*.

Tylecodon Toelken.

Distinguished from *Cotyledon* by the non-waxy leaves arranged in spirals and by the presence of bracts on the flowering stems.

DISTRIBUTION: southern Africa.

Villadia Haw.

A genus that is closely related to *Sedum*, from which it differs in having petals united into a distinct tube.

DISTRIBUTION: Mexico to Peru.

CUCURBITACEAE Juss. (DICOTYLEDONS)

This is a family of fast-growing, climbing plants with tendrils. Several species produce edible fruits. The species cultivated by succulent collectors usually have tuberous rootstocks or swollen bases.

DISTRIBUTION: tropical and warm temperate countries.

Genera Illustrated

Cephalopentandra Chiov.

A monotypic genus.

DISTRIBUTION: Ethiopia, Kenya and Uganda.

Corallocarpus Welw. ex Hook.f.

A genus of about 20 species of plants with climbing or trailing stems arising from a tuberous root. Very few species are of interest to the succulent grower.

DISTRIBUTION: Africa, India and Madagascar.

Gerrardanthus Harv.

A genus of plants with a tuberous rootstock from which climbing stems with tendrils are produced.

DISTRIBUTION: central, eastern and southern Africa.

Ibervillea B.D. Greene

The glabrous stems are swollen at the base, and the climbing branches have tendrils.

DISTRIBUTION: north Mexico and southwest USA.

Kedrostis Medik.

These climbing plants have swollen, caudiciform bases.

DISTRIBUTION: Africa to tropical Asia.

Melothria L.

A genus containing approximately 10 species of climbing- or trailing-stemmed plants with tendrils, very few of which are of interest to the succulent collector.

DISTRIBUTION: tropical and subtropical America.

Momordica L.

About 60 species of climbing plants with fleshy rootstocks. The fruits are more attractive than the flowers.
DISTRIBUTION: Africa.

Seyrigia Keraudren

A genus containing a few species of climbing plants, with slender or succulent, little-branched stems with tendrils.
DISTRIBUTION: Madagascar.

Xerosicyos Humbert

A genus of climbing plants with glabrous or hairy stems and thick, succulent leaves.
DISTRIBUTION: Madagascar.

Zygosicyos Humbert

Climbing stems with tendrils are produced by tuberous roots.
DISTRIBUTION: Asia and Madagascar.

DIDIEREACEAE Drake (DICOTYLEDONS)

This family, which is related to the Cactaceae, contains xerophytic spiny shrubs and small trees.

Genera Illustrated

Alluaudia Drake

A genus of spiny shrubs with erect, spreading branches.
DISTRIBUTION: Madagascar.

Didierea Baill.

The stems have thick, tuberculate branches, which bear narrow leaves and spines.
DISTRIBUTION: Madagascar.

DIOSCOREACEAE R. Br. (MONOCOTYLEDONS)

The plants in this family have large rhizomes or tubers with twining shoots.
DISTRIBUTION: southern Africa and South and Central America.

Genus Illustrated

Dioscorea L.

The very large, spherical caudex is covered with bark, which cracks into polygonal warts. Several species have edible tubers, and some have pharmacological uses.
DISTRIBUTION: southern Africa, Central and South America.

EUPHORBIACEAE Juss. (DICOTYLEDONS)

The Euphorbiaceae family contains about 320 genera and over 8,000 species of geographically widespread plants, which range from annual herbs to large trees. All Euphorbiaceae have a milky sap that may be harmful to the touch. The inflorescence has a complicated structure, based on the cyathium, which consists of an involucre containing one reduced female flower and several male flowers. There are protective bracts and nectaries. The fruit is a capsule, which explodes on reaching maturity.

Genera Illustrated

Euphorbia L.

There are over 2,000 species of very diverse habit, from annual plants to large trees, and including several succulent species. All species contain a poisonous, irritant white latex. Cyathia are enclosed in a five-lobed involucre bearing nectaries and subtended by enlarged, coloured bracts (Fig. 4). Some species make suitable house-plants.
DISTRIBUTION: widespread but the succulent species are more common in Africa and Madagascar.

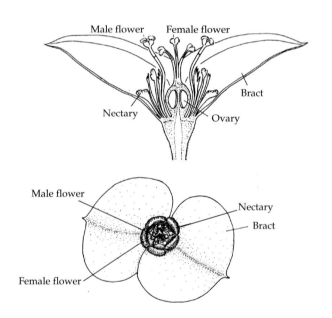

Fig. 4 *In Euphorbiaceae the inflorescence consists of complicated flower structures called cyathia (singular, cyathium). These consist of an involucre (a series of bracts), which contains one reduced female flower and several male ones. The flowers are usually inconspicuous. Pollinators are attracted by the protective bracts (modified leaves), which can be very showy, and by the secretion of the nectaries. The illustration is based on the cyathia of* Euphorbia milii.

Jatropha L.

A genus of trees or shrubs with simple, palmately veined leaves, sometimes covered with hairs. The inflorescence has many branches and bears scarlet flowers.
DISTRIBUTION: tropical and temperate regions.

Monadenium Pax

These succulent shrubs have several species with spirally tuberculate stems. Inflorescences are borne at the stem apices, and the lobes and glands are fused together.
DISTRIBUTION: tropical Africa.

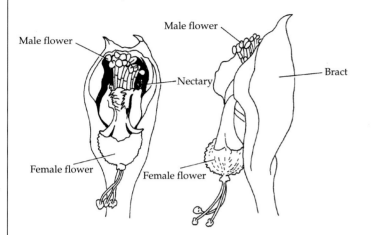

Fig. 5 *A typical* Monadenium *flower.*

Pedilanthus Neck.

A genus of shrubs with several branches and small leaves.
DISTRIBUTION: Central America.

Phyllanthus L.

Trees or shrubs that often have leaf-like stems. The leaves themselves are of variable sizes. The inflorescences are borne from the axils, and the fruit is a capsule containing two seeds.
DISTRIBUTION: tropical regions.

Synadenium Boiss.

A genus of shrubs with thick, succulent stems and large, pale green leaves. The lobes and glands are fused together into a single unit.
DISTRIBUTION: tropical Africa.

FOUQUIERIACEAE DC. (DICOTYLEDONS)

Fouquieriea H.B.& K.

This is the only genus of this family. There are a few species of spiny shrubs or trees with stems over 10 m tall. The genus *Idria* is considered to be a synonym.
DISTRIBUTION: Mexico and southwestern USA.

GERANIACEAE Juss. (DICOTYLEDONS)

The shrubs or herbs in this family usually have aromatic oils in glandular hairs, jointed stems and spirally arranged leaves.
DISTRIBUTION: temperate and tropical regions.

Genera Illustrated

Pelargonium L'Hér.

A genus of low-growing shrub species, some with succulent or swollen stems and roots. The leaves, which may be simple or compound, are often aromatic. Some of the commonly cultivated geraniums are included in *Pelargonium*.
DISTRIBUTION: temperate and tropical regions.

Sarcocaulon (DC.) Sweet.

The succulent stems of the plants within this genus are covered with protective bark. The spreading branches are spiny and have small leaves.
DISTRIBUTION: temperate and tropical regions; most succulent species are common in southern Africa, especially Namibia.

GESNERIACEAE Dumort. (DICOTYLEDONS)

A family of shrubs, herbs or lianas, rarely trees, with opposite leaves and showy flowers. Very few species are of interest to succulent growers.
DISTRIBUTION: widespread.

Genera Illustrated

Rechsteiniea C. Regel

The species within this genus have tuberous roots, velvety or hairy leaves and flowers borne in short panicles.
DISTRIBUTION: South America.

Sinningia Nees

The shrubs in this genus are tuberous and have opposite leaves. The flowers are borne at the axils of the leaves.
DISTRIBUTION: Mexico to Argentina.

ICACINACEAE Miers (DICOTYLEDONS)

The trees, shrubs and lianas in this family have stems that may exhibit peculiar growth forms. Only one genus, *Pyrenacantha* Wright, which is native to eastern Africa, is illustrated in this dictionary.
DISTRIBUTION: tropical and temperate regions.

LABIATAE Juss. (DICOTYLEDONS)

The shrubs and herbaceous plants within this family usually contain fragrant oils. The leaves are simple. Several plants are of interest in horticulture, but few of them are succulents.
DISTRIBUTION: widespread.

Genera Illustrated

Ocimum L.

There are about 35 species of aromatic shrubs and herbaceous plants within the genus. Many species are important for cooking – *O. basilicum* (basil) is one of the best known culinary herbs – or for medicinal purposes. Very few species are suitable for collections of succulent plants, however.
DISTRIBUTION: tropical regions.

Plectranthus L'Hér.

A genus of shrubs or herbs of which only a few species have succulent leaves or stems.
DISTRIBUTION: Africa, Asia and Australia.

LEGUMINOSAE Juss. (DICOTYLEDONS)

A very large family containing over 16,000 species with very diverse habits. Several species are important as cultivated crops. Only one genus, *Dolichos* L., is included in this dictionary.
DISTRIBUTION: widespread.

LILIACEAE Juss. (MONOCOTYLEDONS)

A family of largely herbaceous plants but containing a few tree-like species. Several genera have succulent leaves and are adapted to live in dry conditions.

Genera Illustrated

Aloe L.

A large genus of plants with succulent leaves arranged in spirals. The plants are stemless or have short, rarely woody, stems.
DISTRIBUTION: southern Africa and Madagascar.

Astroloba Uitewaal

A genus containing a few species; closely related to *Haworthia*.
DISTRIBUTION: South Africa.

Bulbine L.

A genus containing plants with succulent leaves and subterranean bulbs.
DISTRIBUTION: southern Africa.

Eriospermum Endl.

Solitary or stoloniferous plants with globose, tuberous roots and with reduced, scale-like leaves and one or more well-developed leaf.
DISTRIBUTION: southern Africa.

Gasteria C.-J. Duval

Stemless plants with succulent leaves that are arranged in rosettes in mature specimens; younger plants have distichous leaves, an arrangement that may persist in mature specimens.
DISTRIBUTION: southern Africa.

Haworthia C.-J. Duval

Plants in dwarf rosettes that may be solitary or clustering. The succulent leaves are very diverse shapes.
DISTRIBUTION: southern Africa and Madagascar.

Poellnitzia Uitewaal

A monotypic genus.
DISTRIBUTION: South Africa.

Scilla L.

A genus of bulbous plants with linear leaves.
DISTRIBUTION: Africa and Europe.

MESEMBRYANTHEMACEAE Baill. (DICOTYLEDONS)

The family of Mesembryanthemaceae consists of about 100 genera with approximately 2,000 species, all of which have succulent leaves. The species range from small shrubs to creeping and the extremely specialized stemless plants. The flowers are usually showy and have many petals. The fruit is a hygroscopic capsule, which opens when wet, so releasing the seeds, and closes when dry. This adaptation is a response to arid environments: the fruit protects the seeds until water is available for germination. The family is widespread in southern Africa, and several species are naturalized in Mediterranean regions. The classification of the genera is based on the characteristics of the fruit, but it is possible to distinguish some by their habit. The great variablity within the family has led to the proliferation of genera and species, and any revision would considerably reduce their number.

In this dictionary the names currently in use in private and public collections as well as in trade catalogues have been followed. More than 50 genera and 296 species are illustrated and described in the alphabetical section.

Genera Illustrated

Aloinopsis Schwantes
Argyroderma N.E. Br.
Aspazoma N.E. Br.
Astridia Dinter & Schwantes
Bergeranthus Schwantes
Biilja N.E. Br.
Carruanthus Schwantes

Cephalophyllum N.E. Br.
Ceroclamys N.E. Br.
Cheiridopsis N.E. Br.
Conophyllum Schwantes
Conophytum N.E. Br.
Cylindrophyllum Schwantes
Dactylopsis N.E. Br.
Delosperma N.E. Br.
Dinteranthus Schwantes
Dracophilus Dinter & Schwantes
Drosanthemum Schwantes
Eberlanzia Schwantes
Enarganthe N.E. Br.
Faucaria Schwantes
Fenestraria N.E. Br.
Gibbaeum Haw.
Glottiphyllum Haw.
Hereroa Dinter & Schwantes
Jordaniella H. Hartmann.
Lampranthus N.E. Br.
Lapidaria Schwantes
Leipoldtia L. Bol.
Lithops N.E. Br.
Machairophyllum L. Bol.
Malephora N.E. Br.
Mestoklema N.E. Br.
Mitrophyllum Schwantes
Monilaria Schwantes
Namaquanthus L. Bol.
Namibia Dinter & Schwantes
Nelia Schwantes
Neoherincia L. Bol.
Odontophorus N.E. Br.
Ophtalmophyllum Dinter & Schwantes
Pleiospilos Dinter & Schwantes
Polymita L. Bol.
Rabiea N.E. Br.
Rhombophyllum Schwantes
Ruschia Schwantes
Ruschianthus L. Bol.
Sceletium N.E. Br.
Schwantesia Dinter
Smicrostigma N.E. Br.
Stomatium Schwantes
Tanquana Hartmann & Liede
Titanopsis Schwantes
Trichodiadema Schwantes
Vanheerdea L. Bol.

MORACEAE Link (DICOTYLEDONS)

The Moraceae family includes about 50 genera and over 1,200 species which are very diverse in habit, ranging from large trees to small herbaceous plants, usually with milky latex. Flowers are small and, in most genera, are wind pollinated. (*Ficus* flowers are pollinated by insects.) The flowers are grouped in inflorescences, with thickened axes forming an invaginated receptacle. The most extreme form is found in *Ficus*: the flowers are actually inside the fig, and the pulp we eat is composed of hundreds of fruits and seeds.

DISTRIBUTION: tropical and temperate regions.

Genera Illustrated

Dorstenia L.

A genus of low-growing plants with slender stems and tuber-like rhizomes. Inflorescences are solitary and may be regarded as a fig inflorescence that is not enclosed (Fig. 6).

DISTRIBUTION: tropical Africa and America.

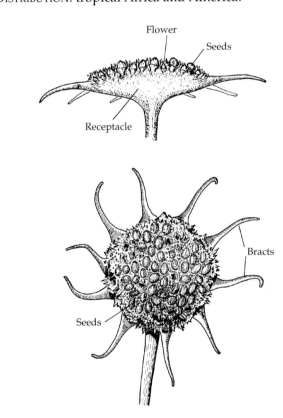

Fig. 6 *The members of the Moraceae family have small flowers. In most genera these are wind pollinated, although those of the* Ficus *are insect pollinated. The flowers are grouped in inflorescences, with thickened axes forming an invaginated receptacle. The most extreme form is found in* Ficus: *the flowers are actually inside the fig and the pulp we eat is formed by hundreds of fruits and seeds. In* Dorstenia *the inflorescence may be regarded as resembling the inflorescence of a fig that is not enclosed. The illustration is based on the flowers of* Dorstenia.

Ficus L.

The trees or climbing vines within this genus contain latex. The leaves are simple, and the flowers are very small, with up to several thousands enclosed in a single receptacle.

DISTRIBUTION: tropical and temperate regions.

OXALIDACEAE R.Br. (DICOTYLEDONS)

The small trees or herbs within this family have tubers and trifoliate leaves. The fruit is a capsule.

DISTRIBUTION: tropical and temperate regions.

Genus Illustrated

Oxalis L.

A genus of stemless herbaceous plants with tuberous roots. The trifoliate, long-stalked leaves are usually lowered at night. The flowers are yellow. Fruits explode when they achieve maturity, dispersing the seeds over considerable distances.

DISTRIBUTION: southern Africa and South America; some species are naturalized in Europe and have become pernicious weeds.

PASSIFLORACEAE Juss. (DICOTYLEDONS)

Lianas, shrubs or trees with lobed leaves arranged in spirals.

Genus Illustrated

Adenia Forsk.

A genus of herbaceous climbers with tendrils. The species of interest to succulent enthusiasts have swollen roots.

DISTRIBUTION: Africa to Asia.

PEDALIACEAE R.Br. (DICOTYLEDONS)

A family of shrubs or herbs with opposite, usually hairy, leaves. The flowers are campanulate, and the fruit is a capsule, often armed with spines or prickles.

DISTRIBUTION: temperate and warm regions.

Genera Illustrated

Pterodiscus Hook.

A genus containing species of small herbaceous plants and shrubs with succulent, swollen caudices and tuberous roots. The leaves, which have undulate margins, are variable in shape. Flowers arise from the leaf axils.

DISTRIBUTION: Angola, Namibia and South Africa.

Sesamothamnus Welw.

A few species of spiny shrubs or small trees, with short leafy shoots in the axils of the thorns.

DISTRIBUTION: Angola, Botswana, Ethiopia, Namibia and Somalia.

Uncarina Stapf

A genus of nine species found in the dry to arid regions of south Madagascar. The flowers are yellow or maroon to pink.

DISTRIBUTION: Madagascar.

PIPERACEAE C. Agardh (DICOTYLEDONS)

The Piperaceae family contains species ranging from herbaceous plants to small trees, many of which are aromatic. The leaves are simple, and there are small flowers. Pepper is obtained from *Piper nigrum*, a member of this family.

DISTRIBUTION: tropical regions.

Genus Illustrated

Peperomia Ruiz & Pav.

A genus of small succulent herbs with minute flowers.

DISTRIBUTION: tropical regions.

PORTULACACEAE Juss. (DICOTYLEDONS)

This family contains more than 20 genera and 400 species of shrubs and herbaceous plants with succulent leaves. The leaves are entire and often bear long hairs at their base. The flowers are small, but they may be very showy in some species. The family is widespread in tropical and temperate regions.

Genera Illustrated

Anacampseros L.

The genus contains dwarf plants that have papery stipules covering the small leaves or hair-like stipules among the succulent leaves.

DISTRIBUTION: Argentina (one species), Australia (one species), Namibia and South Africa.

Ceraria Pearson & Stephens.

A genus of shrubs and branches with reduced leaves. The inflorescence has from two to six small pink flowers.

DISTRIBUTION: Namibia and South Africa.

Lewisia Pursh

A group of low-growing plants with fleshy taproots and leaves arranged in rosettes.

DISTRIBUTION: west to north North America.

Portulaca L.
Trailing herbs with opposite leaves and tufts of bristles in the axils. The purple or yellow flowers open only in direct sunshine.
DISTRIBUTION: tropical regions.

Portulacaria Jacq.
A genus of plants with branches covered with succulent leaves. The small flowers are pink.
DISTRIBUTION: Mozambique, Namibia and South Africa.

Talinum Adans.
Plants with fleshy roots and annual, shrubby branches. The flowers have two-keeled sepals.
DISTRIBUTION: tropical regions.

RUBIACEAE Juss. (DICOTYLEDONS)

A large family of trees, shrubs and lianas, although very few genera are of interest to succulent collectors. *Coffea* species (coffee) belong to this family.
DISTRIBUTION: Africa, Asia and Europe.

Genus Illustrated

Myrmecodia Jack
A genus of woody shrubs with large tubers, which are usually inhabited by ants in the wild. The tuber contains a series of cavities, filled with dead plant material. The ants remove the dead material and use the cavities as nests. There are several advantages to the plants for this symbiosis, the main one being defence: the ants keep potential predators away from the plants. Another advantage is the re-use of the carbon dioxide produced by the respiration of the ants.
DISTRIBUTION: Indonesia and New Guinea.

STERCULIACEAE Bartal. (DICOTYLEDONS)

A family of trees and shrubs, but with no true succulent plants. Some species are cultivated for their bonsai or caudiciform aspect.
DISTRIBUTION: tropical regions.

Genus Illustrated

Brachychiton Schott and Endl.
A genus of trees with swollen trunks and entire or deeply palmate leaves.
DISTRIBUTION: Australia and Papua New Guinea.

VITACEAE Juss. (DICOTYLEDONS)

A family containing about 12 genera and 700 species of lianas with tendrils or small trees. Only two genera are of interest to the succulent collector. Included in this family is the grapevine, *Vitis vinifera*.
DISTRIBUTION: widespread in tropical regions.

Genera Illustrated

Cissus L.
A genus of climbing plants with tendrils and opposite leaves. A few species have succulent roots and leaves.
DISTRIBUTION: tropical and subtropical regions.

Cyphostemma (Planch.) Alston
There are approximately 150 species of caudiciform shrubs or trees within this genus. The leaves are clustered at the apices of stems. Succulent species may achieve huge dimensions.
DISTRIBUTION: southern and eastern Africa and Madagascar.

WELWITSCHIACEAE Markgr. (GYMNOSPERMS)

A monotypic family belonging to the Gymnosperms group, together with cycads and conifers. The pollen is dispersed by the wind.
DISTRIBUTION: Angola and Namibia.

Welwitschia Hook.f.
A monotypic genus.

ILLUSTRATED A-Z
OF SPECIES

Abromeitiella brevifolia (Griseb.) A. Cast.
BROMELIACEAE

Rosettes forming clumps over 1 m in diameter; green, triangular leaves to 3 cm long with terminal spine but spineless margins; greenish flowers 3-4 cm long.

Argentina, Bolivia

Abromeitiella chlorantha (Speg.) Mez
BROMELIACEAE

Small, narrow rosettes of elongated triangular leaves to 2 cm long, with small terminal spine and dentate margins; small, greenish flowers.

Abromeitiella pulvinata Mez

Argentina

Abromeitiella lorentziana (Mez) A. Cast.
BROMELIACEAE

Rosettes forming dense clumps to 1 m in diameter; triangular, grey-green leaves, 4–15 cm long, with terminal spine and spined margins; greenish flowers.

Argentina

Abromeitiella scapigera Rauh & H. Hrom.
BROMELIACEAE

Rosettes; leaves, 15–25 cm long, end in sharp spine and margins have small spines; greenish flowers.

Bolivia

Adenia aculeata Engl.
PASSIFLORACEAE

Shrub to 1.5 m tall; large, tuberous caudex from which arise 4-angled climbing stems with conical spines at edges; pale green to yellow flowers.

Somalia

Adenia digitata Engl.
PASSIFLORACEAE

Spherical caudex, tapering upwards into erect stem, to 3 m tall, with tendrils and digitate leaves; pale green to yellow flowers.

Adenia angustisecta Burtt-Davy; *A. buchannannii* Harms; *A. multiflora* Potts

South Africa (Transvaal)

Adenia glauca Schinz
PASSIFLORACEAE

Large, irregular swollen stem with taproot; climbing branches with compound leaves are produced during growing season; branches dry out in dry season; pale yellow flowers.

Botswana, South Africa (Transvaal)

Adenia pechuelii (Engl.) Harms
PASSIFLORACEAE

Plant to 1 m tall with large, fleshy caudex to 50 cm in diameter with several branches; lanceolate, caducous leaves; small inflorescence; pale green to yellow flowers.

Echinothamnus pechuelii Engl.

Namibia

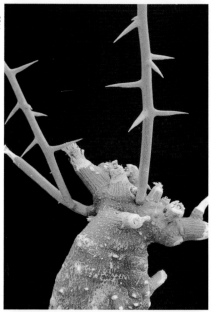

Adenia globosa Engl.
PASSIFLORACEAE

Caudex to 1 m high with several thin branches armed with thorns; small leaves during rainy season; bright red flowers.

Tanzania

Adenia perrieri Burtt Davy
PASSIFLORACEAE

Branches to 1 m long; stems and branches bear attractive, compound, green leaves; greenish-yellow flowers.

Southern Africa

Adenia keramanthus Harms
PASSIFLORACEAE

Thick caudex 8–10 cm in diameter and 50 cm high; erect branches with ovate to rounded leaves; yellowish flowers.

Tanzania

Adenia sp.
PASSIFLORACEAE

An attractive but so far unidentified *Adenia* found in several collections; caudex is 10–15 cm in diameter, with several leafy stems; greenish-yellow flowers.

Adenia spinosa Burtt Davy

PASSIFLORACEAE

Large, branching caudex, diameter to 2 m and to 50 cm high; branches armed with straight spines; numerous small leaves; creamy-yellow flowers.

South Africa (Transvaal)

Adenium obesum Balf.f.

APOCYNACEAE

Shrub to 2 m high with thick caudex and many short branches; leaves at ends of branches; pink flowers.

Kenya, Tanzania, Zimbabwe

Adenium oleifolium Stapf

APOCYNACEAE

Plant 1–1.5 m tall; subter-ranean caudex with thin aerial shoots and long, glaucous green leaves; pink to red flowers. Possibly a variety of A. obesum.

Botswana, Namibia

Adenium somalense Balf.f.

APOCYNACEAE

Thick, fleshy caudex with short branches; root thick and swollen above ground; blue-green leaves 6–15 cm long at branch ends; inflorescence with 2–10 white to pink flowers. The photograph shows var. *crispum*.

Kenya, Somalia, Tanzania

Adenium swazicum Stapf

APOCYNACEAE

Large shrub with stems 10–15 cm in diameter buried in the soil; greenish branches bear clusters of leaves to 15 cm long; pink flowers.

Mozambique, South Africa (Transvaal), Swaziland

Adromischus alveolatus Hutchison

CRASSULACEAE

Tuberous root; stem 2–3 cm long; leaves 3–4 cm long and 2 cm wide, grey-green to yellowish-green but variable in colour; inflorescence to 17 cm high. Considered to be a form of A. marianae var. antidorcatum.

South Africa (Cape Province)

Adromischus antidorcadum Poelln.
CRASSULACEAE
Stem branched; dark red to brownish-red leaves 3–4 cm long with greyish-green spots; grey-green inflorescence to 10 cm high. Considered to be a variety of *A. marianae*.
South Africa (Cape Province)

Adromischus cooperi
CRASSULACEAE
The pink flowers borne on the tall inflorescence.

Adromischus caryophyllaceus (Burm.f.) Lem.
CRASSULACEAE
Dwarf shrub; glossy green leaves 4–5 cm long and to 2 cm wide; inflorescence 20–30 cm tall; pink flowers.
South Africa (Cape Province)

Adromischus cristatus (Haw.) Lem.
CRASSULACEAE
Short branching stems; green leaves 2–4 cm long, convex on both sides and covered with soft hairs; inflorescence to 2 cm long; whitish-red flowers.
South Africa (Cape Province)

Adromischus cooperi (Baker) A. Berger
CRASSULACEAE
Short, spreading branches densely covered with truncate leaves, variable in colour; inflorescence to 35 cm tall; pink flowers.
Adromischus cuneatus Poelln.; *A. festivus* C.A. Sm.; *A. halesowensis* Uitewaal
South Africa (Cape Province)

Adromischus herrei (W.F. Barker) Poelln.
CRASSULACEAE
Rootstock thick; no more than 7 red-brown leaves, which are coated with wax and papillae; red flowers. Considered to be a form of *A. marianae* var. *antidorcadum*.
South Africa (Cape Province)

Adromischus humilis (Marloth) Poelln.
CRASSULACEAE
Stemless plants; thick roots; grey leaves 1.5 cm long and 8 mm wide, concave on upper surface and arranged in dense rosettes; red flowers.
South Africa (Cape Province)

Adromischus marianae (Marloth) A. Berger
CRASSULACEAE
Small clumps; flat, dark grey-green to bright brownish-green leaves, 1.5 cm long with brownish markings; green flowers with red tips.
South Africa (Cape Province)

Adromischus kubosensis Uitewaal
CRASSULACEAE
Reddish-brown stems 8–10 cm high and coated with wax; erect, club-shaped leaves, tapering at end, green when young, becoming pruinose with age; purple flowers.
South Africa (Cape Province)

Adromischus rhombifolius (Haw.) Lem.
CRASSULACEAE
Shrub; grey-green leaves 5–9 cm long and 3–5 cm wide, convex on lower surface, cartilaginous margins and short tips; pink flowers.
South Africa (Cape Province)

Adromischus maculatus (Salm-Dyck) Lem.
CRASSULACEAE
Purple-spotted, obovate-spatulate leaves to 5 cm, constricting at base; pink flowers.
South Africa (Transvaal)

Adromischus roaneanus Uitewaal
CRASSULACEAE
Erect, freely branching stems; grey-green leaves 3 cm long with numerous waxy markings; flowers light green with pink tips.
South Africa (Cape Province)

Adromischus tricolor
C.A. Sm.
CRASSULACEAE
Erect stems to 35 cm high, prostrate when longer; green to grey-green leaves 4–8 cm long with purple spots; purplish-red flowers.
South Africa (Cape Province)

Aeonium canariense Webb & Berth.
CRASSULACEAE
Short stems with large, offsetting rosettes to 50 cm in diameter; leaves green, covered with hairs; pale green flowers.
Canary Islands (Tenerife)

Adromischus triflorus (L.f.) A. Berger
CRASSULACEAE
Stems to 10 cm with few branches at base; leaves convex on both sides and pale green with waxy dots; inflorescence to 35 cm; pale pink flowers.
Adromischus procurvus C.A. Sm.; *A. subcompressus* Poelln.; *A. subpetiolaris* Poelln.
South Africa (Cape Province)

Aeonium glandulosum Webb & Berth.
CRASSULACEAE
Rosettes with rhomboidal leaves covered by soft hairs; yellow flowers.
Aeonium meyerheimii Bolle
Madeira

Aeonium arboreum var. atropurpureum (W.A. Nicholson) A. Berger
CRASSULACEAE
Erect stems to 1 m high with dense rosettes 20 cm in diameter; leaves dark purple (light green in the type species); inflorescence to 30 cm tall; yellow flowers.
Canary Islands, Morocco; naturalized (?) in several Mediterranean countries

Aeonium glutinosum (Aiton) A. Berger
CRASSULACEAE
Low shrub with red branches; light green leaves with finely ciliate margins, sometimes with reddish stripes, in open rosettes 5–6 cm in diameter; inflorescence 30 cm tall; yellow to white flowers.
Madeira

Aeonium gomerense Praeger
CRASSULACEAE
Bush to 50 cm high with many side branches; leaves arranged in rosettes 6 cm in diameter; white flowers.
Canary Islands (Gomera)

Aeonium simsii (Sweet) Stearn
CRASSULACEAE
Broad rosettes forming low clumps; leaves green with reddish lines; yellow flowers.
Canary Islands (Tenerife)

Aeonium lindleyi Webb & Berth.
CRASSULACEAE
Hemispherical bush to 30 cm high, with several thin branches ending in small rosette; leaves hairy and light green; yellow flowers.
Canary Islands

Aeonium smithii (Sims) Webb & Berth.
CRASSULACEAE
Branched stems to 60 cm long covered with white hairs; rosettes 10 cm in diameter; green leaves with reddish lines; yellow flowers.
Canary Islands (Tenerife)

Aeonium sedifolium Pit. & Proust
CRASSULACEAE
Bush to 15 cm high; rosettes of green to yellowish-green leaves with red stripes; yellow flowers.
Canary Islands (La Palma, Tenerife)

Aeonium spathulatum Praeger
CRASSULACEAE
Branches to 90 cm high with small rosettes; leaves 3–4 cm long with cartilaginous margins; yellow flowers.
Canary Islands

Aeonium subplanum Praeger
CRASSULACEAE
Similar to *A. canariense* but the rosettes are flatter and to 50 cm in diameter; green, spatulate leaves 30 cm long.
Canary Islands (Gomera)

Aeonium viscatum Bolle
CRASSULACEAE
Stems thin; pale green, sticky leaves 4–5 cm long and 4 mm thick; numerous yellow flowers.
Canary Islands (Gomera)

Aeonium tabulaeforme (Haw.) Webb & Berth.
CRASSULACEAE
Low stems with large rosettes to 50 cm in diameter; leaves green; branching inflorescence to 60 cm high; yellow flowers. The rosette dies after flowering.
Aeonium bertoletianum Bolle; *A. macrolepum* Webb
Canary Islands (Tenerife)

Agave americana var. marginata Trel.
AGAVACEAE
Offsetting, stemless rosettes with 20–30 leaves to 1.4 m long and 25 cm wide, ending in thick spine 3 cm long and with several marginal spines; branching inflorescence to 9 m high; yellow flowers 8–10 cm long. This variety has yellow leaf margins.
Mexico; naturalized in several Mediterranean countries

Aeonium urbicum Webb & Berth
CRASSULACEAE
Stems to 1 m high, branching from base; oblong leaves in rosettes to 25 cm in diameter; greenish-white or whitish-pink flowers borne in large pyramid.
Canary Islands (Tenerife)

Agave americana var. mediopicta Trel.
AGAVACEAE
Variegated form; green leaves have yellowish central stripes.
Mexico

Agave americana var. mediopicta f. alba Hort.

AGAVACEAE

Variegated form with white stripes in centre of leaves.

Mexico

Agave bracteosa S. Watson

AGAVACEAE

Stemless, offsetting rosettes, 80 cm in diameter; yellow-green leaves to 40 cm long, recurved at tip; inflorescence to 2 m tall with numerous white to pale yellow flowers.

Mexico

Agave angustifolia var. marginata Hort.

AGAVACEAE

Stem to 40 cm high with offsets; rosettes 1 m in diameter with several leaves 50–80 cm long and ending in 18 mm long terminal spine; inflorescence to 2.7 m tall. This variety has white leaf margins.

From Costa Rica to Mexico (Sonora)

Agave celsii var. albicans (Jacobi) Gentry

AGAVACEAE

Rosettes of pale green, undulate leaves to 70 cm long and armed with 3 mm long teeth and brown terminal spines 2 cm long; inflorescence 2–3 m tall; yellow to reddish flowers.

A. mitis Jacobi

Mexico

Agave attenuata Salm-Dyck

AGAVACEAE

Stem to 1.5 m high and 10 cm thick; rosettes with 20–25 spineless, glaucous grey to pale yellowish-green leaves 70 cm long; pendent inflorescence to 2 m long; greenish-yellow flowers.

Agave glaucescens Hook.

Mexico

Agave colimana Gentry

AGAVACEAE

Short-stemmed rosettes; green leaves, 50–70 cm long, with brown margins and dark brown terminal spines 8 mm long; inflorescence to 3 m tall; yellow flowers. The specimen illustrated is young. It is sometimes cultivated under the name *A. nigra* or *A. nigrans*.

Mexico

Agave echinoides Jacobi
AGAVACEAE
A small species; rosettes to 30 cm across with numerous leaves, 15 cm long and ending in brown terminal spine; inflorescence to 2 m tall; yellow or red flowers. Gentry considers this to be a synonym of *A. striata*.
Mexico

Agave ferox C. Koch
AGAVACEAE
Stemless rosettes of 20–30 leaves to 1 m long and 35 cm wide with black, marginal spines 2–3 cm long and hooked, terminal spines to 9 cm long; inflorescence to 10 m high; yellow flowers.
Agave coelum Hort.; possibly a variety of *A. salmiana*
Mexico

Agave ellemeetiana Jacobi
AGAVACEAE
Stemless rosettes to 1 m in diameter with few spineless, bright green leaves to 20 cm long; inflorescence to 5 m tall; greenish-yellow flowers.
Mexico

Agave filifera Salm-Dyck
AGAVACEAE
Stemless rosettes to 65 cm in diameter with lateral shoots; numerous shiny green leaves to 25 cm long and 3 cm wide with white lines and filiferous margins; inflorescence to 3 m tall; greenish-yellow flowers.
A. filamentosa Salm-Dyck
Mexico

Agave ferdinandi-regis A. Berger
AGAVACEAE
Small rosettes of folded leaves to 13 cm long with horny stripes in lower part and black, terminal spine 15 mm long; inflorescence to 4 m tall; varicoloured flowers tinged with red or purple. Gentry considers this to be a synonym of *A. victoriae-reginae*.
Mexico   CITES App. II

Agave geminiflora Ker Gawl.
AGAVACEAE
Stemless, branching rosettes of more than 100 leaves to 50 cm long and 5 mm wide with 4 mm long terminal spine and filiferous margins; inflorescence to 4 m high; flowers greenish below, flushed with red above.
Agave angustissima Engelm.
Mexico

Agave ghiesbreghtii C. Koch
AGAVACEAE
Stemless, offsetting rosettes with dark green, strongly armed leaves to 40 cm long; inflorescence to 3 m tall; greenish-brown to purplish flowers.
Mexico

Agave kerchovei Lem.
AGAVACEAE
Rosettes to 70 cm in diameter and 40 cm high; green-grey leaves 30–40 cm long with horny edges and ending in 4 cm long terminal spine; inflorescence 2.5–5 m high; greenish-purple flowers.
Mexico

Agave horrida Lem.
AGAVACEAE
Strongly armed, solitary rosettes; numerous, dark green to yellow-green leaves with grey teeth 1.5 cm long and terminal spine to 4 cm long, grey with darker tip; inflorescence to 2.5 m tall; pale yellow-green flowers.
Mexico

Agave lechuguilla Torr.
AGAVACEAE
Suckering rosettes 50–60 cm in diameter; light green leaves to 30 cm long; inflorescence to 3 m tall; yellow flowers often tinged with red.
Mexico, USA (New Mexico, Texas)

Agave karwinskii Zucc.
AGAVACEAE
Stems to 4 m high; green leaves to 70 cm long and 4 cm wide, with dark brown terminal spine 5 cm long; inflorescence to 6 m high; greenish to pale yellow flowers.
Agave bakeri Ross; *A. coredoray* Baker
Mexico

Agave x leopoldii Hort.
AGAVACEAE
Rosettes with numerous, filiferous leaves 30–40 cm long with 5 mm long terminal spine; inflorescence 2–4 m tall; greenish-yellow flowers. Garden hybrid: *A. filifera* x *A. schidigera*.

Agave lophantha Schiede
AGAVACEAE

Short-stemmed rosettes; pale or yellow-green leaves 50–70 cm long with horny margins and grey-brown terminal spine 2 cm long; inflorescence 3–4 m tall; glaucous green to yellow flowers.

Mexico

Agave macroacantha Zucc.
AGAVACEAE

Stemless or short-stemmed rosettes; leaves can be to 55 cm long (average length 15–30 cm) with 3 cm long terminal spine; inflorescence to 3 m tall; numerous reddish flowers flushed with grey.

Mexico (Oaxaca, Tehuacán)

Agave marmorata Roezl
AGAVACEAE

Stemless rosettes to 2 m in diameter with 30–50 leaves to 1 m long and to 30 cm wide at base, their margins armed with curved spines and terminal spine 2–3 cm long; inflorescence to 6 m tall; golden yellow flowers.

Agave todaroi Baker

Mexico

Agave palmeri Engelm.
AGAVACEAE

Rosettes to 120 cm in diameter; glaucous green or pale green leaves armed with teeth and brown terminal spine 4–6 cm long; inflorescence 4–5 m tall; greenish-yellow flowers.

Mexico, USA (Arizona, New Mexico)

Agave parrasana A. Berger
AGAVACEAE

Dense rosettes 60 cm in diameter, rarely offsetting; blue-grey leaves to 30 cm long and 10–15 cm wide, with terminal spine 2.5 cm long; inflorescence 3–4 m tall; flowers yellow, flushed with red.

A. wislizeni Engelm.

Mexico (Coahuila)

Agave parryi Engelm.
AGAVACEAE

Compact rosettes 50–80 cm in diameter; grey to light green leaves to 30 cm long and 6–10 cm wide; inflorescence 2–3 m tall; greenish-yellow flowers.

Agave chihuahuana Trel.; *A. patoni* Trel.

Mexico, USA (Arizona, New Mexico)

Agave parryi var. couesii Gentry
AGAVACEAE
This variety has broader leaves.
Mexico

Agave potatorum var. verschaffeltii (Lem.) A. Berger
AGAVACEAE
Similar to the type species; whitish-grey leaves with short, red-brown or yellow-brown spines.
Mexico (Oaxaca, Puebla)

Agave parviflora Torr.
AGAVACEAE
Small rosettes 15–25 cm in diameter and 10–15 cm high, with numerous, dark green leaves to 10 cm long with 5 mm long terminal spine and filiferous margins; inflorescence 1–1.5 m tall; pale yellow flowers.
Mexico, USA (Arizona)   CITES App. I

Agave pumila De Smet ex Baker
AGAVACEAE
In the juvenile stage, which may persist for several years, rosettes are 3–4 cm in diameter with 5–8 short, thick leaves. Inflorescence unknown. When cultivated in the ground plants lose their dwarf habit. It could be a hybrid of *A. lechuguilla* Torr.
Mexico

Agave potatorum Zucc.
AGAVACEAE
Rosette with 30–80 glaucous green to white leaves 30 cm long and 11 cm wide at base, armed with sharp spines and terminal spine to 4 cm long; inflorescence 3–6 m tall; light green to yellowish flowers.
Agave saundersii Hook.f.; *A. scolymus* Karw.
Mexico

Agave schidigera Lem.
AGAVACEAE
Solitary rosettes with green or yellowish-green leaves 30–40 cm long and 7 cm wide and with terminal spine 1.5 cm long; inflorescence 3–4 m tall; green to yellow flowers. Considered by Ulrich to be a variety of *A. filifera* Salm-Dyck.
Agave disceptata Drum; *A. vestita* S. Watson
Mexico

Agave sisalana Perrine
AGAVACEAE
Stems to 1 m high, offsetting; green leaves 1.5 m long and 7–8 cm wide with short terminal spine; inflorescence 5–7 m tall; greenish-yellow flowers. Cultivated for fibre production in warm climates.
Mexico

Agave stricta 'Nana'
AGAVACEAE
Offsetting rosettes with several leaves; this cultivar is smaller than the type species; inflorescence not seen.
Garden origin

Agave sp. FO 076
AGAVACEAE
A dwarf species, strongly armed with brown teeth and terminal spine. It is common in cultivation under the name *A. titanota*.
Mexico (Sierra Mixteca)

Agave toumeyana Trel.
AGAVACEAE
Rosettes to 30 cm in diameter with stiff leaves to 25 cm long with filiferous margins and 15 mm terminal spine; inflorescence 1.5–2.5 m tall; whitish-green flowers.
USA (Arizona)

Agave stricta Salm-Dyck
AGAVACEAE
Spherical rosette 60–110 cm in diameter forming thick, branched stem with many leaves; green leaves about 35 cm long, thick at base then narrowing, with terminal spine 2 cm long; inflorescence 2 m tall; red to purplish flowers.
Mexico (Tehuacán)

Agave triangularis Jacobi
AGAVACEAE
Olive-green, deltoid leaves 30–50 cm long with terminal spine 2 cm long and marginal spines 5–7 mm long; leaves variable in size and shape.
Mexico

Agave univittata Haw.
AGAVACEAE

Offsetting rosettes with 30–50 leaves; glossy green leaves to 1 m long with darker longitudinal stripes, marginal hooked spines and 3 cm long terminal spine; inflorescence 4 m tall; light grey-green to yellow flowers. Considered by Gentry to be a synonym of *A. lophanta* Schiede.

Mexico

Agave utahensis var. nevadendis Engelm.
AGAVACEAE

Similar to *A. utahensis* but smaller and with more erect rosettes, 15–25 cm tall.

USA (California, Nevada)

Agave utahensis Engelm.
AGAVACEAE

Rosettes 25–40 cm in diameter with 70–80 grey-green leaves to 17 cm long with noticeable terminal spine; inflorescence to 2.5 m tall; yellow flowers. A hardy species.

USA (Arizona)

Agave victoriae-reginae T. Moore
AGAVACEAE

Solitary, spherical rosettes with numerous green leaves 10–15 cm long with white margins and terminal spine 2 mm long; inflorescence to 4 m tall; vari-coloured flowers, often tinged with red.

Agave consideranti Duch.; *A. nickelsii* R. Gosselin

Mexico   CITES App. II

Agave utahensis var. discreta M.E. Jones
AGAVACEAE

Similar to type species but with slight differences in colour and rosette shape. Although it should be considered a synonym of *A. utahensis*, it is still found in cultivation under the varietal name.

USA (Arizona)

Agave victoriae-reginae x asperrima
AGAVACEAE

Stemless rosettes with numerous grey-green to light green leaves to 18 cm long with terminal spine 4 cm long; inflorescence 2–3 m tall; yellow flowers. A natural hybrid.

Mexico

Agave victoriae-reginae x lechuguilla
AGAVACEAE

A compact hybrid; grey-green leaves with brown teeth and stout terminal spine; inflorescence 2–3 m tall; flowers variable in colour.

Mexico

Agave xylonacantha Salm-Dyck
AGAVACEAE

Short-stemmed rosettes 50–60 cm in diameter; numerous leaves to 20 cm long with 3–4 cm long terminal spines; inflorescence to 4 m tall; greenish to pale yellow flowers.

Agave carchariodontha Pamp.

Mexico

Aichryson bethencourtianum Webb
CRASSULACEAE

Low shrub 20–30 cm high with hairy branches ending in small rosettes; leaves 2 cm long and 1 cm wide; yellow flowers.

Canary Islands

Alluaudia adscendens Drake
DIDIEREACEAE

Thick stems with few branches to 15 m high; thorns 15 mm long; leaves 13–25 mm long and 13–22 mm wide; small, white to reddish flowers borne on 5–10 cm stalk.

Didierea adscendens Drake

Madagascar

CITES App. II

Alluaudia comosa Drake
DIDIEREACEAE

In the juvenile stage this is a shrub, but at maturity it forms a short, thick stem, 1 m high, branching into secondary stems; thorns 3.5 cm long in pairs; leaves 1.5–2 cm long and 1–1.5 cm wide; small, white flowers.

Madagascar   CITES App. II

Alluaudia dumosa Drake
DIDIEREACEAE

A shrub in the juvenile stage but growing to 10 m at maturity, with several ascending branches and few thorns; leaves very small and caducous; whitish flowers.

Madagascar   CITES App. II

41

Alluaudia humbertii Choux

DIDIEREACEAE

Branched shrub to 7 m high; oval leaves 7–15 mm long and 5–10 mm wide, borne in pairs below the thorns; inflorescence 10 cm long; small flowers: male flowers greenish, female flowers white.

Madagascar   CITES App. II

Alluaudia montagnacii Rauh

DIDIEREACEAE

Similar in habit to *A. adscendens* but small, white flowers borne laterally on branches. Possibly a natural hybrid.

Madagascar

CITES App. II

Alluaudia procera Drake

DIDIEREACEAE

Tree 3–15 m tall with few branches armed with conical thorns; ovate leaves to 2.5 cm long and 5–10 mm wide; inflorescence 30 cm long; small yellowish- or whitish-green flowers.

Madagascar

CITES App. II

Aloe albiflora Guill.

LILIACEAE

Stemless rosettes; grey-green leaves to 15 cm long with many white spots; inflorescence 60 cm high; white flowers.

Madagascar   CITES App. II

Aloe aristata Haw.

LILIACEAE

Up to 12 rosettes, each with 100–150 dark green leaves 8 cm long, ending in transparent spinous process and with soft spines, especially on underside; leaf margins with horny teeth; inflorescence to 50 cm tall with several orange-red flowers.

Aloe ellenbergeri Guill.; *A. longiaristata* Roem. & Schult.

South Africa (Cape Province, Natal, Orange Free State)   CITES App. II

Aloe bakeri Scott-Elliot

LILIACEAE

Green leaves 8–10 cm long with white markings and white marginal spines; leaves sometimes tinged with reddish-pink.

Madagascar   CITES App. II

Aloe bellatula Reynolds
LILIACEAE
Rosettes freely suckering from base and forming dense groups; green leaves 15–20 cm long with pale green areas; inflorescence about 50 cm tall; coral-red flowers.
Madagascar   CITES App. II

Aloe bowiea Roem. & Schult.
LILIACEAE
Stemless rosettes; slender, green to pale green leaves with white spots and soft prickles along centre; inflorescence 25 cm tall; greenish flowers.
South Africa (Cape Province)   CITES App. II

Aloe brevifolia Mill.
LILIACEAE
Stemless rosettes 8 cm in diameter with several offshoots from base forming large clumps; leaves 6 cm long and 2 cm wide at base with little white teeth; inflorescence 40 cm tall; pale scarlet flowers.
Aloe prolifera Haw.
South Africa (Cape Province)   CITES App. II

Aloe broomii Schönland
LILIACEAE
Solitary rosettes to 1 m in diameter; leaves bright green with horny edges; inflorescence to 1.5 m tall; yellow flowers.
South Africa (Cape Province)   CITES App. II

Aloe cameronii Hemsl.
LILIACEAE
Stems to 1 m high, branching from base; leaves green to copper-red during dry season, 40–50 cm long, 5–7 cm wide at base and narrowing towards leaf apex, margins armed with teeth 2–3 mm long; inflorescence to 1 m tall; red flowers. Plant photographed in habitat.
Malawi, Mozambique, Zimbabwe

CITES App. II

Aloe ciliaris Haw.
LILIACEAE
Long stems with leaves on terminal portion; leaf base covered with white cartilaginous teeth; red flowers.
South Africa (Cape Province)   CITES App. II

43

Aloe concinna Baker
LILIACEAE

Short-stemmed rosettes; light green leaves 10–15 cm long with white markings and dentate margins; red flowers.

Distribution unknown   CITES App. II

Aloe cooperi Baker
LILIACEAE

Stem to 15 cm long, solitary or offsetting from base; spotted green leaves 30–50 cm long and 6 cm wide at base with cartilaginous margins; inflorescence to 1 m tall; pink flowers.

Aloe. schmidtiana Regel

South Africa (Natal)   CITES App. II

Aloe confusa Engl.
LILIACEAE

Branched stem to 1 m high; spreading leaves, spirally arranged, 20–30 cm long with dentate margins; red flowers.

Tanzania   CITES App. II

Aloe cryptopoda Baker
LILIACEAE

Stemless or short-stemmed rosettes of 20–30 leaves; glossy green leaves to 60 cm long with pinkish marginal teeth; red flowers.

Mozambique, Zambia, Zimbabwe   CITES App. II

Aloe conifera H. Perrier
LILIACEAE

Stemless or short-stemmed rosettes; 15–20 leaves armed with short teeth; inflorescence to 50 cm long; yellow flowers.

Madagascar   CITES App. II

Aloe descoingsii Reynolds
LILIACEAE

Stemless rosette forming dense groups; dull green, recurved leaves 3 cm long and 1.5 cm wide at base with white excrescences giving leaves appearance of being covered with white spots; inflorescence 15 cm tall; scarlet-orange flowers.

Madagascar   CITES App. II

Aloe dichotoma L.f.
LILIACEAE

Dichotomously branching tree to 10 m high and 1 m across; leaves 20–30 cm long arranged in rosettes at ends of branches; yellow flowers. Plant photographed in habitat.

Namibia, South Africa (Cape Province)

CITES App. II

Aloe ferox Mill.
LILIACEAE

Tall, single stems; remains of old leaves persistent; leaves to 1 m long with spiny upper surface; young plants are always spiny; orange-red flowers.

South Africa   CITES App. II

Aloe erinacea Hardy
LILIACEAE

Rosettes forming large clumps; greyish-green, spreading leaves, well armed with black spines, which are white on younger leaves; inflorescence 1 m tall; red flowers.

Namibia   CITES App. II

Aloe gariepensis Pillans
LILIACEAE

Branching stems to 1 m high form small groups; dark green leaves with white spots and horny edges are arranged in rosettes; persistent dry leaves cover stems; inflorescence to 1.2 m tall; yellow flowers.

Aloe gariusana Dinter

Namibia, South Africa (Cape Province)

CITES App. II

Aloe eru A. Berger
LILIACEAE

Branching stems 40–50 cm long; dark green leaves to 50 cm long with white spots and 4–5 mm long marginal teeth; inflorescence 1 m tall; orange flowers.

Aloe abyssinica Baker

Ethiopia   CITES App. II

Aloe globuligemma
Pole-Evans
LILIACEAE

Creeping stems to 50 cm long; bluish leaves 40 cm long with white marginal teeth 1 cm apart; inflorescence 1 m high; yellow flowers.

South Africa (Transvaal)

CITES App. II

Aloe haworthioides Baker
LILIACEAE
Stemless rosettes 3–5 cm in diameter; leaves 4 cm long with terminal spine and marginal spines; inflorescence 30 cm tall; red flowers.
Madagascar   CITES App. II

Aloe hemmingii Reynolds
LILIACEAE
Stemless or short-stemmed rosettes; recurved brownish-green leaves 10–14 cm long and 3 cm wide at base with dull white streaks and marginal spines; inflorescence 35 cm tall; rose-red flowers.
Somalia   CITES App. II

Aloe hereroensis Engl.
LILIACEAE
Short-stemmed rosettes; grey-green leaves 25–35 cm long with scattered spots and red-brown teeth; inflorescence 1–2 m tall; orange to scarlet flowers.
Namibia, South Africa (Cape Province, Orange Free State)

CITES App. II

Aloe hereroensis var. lutea A. Berger
LILIACEAE
A yellow-flowering variety.
Central Namibia

CITES App. II

Aloe humilis (L.) Mill.
LILIACEAE
Offsetting, clump-forming rosettes; green leaves 10 cm long and 10–15 mm wide, tuberculate with whitish teeth; inflorescence 40 cm tall; coral-red flowers.
Aloe. humilis var. *candollei* Mill.; *A. perfoliata* var. *humilis* L.
South Africa (Cape Province)   CITES App. II

Aloe humilis var. echinata (Willd.) Baker
LILIACEAE
A smaller variety with fleshy spines on upper surface of leaves.
Aloe echinata Willd.; *A. tuberculata* Haw.
South Africa (Cape Province)   CITES App. II

Aloe jucunda Reynolds
LILIACEAE
Short-stemmed, dense rosettes 8 cm in diameter; recurved, dark green leaves 4 cm long and 2–5 cm wide with numerous transparent spots and 2 mm long marginal teeth; inflorescence 35 cm tall; pale rose- to coral-pink flowers.
Somalia

CITES App. II

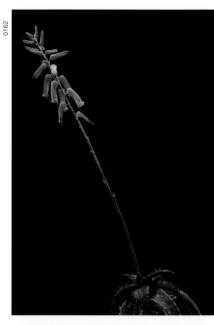

Aloe littoralis Baker
LILIACEAE
Unbranched stem to 4 m high; numerous leaves arranged in rosettes; grey-green leaves to 60 cm long with brown marginal teeth; inflorescence to 1.5 m tall; pink to red flowers. Plant photographed in habitat.
Angola, Botswana, Mozambique, Namibia, South Africa (Transvaal), Zambia

CITES App. II

Aloe melanacantha A. Berger
LILIACEAE
Stemless rosettes; brownish-green leaves to 20 cm long with sharp black thorns (white in younger specimens); inflorescence to 1 m tall; flowers variable in colour.
Namibia   CITES App. II

Aloe microstigma Salm-Dyck
LILIACEAE
Stems, solitary or branched, to 50 cm long and covered with remains of old leaves; leaves 30 cm long and 6 cm wide at base with whitish, H-shaped markings on both surfaces; orange flowers.
Namibia, South Africa (Cape Province)   CITES App. II

Aloe mcloughlinii Christian
LILIACEAE
Stemless or short-stemmed rosettes; green leaves about 40 cm long with numerous pale green markings and marginal teeth; inflorescence 1 m high; red flowers.
Ethiopia   CITES App. II

Aloe millottii Reynolds
LILIACEAE
Stems 20–25 cm long, branched from base; leaves 8–10 cm long and 7 mm wide with white markings and white, cartilaginous, marginal teeth; pink to red flowers.
Madagascar   CITES App. II

Aloe obscura Mill.
LILIACEAE

Short-stemmed rosettes; leaves 20–25 cm long with oblong spots and triangular marginal teeth; inflorescence 20 cm tall; red flowers.

Aloe maculosa Lam.; *A. picta* Thunb.

Namibia   CITES App. II

Aloe pachygaster Dinter
LILIACEAE

Stemless rosettes 20 cm in diameter with spirally arranged grey-green leaves 12–16 cm long with yellow marginal teeth; inflorescence 90 cm tall; red flowers.

Namibia   CITES App. II

Aloe parvula A. Berger
LILIACEAE

Small plants, solitary or forming small groups; bluish-grey, thick and fleshy leaves 10 cm long armed with cartilaginous, white, marginal teeth; reddish flowers.

Aloe sempervivoides H. Perrier

Madagascar   CITES App. II

Aloe plicatilis (L.) Mill.
LILIACEAE

Tree-like species to 5 m high with short, dichotomously branching stems; 10–16 leaves at branch apices; dull green leaves 30 cm long and 4 cm wide with flat margins with slightly cartilaginous edges; inflorescence 50 cm tall; scarlet flowers.

Aloe lingua Thunb.; *A. linguae-formis* L.; *A. tripetala* Medik.

South Africa (Cape Province)

CITES App. II

Aloe ramosissima Pillans
LILIACEAE

Shrubs to 2 m high with freely branching, dichotomous stems covered with waxy white powder; inflorescence 20 cm high; greenish-yellow flowers.

Namibia, South Africa (Cape Province)

CITES App. II

Aloe rauhii Reynolds
LILIACEAE

Stemless or short-stemmed rosettes 10 cm in diameter forming dense groups; grey-green leaves, sometimes with brownish tinge, 10 cm long, 2 cm wide at base and narrowing to acute point at apex with white spots and small marginal spines; inflorescence 30 cm tall; scarlet flowers.

Madagascar   CITES App. II

Aloe saponaria Haw.
LILIACEAE
Stemless rosettes; light green leaves 15–20 cm long with horny, dark brown, marginal teeth; orange flowers.
Lesotho, South Africa (Cape Province, Natal), Zimbabwe   CITES App. II

Aloe squarrosa Baker
LILIACEAE
Thin stems 20 cm long with leaves in loose rosette; green leaves 8 cm long and 2 cm wide with spots and bands and sharp marginal teeth; inflorescence 10–15 cm long; red flowers.
South Yemen (Socotra)   CITES App. II

Aloe somalensis Watson
LILIACEAE
Stemless rosettes of 12–16 leaves; brownish-green leaves about 20 cm long with numerous spots and reddish-brown marginal teeth; pink flowers.
Somalia   CITES App. II

Aloe striata Haw.
LILIACEAE
Stemless rosettes; leaves 40–50 cm long and 10–15 cm wide with white marginal teeth; inflorescence branching; coral-red flowers.
Aloe albo-cincta Haw.; *A. hanburyana* Naudin; *A. paniculata* Jacq.; *A. rhodocincta* Hort.
Namibia   CITES App. II

Aloe spinosissima Hort.
LILIACEAE
A hybrid, *A. humilis* x *A. arborescens*, with stems over 1 m high; leaves 25–30 cm long with horny marginal teeth; orange-red flowers.
     CITES App. II

Aloe striata subsp. karasbergensis Glen & D.S. Hardy
LILIACEAE
Leaves conspicuously veined; flowers paler and tipped with green.
Namibia, South Africa (Cape Province)   CITES App. II

Aloe suprafoliata Pole-Evans
LILIACEAE
Solitary, stemless rosettes; greyish-green or bluish-green leaves. Young plants (like the illustrated specimen) are distichous.
South Africa (Natal, Swaziland)   CITES App. II

Aloe variegata L.
LILIACEAE
Stemless, elongated rosettes to 20 cm high, offsetting and forming dense groups; dark green leaves to 15 cm long and 4 cm wide at base with white spots arranged in bands; inflorescence 30 cm tall; pink flowers.
Aloe punctata Haw.
South Africa (Cape Province)   CITES App. II

Aloe vera L.
LILIACEAE
Plant with short stems, suckering and forming dense groups; green leaves to 50 cm long with or without white spots; yellow flowers. Long known in cultivation for its pharmaceutical properties.
Aloe barbadensis Mill.; *A. indica* Royle; *A. lanzae* Tod.; *A. vulgaris* Lam.
Canary Islands, Cape Verde Islands; widely naturalized in temperate regions
                                       CITES App. II

Aloinopsis hilmari L. Bol.
MESEMBRYANTHEMACEAE
Large taproot; branches with 2–4 leaves, forming clumps to 7 cm in diameter; grey-green, erect leaves 2 cm long and 1 cm wide; yellow flowers 3 cm in diameter.
Cheiridopsis hilmari L. Bol.
South Africa (Cape Province)

Aloinopsis luckhoffii L. Bol.
MESEMBRYANTHEMACEAE
Large taproot; bluish-green leaves 20 cm long with triangular apex and greyish tubercles; yellow flowers 2.5 cm in diameter.
Titanopsis luckhoffii L. Bol.; *Nananthus luckhoffii* L. Bol.
South Africa (Cape Province)

Aloinopsis malherbei L. Bol.
MESEMBRYANTHEMACEAE
Erect, lanceolate, glaucous green leaves 2 cm long covered with small tubercles more evident at margins; yellow flowers 2.5 cm in diameter.
Nananthus malherbei L. Bol.
South Africa (Calvinia District)

Aloinopsis orpenii (N.E. Br.) L. Bol.
MESEMBRYANTHEMACEAE
Dense clumps of bluish-green leaves 15–20 cm long with dark dots; yellow flowers 3.5 cm in diameter.
Nananthus orpenii L. Bol.
South Africa (Cape Province)

Ammocharis coranica Herb.
AMARYLLIDACEAE
Ovoid bulb to 20 cm in diameter; 5–20 striated leaves, ranging in length from 10 to 80 cm; inflorescence to 35 cm tall; pink flowers.
Amaryllis coranica Ker Gawl.
Angola, Namibia, Zimbabwe

Aloinopsis schooneesii L. Bol.
MESEMBRYANTHEMACEAE
Small plants with tuberous roots and small, bluish-green leaves; silky, yellowish-red flowers 1–2 cm in diameter.
Nananthus schooneesii L. Bol.
South Africa (Cape Province)

Anacampseros albissima Marloth
PORTULACACEAE
Several thin stems 40 cm high with tuberous root; small leaves covered by papery, white stipules; white flowers.
Namibia   CITES App. II

Aloinopsis setifera L. Bol.
MESEMBRYANTHEMACEAE
Rosettes 2–3 cm wide forming clumps; leaves 2 cm long, triangular at end and covered with small white tubercles, upper part with 5–10 teeth 1 mm long; yellow flowers 2.5 cm in diameter.
Titanopsis setifera L. Bol.
South Africa (Cape Province)

Anacampseros alstonii Schönland
PORTULACACEAE
Caudex to 6 cm in diameter with numerous branches 2 cm long; leaves in rows covered with silvery stipules; white flowers.
Namibia   CITES App. II

Anacampseros buderiana Poelln.
PORTULACACEAE

Tuberous root with many prostrate branches 30 cm long and 6 mm thick; leaves covered by white stipules; white flowers.

Namibia/South Africa (Namaqualand)   CITES App. II

Anacampseros densifolia Dinter
PORTULACACEAE

Branching plants with stems to 5 cm long; obovate leaves to 8 mm long with hairs from axils; pink flowers.

Namibia   CITES App. II

Anacampseros comptonii Pillans
PORTULACACEAE

Small caudex 1–2 cm in diameter with short branches bearing 2–4 opposite leaves 3–5 cm long and covered with white hairs; red flowers.

Namibia, South Africa (Cape Province)   CITES App. II

Anacampseros filamentosa (Haw.) Sims
PORTULACACEAE

Tuberous root with stem to 5 cm long; thick leaves ovoid to spherical 6–10 mm long with long white hairs; pink flowers.

Anacampseros intermedia G. Nicholson

Namibia, South Africa (Cape Province)   CITES App. II

Anacampseros crinita Dinter
PORTULACACEAE

Stems with small branches 8 cm long and 1 cm thick; light green leaves 4 mm long covered with hairs to 15 mm long; flowers carmine with white margins.

Namibia/South Africa (Namaqualand)   CITES App. II

Anacampseros papyracea E. Mey.
PORTULACACEAE

Tuberous root with many prostrate branches 5 cm long and 1 cm thick; leaves completely hidden by white hairs; white flowers.

Namibia/South Africa (Namaqualand), South Africa (Karoo)   CITES App. II

Anacampseros retusa Poelln.

PORTULACACEAE

Branches to 4 cm long; rosettes of compressed, hairy, brownish leaves 1.5 cm long; pink flowers.

South Africa (Cape Province)　　　　　CITES App. II

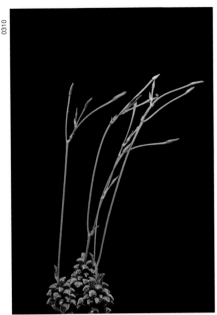

Anacampseros tomentosa A. Berger

PORTULACACEAE

Brownish-green leaves, ovate to roundish and to 2 cm long, with few hairs; inflorescence 15 cm tall; pink flowers.

Anacampseros poelnitziana Dinter

Namibia

CITES App. II

Anacampseros rufescens (Haw.) Sweet

PORTULACACEAE

Tuberous root; dichotomously branched stems 5–10 cm long; green leaves 2 cm long with reddish lower surface and covered with bristly hairs; pink flowers.

Anacampseros arachnoides Hort.

South Africa (Cape Province)　　　　　CITES App. II

Argyroderma fissum (Haw.) L. Bol.

MESEMBRYANTHEMACEAE

Leaves 3–5 cm long, forming clumps; older plants form short stems; red flowers.

South Africa (Cape Province)

Anacampseros telephiastrum DC.

PORTULACACEAE

Several stems to 5 cm high arising from thickened root; green or brownish leaves 1 cm long and 8 mm wide, covered with bristly hairs; pink flowers.

South Africa (Cape Province)　　　　　CITES App. II

Argyroderma schuldtii Schwantes

MESEMBRYANTHEMACEAE

Solitary plants; leaves 1–2 cm long and 3 cm wide, rounded at apex; pink flowers.

South Africa (Cape Province)

53

Argyroderma subalbum (N.E. Br.) N.E. Br.
MESEMBRYANTHEMACEAE
Whitish leaves 1.5–2 cm long and wide borne in pairs with short stems, forming clumps with age; white flowers.
South Africa (Cape Province)

Astridia hallii L. Bol.
MESEMBRYANTHEMACEAE
Shrub to 30 cm high; leaves 5–8 cm long and 3 cm in diameter narrowed towards tip; white flowers.
Namibia

Argyroderma testiculare (Aiton) N.E. Br.
MESEMBRYANTHEMACEAE
Pairs of equal sized green to yellow-green or glaucous green leaves 2–3 cm long; white or purple flowers.
South Africa (Cape Province)

Astridia velutina var. lutata L. Bol.
MESEMBRYANTHEMACEAE
Shrub to 30 cm high; arcuate leaves 3–3.5 cm long; white flowers. Type species has grey-green leaves; this variety has yellowish leaves.
Namibia

Aspazoma amplectens (L. Bol.) N.E. Br.
MESEMBRYANTHEMACEAE
Shrubs to 15 cm high; leaves 1–3 m long; yellow flowers.
South Africa (Cape Province)

Astroloba pentagona (Haw.) Uitewaal
LILIACEAE
Rosette to 8 cm in diameter; stem about 25 cm high; light green, triangular leaves to 4 cm long; yellow flowers.
Haworthia pentagona Haw.
South Africa (Cape Province)

Bergeranthus glenensis N.E. Br.

MESEMBRYANTHEMACEAE

Freely branching plant with stems 5 cm long; leaves 3–4 cm long with dark green dots; yellowish flowers.

South Africa (Orange Free State)

Bergeranthus scapiger (Haw.) N.E. Br.

MESEMBRYANTHEMACEAE

Green leaves to 12 cm long and with cartilaginous edges, borne in pairs; yellow flowers.

South Africa (Cape Province)

Biilja cana N.E. Br.

MESEMBRYANTHEMACEAE

Rosettes of 4–6 leaves 3 cm long and 1.2 cm wide; yellow flowers 3.5 cm in diameter.

South Africa (Cape Province)

Bombax ellipticum
H.B. & K.

BOMBACACEAE

Tree with clavate to spherical, large, grey-brown caudex covered with leaf-scars; several short stems arise from tuberous caudex; caducous, cordate, green leaves 8–15 cm long appear in late spring and fall in autumn (dry season); purplish flowers.

Mexico

Boussingaultia cordifolia Ten.

BASELLACEAE

Tuberous root; twining stems to 6 m; green leaves 10 cm long and 2.5 cm wide; white flowers.

Anredera cordifolia (Ten.) Steenis

Argentina

Bowiea volubilis Harv.

LILIACEAE

Large, light green, spherical bulbs to 30 cm in diameter, producing long, twining shoots; short, caducous, green leaves; greenish-white flowers 8 mm long.

Schizobasopsis volubilis J.F. Macbr.

Southern Africa

Brachychiton rupestris
Schum.

STERCULIACEAE

Bottle-shaped tree; leaves digitate on young plants, simple on mature trees; cultivated as caudiciform plant.

Australia (Queensland)

Brachystelma circinatum
E. Mey.

ASCLEPIADACEAE

Caudex to 13 cm in diameter; stems 25 cm long branching from base; caducous leaves 10–20 cm long; flowers of variable colour borne in clusters.

Namibia, South Africa (Cape Province)

Brachystelma barberae Harv. ex Hook.

ASCLEPIADACEAE

Flat caudex 10 cm or more in diameter; short stems with caducous leaves 10–20 cm long; malodorous, dirty purple flowers with yellow centres.

South Africa (Cape Province, Natal, Transvaal), Zimbabwe

Brachystelma dinteri Schltr.

ASCLEPIADACEAE

Caudex 3–5 cm in diameter; stems to 20 cm long; hairy, pale green, caducous leaves 4 cm long and 1–2 mm wide; brown flowers.

South Africa (Cape Province)

Brachystelma brevipedicellatum
Turrill

ASCLEPIADACEAE

Tuber 5–6 cm in diameter; 2–4 stems to 10 cm long; caducous, green leaves 2–4 cm long and 1–2 cm wide with hairs on lower surface only; flowers brown.

South Africa (Transvaal)

Brachystelma pygmaeum (Schltr.) N.E. Br.

ASCLEPIADACEAE

Caudex napiform (turnip-shaped) with flattened apex; stems 5–10 cm long; caducous, green leaves 2 cm long; yellow flowers.

South Africa (Transvaal)

Brachystelma swazicum R.A. Dyer

ASCLEPIADACEAE

Caudex 5–8 cm in diameter with 2–3 prostrate stems to 30 cm long; caducous, green leaves 2 cm long and wide with reddish lower surface; dark purple flowers.

South Africa (Transvaal), Swaziland

Bulbine margarethae L.I. Hall

LILIACEAE

Caudex 2–4 cm in diameter, offsetting; erect, light green leaves 3–5 cm long; yellow flowers.

South Africa (Cape Province)

Bulbine sp.

LILIACEAE

Caudex to 2 cm in diameter; green leaves 1–4 cm long and spirally arranged; inflorescence 15 cm tall; yellow flowers.

Namibia, South Africa (Cape Province)

Bursera fagaroides var. elongata McVaugh & Rzed.

BURSERACEAE

Shrub or small tree to 5 m high; bark of trunk pale reddish-orange; pinnate leaves 5–7 cm long; white flowers.

Bursera odorata Brandegee

Mexico

Bursera hindsiana (Benth.) Engl.

BURSERACEAE

Small tree to 3 m high with reddish bark on trunk; younger branches reddish; green, oval leaves 4.5 cm long with rounded tips; white flowers.

Mexico (Baja California)

Bursera microphylla (Rose) A. Gray.

BURSERACEAE

Freely branching shrub or tree 2–5 m high (to 10 m in Mexico), covered with papery, white bark; leaflets in pairs of 8–18; leaves 5–10 cm long and 1–2 mm wide; white flowers in small clusters.

Mexico, USA (California)

Calibanus hookeri Trel.
AGAVACEAE

Hemispherical caudex 40–50 cm in diameter and covered with corky bark; several branches bearing grass-like leaves 40 cm long; branched inflorescence to 60 cm tall; insignificant pinkish-purple flowers.

Calibanus caespitosum Rose

Mexico (Jaumave)

Callisia repens L.
COMMELINACEAE

Creeping stems forming mats; glabrous, variable leaves to 4 cm long and 1–2 cm wide; spike-like inflorescence; small white flowers.

USA (Texas), West Indies to Argentina

Caralluma burchardii N.E. Br.
ASCLEPIADACEAE

Olive-green or grey-green, 4-angled stems 20–40 cm long; small, caducous leaves; reddish-brown flowers borne in clusters.

Canary Islands, Morocco

Caralluma dummeri (N.E. Br.) A.C. White & Sloane
ASCLEPIADACEAE

Roundish or 4-angled stem 10 cm long; grey-green teeth 1.5 cm long and 5 mm wide at base with red stripes; olive-green, hairy flowers borne on short stalks. Transferred by M.G. Gilbert to the genus *Pachycymbium*.

Stapelia dummeri N.E. Br.

Kenya, Tanzania, Uganda

Caralluma europaea (Guss.) N.E. Br.
ASCLEPIADACEAE

Grey-green, 4-angled branches 1–2 cm thick with reddish spots; small, caducous leaves; 6–10 red-brown flowers with yellow stripes.

Stapelia europaea Guss.

Algeria, Italy (Lampedusa Island), Morocco, southern Spain, Tunisia

Caralluma europaea (Guss.) N.E. Br.
ASCLEPIADACEAE

A flowering stem, photographed in habitat.

Caralluma europaea
(Guss.) N.E. Br.
ASCLEPIADACEAE
A mature follicle releasing seeds.

Caralluma hesperidum Maire
ASCLEPIADACEAE
Green, 4-angled stems, branching from base and with spine-like teeth; purple-brown flowers. Transferred by M.G. Gilbert to the genus *Pachycymbium*.
Caralluma commutata subsp. *hesperidium* (Maire) Maire
Morocco

Caralluma luntii N.E. Br.
ASCLEPIADACEAE
Grey to green, 4-angled stems 10–20 cm high with red dots and conical teeth; flowers greenish-yellow at base and brown above. Transferred by M.G. Gilbert to the genus *Pachycymbium*.
South Yemen

Caralluma petraea
Lavranos
ASCLEPIADACEAE
Freely branching, 4-angled, green stems to 20 cm high and 10–15 mm thick with rounded teeth; small, caducous green leaves; flowers dark brown or yellowish with brown dots.
Saudi Arabia, Yemen

Caralluma priogonium
Schum.
ASCLEPIADACEAE
Brown stems 20–50 cm long with 4 acute angles bearing sharp teeth; leaves to 4 mm long; flowers purple with white spots.
Caralluma elata Chiov.
Ethiopia, Kenya, Somalia, Tanzania, Uganda

Caralluma socotrana
(Balf.f.) N.E. Br.
ASCLEPIADACEAE
Freely branching, 4-angled, erect, glaucous grey to reddish stems 15 cm high with deltoid teeth; dark red flowers.
Caralluma corrugata N.E. Br.; *C. rivae* Chiov.
Ethiopia, Kenya, Somalia, South Yemen (Socotra)

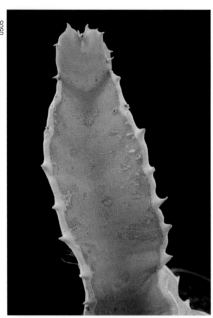

Caralluma speciosa
(N.E. Br.) N.E. Br.

ASCLEPIADACEAE

Clump-forming, 4-angled stems to 1 m high; dark brown flowers 5 cm in diameter with orange to yellow tubes.

Caralluma codonoides K. Schum.

Ethiopia, Kenya, Somalia, Sudan, Tanzania, Uganda

Caralluma turneri
E.A. Bruce.

ASCLEPIADACEAE

Branching, intensely green stems with purple spots to 50 cm long; several inflorescences bearing clusters of 2–4 brown flowers.

Caralluma dicapuae subsp. *turneri* (E.A. Bruce) P.R.O. Bally

Ethiopia, Kenya, Uganda

Caralluma stalagmifera
C. Fisch

ASCLEPIADACEAE

Erect, 4-angled stems 5 mm thick with angular branches; dark red flowers with hairs.

India

Caralluma ubomboensis
I. Verd.

ASCLEPIADACEAE

Branching and clump-forming green stems 4–5 cm long with 4 dentate angles; small, erect leaves; dark purple flowers. Transferred by M.G. Gilbert (1990) to the genus *Pachycymbium*.

South Africa (Natal, Transvaal), Zimbabwe

Caralluma stalagmifera C. Fisch

ASCLEPIADACEAE

A flowering stem.

Carruanthus peersii L. Bol.

MESEMBRYANTHEMACEAE

Short, branched stems; leaves 5 cm long and narrowed towards apex with few teeth on margins; yellow flowers.

South Africa (Cape Province)

Cephalopentandra ecirrhosa (Chiov.) C. Jeffrey
CUCURBITACEAE

Tuberous root with climbing stems; elliptical leaves 3–9 cm long; yellow flowers.

Ethiopia, Kenya, Uganda

Cephalophyllum numeesense
H.E.K. Hartmann

MESEMBRYANTHEMACEAE

Short stems; grey-green, cylindrical, erect leaves 6–8 cm long, united at base to form spherical body; yellow flowers.

South Africa (Cape Province)

Cephalophyllum regale L. Bol.
MESEMBRYANTHEMACEAE

Low-growing plant with elongated branches; leaves 7–10 cm long and 8 mm wide are borne in pairs; purple-pink flowers.

South Africa (Cape Province)

Ceraria namaquensis (Sonder) Pearson & Stephens
PORTULACACEAE

Shrub to 2 m high with numerous grey-white branches, covered with small, succulent leaves; white flowers.

Namibia

Ceraria pygmaea (Pillans) Pillans
PORTULACACEAE

Branched shrub to 20 cm high; stem woody at base; fleshy, dichotomous branches; leaves 1.5 cm long and 4 mm thick; inflorescence with small white flowers with pink outer petals.

South Africa (Cape Province)

Cerochlamys pachyphylla L. Bol.
MESEMBRYANTHEMACEAE

Stemless, clump-forming leaves 6 cm long in 2 pairs; purple-red flowers.
South Africa (Cape Province)

Ceropegia africana R. Br.
ASCLEPIADACEAE
Small tubers with trailing, proliferous stems; leaves 2 cm long; green flowers with hairs inside.
South Africa (Cape Province)   CITES App. II

Ceropegia bulbosa Roxb.
ASCLEPIADACEAE
Tuberous roots; thin, twining stems; green leaves with white marbling 2–8 cm long; flowers greenish in basal part and purple above.
West Indies   CITES App. II

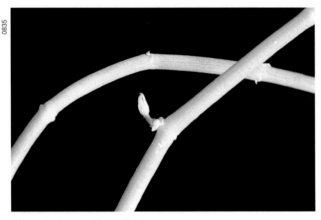

Ceropegia ampliata E. Mey.
ASCLEPIADACEAE
Fusiform roots with thin, leafless, grey-green stems to 2 m long; pale green flowers with transverse purple band inside.
South Africa (Cape Province)   CITES App. II

Ceropegia conrathii
Schltr.
ASCLEPIADACEAE
Tuberous roots to 10 cm in diameter and 2–7 cm high, with several stems 10–15 cm long; leaves 3 cm long and 1 cm wide; yellowish-brown flowers.
South Africa (Natal, Transvaal)

CITES App. II

Ceropegia armandii Rauh
ASCLEPIADACEAE
Erect or prostrate green stems 10–15 cm long and 2 cm thick, with black spots; caducous leaves 5–7 mm long; grey-green flowers.
Madagascar   CITES App. II

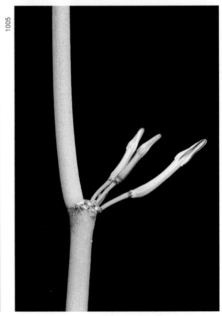

Ceropegia dichotoma
Haw.
ASCLEPIADACEAE
Dichotomously branching stems to 1 m tall; erect, linear, grey-green leaves to 4 cm long and 2–3 mm wide; yellow flowers with lobes remaining attached.
Ceropegia hians Svent.
Canary Islands (Tenerife)

CITES App. II

Ceropegia dimorpha Humbert

ASCLEPIADACEAE

Erect, green stem 15 cm tall and 15 mm thick; green leaves to 3.5 cm long; purplish-white flowers.

Madagascar

CITES App. II

Ceropegia linearis subsp. debilis (N.E. Br.) H.Huber

ASCLEPIADACEAE

A flowering stem.

Ceropegia fusca Bolle

ASCLEPIADACEAE

Erect stems to 1 m high with several spreading, greyish or purplish, cylindrical branches; leaves 4 cm long and 3 mm wide borne only during growing season; brown flowers.

Canary Islands   CITES App. II

Ceropegia multiflora Baker

ASCLEPIADACEAE

Tubers 10 cm in diameter; twining stems to 90 cm long die back each year; leaves 3 cm long; greenish flowers.

South Africa (Transvaal)   CITES App. II

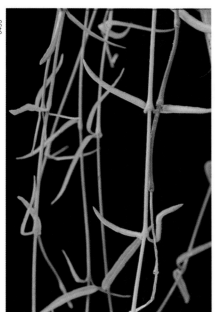

Ceropegia linearis subsp. debilis (N.E. Br.) H. Huber

ASCLEPIADACEAE

Twining, pendent stems forming tubers at nodes; linear leaves 3 cm long and 3 mm wide; flowers greenish outside with dark purple-brown lobes.

Ceropegia debilis N.E. Br.

South Africa (Cape Province), Zimbabwe

CITES App. II

Ceropegia nilotica Kotschy

ASCLEPIADACEAE

Twining stems to 1 m or longer, 4-angled or roundish with thickened nodes; dentate, ovate leaves tapering gradually; dark brown flowers.

Kenya, Sudan   CITES App. II

Ceropegia pachystelma Schltr.
ASCLEPIADACEAE
Tuber 10 cm in diameter; stems twining; broad, fleshy leaves 1–3 cm long; yellow-green flowers.
Mozambique, Namibia, South Africa (Natal, Transvaal) CITES App. II

Ceropegia stapeliiformis Haw.
ASCLEPIADACEAE
Succulent, trailing, rounded stems to 1.5 m long and 15 mm thick; small leaves; brownish flowers with whitish spots.
South Africa (Cape Province) CITES App. II

Ceropegia radicans Schltr.
ASCLEPIADACEAE
Creeping stems; elliptical, succulent leaves 1–2 cm long; pale greenish-white flowers.
South Africa (Cape Province) CITES App. II

Ceropegia woodii Schltr.
ASCLEPIADACEAE
Creeping, filamentous branches with tubers at nodes; dark green, heart-shaped leaves with white marks; brown flowers. Some authors consider this to be a variety of *C. linearis* E. Mey.
South Africa (Natal), Zimbabwe CITES App. II

Ceropegia sandersonii Decne. ex Hook.f.
ASCLEPIADACEAE
Succulent, twining stems; leaves 4–5 cm long and 3 cm wide; green flowers.
Mozambique, South Africa (Natal, Transvaal) CITES App. II

Cheiridopsis acuminata L. Bol.
MESEMBRYANTHEMACEAE
Stem to 1 cm thick with 2–3 pairs of leaves 5–7 cm long; yellow flowers.
South Africa (Cape Province)

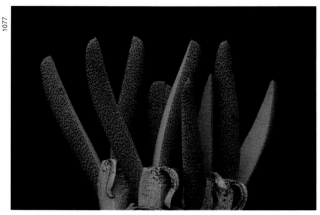

Cheiridopsis bibracteata (Haw.) N.E. Br.
MESEMBRYANTHEMACEAE
Stemless plants; leaves to 8 cm long and united at base; yellow flowers.
South Africa (Cape Province)

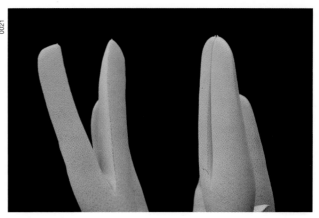

Cheiridopsis candidissima (Haw.) N.E. Br.
MESEMBRYANTHEMACEAE
One of the largest species of the genus with branches 20–30 cm long and 2 cm in diameter; stems to 9 cm long and 1 cm in diameter; whitish-grey leaves 8–10 cm long limited to 1 pair to each stem; white flowers.
Namibia, South Africa (Cape Province)

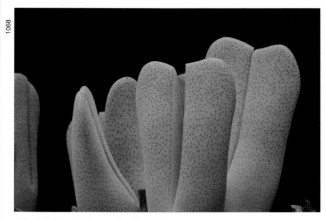

Cheiridopsis borealis L. Bol.
MESEMBRYANTHEMACEAE
Clumps of 4-leaved branches; leaves to 3 cm long and united at base; yellow flowers.
Namibia

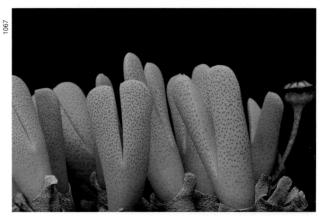

Cheiridopsis caroli-schmidthii (Dinter & A. Berger) N.E. Br.
MESEMBRYANTHEMACEAE
Stems with several pairs of leaves united at base, leaf pairs being of unequal length; light green leaves 2–3 cm and with darker spots; yellow flowers.
Namibia

Cheiridopsis brownii Tischer
MESEMBRYANTHEMACEAE
Clumps 5–10 cm in diameter; green leaves 3–5 cm long with darker green dots, united to form body; yellow flowers.
South Africa (Cape Province)

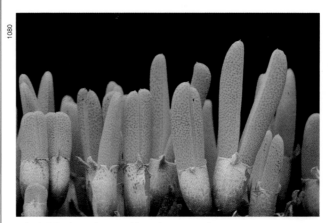

Cheiridopsis cigarettifera (A.Berger) N.E. Br.
MESEMBRYANTHEMACEAE
Stems with 2–4 pairs of leaves of unequal size, the longest pair being 3–6 cm long; leaves grey-green or green with translucent spots; yellow flowers.
South Africa (Cape Province)

Cheiridopsis cuprea (L. Bol.) N.E. Br.
MESEMBRYANTHEMACEAE
Large clumps of stems with 2 pairs of greenish leaves 3–4 cm long and united at base; flowers yellow.
South Africa (Cape Province)

Cheiridopsis meyeri var. minor N.E. Br.
MESEMBRYANTHEMACEAE
Similar to the type species but smaller.
South Africa (Cape Province)

Cheiridopsis inspersa (N.E. Br.) N.E. Br.
MESEMBRYANTHEMACEAE
Stemless leaves, glaucous or tinged with purple, 5–7 cm long and united for one-third of their length to form body; yellow flowers.
South Africa (Cape Province)

Cheiridopsis peculiaris N.E. Br.
MESEMBRYANTHEMACEAE
Small plants; grey-green leaves with darker dots borne in 2 pairs; yellow flowers.
Namibia/South Africa (Little Namaqualand)

Cheiridopsis meyeri N.E. Br.
MESEMBRYANTHEMACEAE
Small plants; grey-green leaves with darker dots borne in 2 pairs; yellow flowers.
Namibia/South Africa (Little Namaqualand)

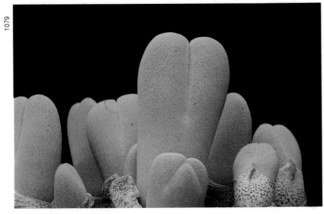

Cheiridopsis pillansii L. Bol.
MESEMBRYANTHEMACEAE
Short, clump-forming stems; stems with 1–2 pairs of leaves 3–4 cm long and united for one-third of their length; grey-green leaves with darker spots; yellow flowers.
South Africa (Cape Province)

Cheiridopsis pulverulenta L. Bol.

MESEMBRYANTHEMACEAE

Short branches with 2 pairs of pale green leaves covered with minute papillae; yellow flowers.

South Africa (Cape Province)

Cheiridopsis rostrata (L.) N.E. Br.

MESEMBRYANTHEMACEAE

Stemless plants with 4–6 unequally sized, grey- or blue-green leaves with darker spots; leaves 4–5 cm long and 17 mm wide, united at base for 9 mm; yellow flowers.

South Africa (Cape Province)

Cheiridopsis purpurea N.E. Br.

MESEMBRYANTHEMACEAE

Stems with grey- to blue-green leaves to 6 cm long; yellow flowers.

Namibia/South Africa (Little Namaqualand)

Cheiridopsis truncata L. Bol.

MESEMBRYANTHEMACEAE

Plant growing in clumps with branches consisting of 1–2 pairs of opposite, glaucous leaves, to 4 cm long and 1 cm wide; yellow flowers.

South Africa (Cape Province)

Cheiridopsis robusta (Haw.) N.E. Br.

MESEMBRYANTHEMACEAE

Short stems with 4 velvety, unequal sized leaves 4–5 cm long; yellow flowers.
South Africa (Cape Province)

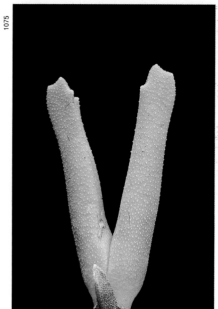

Cheiridopsis umdauensis L. Bol.

MESEMBRYANTHEMACEAE

Elongated branches 13 mm long with 1–2 pairs of green leaves 3–4 cm long and united at base; leaf apex bears few teeth.

South Africa (Cape Province)

67

Chorisia insignis Kunth
BOMBACACEAE

Tree to 15 m tall; bottle-shaped, spineless trunk to 2 m in diameter; leaves 10–15 cm long; white to yellow flowers. Seedlings are cultivated for their caudiciform appearance.

Argentina

Cissus cactiformis Gilg
VITACEAE

Climbing 4- or 5-angled stems 4–5 cm in diameter; stems winged and constricted at nodes from which adventitious roots develop; leaves caducous; inflorescence 20 cm long; yellowish-green flowers.

Southern and tropical Africa

Cissus olearacea L. Bol.
VITACEAE

Subterranean rhizomes to 10 cm in diameter forming several tubers; numerous stems to 60 cm long; leaves 20 cm long and 15 cm wide; inflorescence branched; greenish flowers with pink tips.

Southern Africa

Cissus quadrangularis L.
VITACEAE

Succulent, 4-angled, climbing stems, much branched and winged; stems constricted at nodes; leaves borne on growing portions of the stems; inflorescence 5 cm long; green to yellow flowers.

Tropical Africa, southern Asia, Malaysia

Cissus quinquangularis Chiov.
VITACEAE

Similar to *C. quadrangularis* but with 5-angled stems and larger, caducous leaves.

Somalia

Cissus rotundifolia (Forssk.) Vahl
VITACEAE

Thin, cylindrical, 4- or 5-angled stems; thick, fleshy leaves 4–6 cm long; small, greenish flowers.

East Africa to Yemen

Cissus sicoydes L.

VITACEAE

Climbing stem; large leaves deep green above, paler beneath; inflorescence about 5 cm long; yellow or white flowers.
Wide distribution: central Africa, Ecuador (Galapagos Islands), Mexico

Commiphora sp.

BURSERACEAE

Thick, tuberous caudex with erect branches; small, bilobate leaves.
Namibia

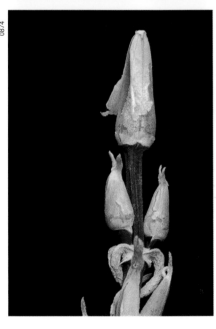

Conophyllum dissitum
(N.E. Br.) Schwantes

MESEMBRYANTHEMACEAE

Brown stem to 30 cm tall; 2 types of leaves: 1 type united to form fleshy, conical body 2–4 cm long, the other type united at base and 2–4 cm long, narrowing towards tips, both types grey-green with remains of old leaves; pink flowers.

Mitrophyllum dissitum (N.E. Br.) N.E. Br.

South Africa (Cape Province)

Conophyllum framesii
(L. Bol.) L. Bol.

MESEMBRYANTHEMACEAE

Similar to *C. dissitum* but with shorter stems and leaves.
Mitrophyllum framesii L. Bol.
South Africa (Cape Province)

Conophyllum obtusipetalum L. Bol.

MESEMBRYANTHEMACEAE

Stems 30–40 cm high; leaves to 9 cm long and covered with remains of old leaves; white flowers.
South Africa (Cape Province)

Conophyllum proximus (N.E. Br.) Schwantes

MESEMBRYANTHEMACEAE

Stems 20–30 cm high; 2 types of leaves: 1 type 3–7 cm long and almost completely united, the other type united at base and 2–6 cm long, narrowing towards apex, both types light green and covered with remains of old leaves; yellow flowers.
Mitrophyllum proximus N.E. Br.
South Africa (Cape Province)

Conophytum apiatum (N.E. Br.) N.E. Br.
MESEMBRYANTHEMACEAE
Elongated body to 4 cm long, separated above into 2 lobes; body whitish-green with dark green spots; flowers yellow. Probably a variant of *C. bilobum* N.E. Br.
Namibia/South Africa (Little Namaqualand)

Conophytum avenantii L. Bol.
MESEMBRYANTHEMACEAE
Obconical bodies 1.5–2 cm in diameter, narrowing below; bodies pale green or blue-green scattered with grey dots and covered with persistent sheath; white flowers with long tube.
South Africa (Cape Province)

Conophytum areolatum Littlew.
MESEMBRYANTHEMACEAE
Small bodies with opaque windows and ciliate fissures; white to pink flowers. Similar to *C. pellucidum* Schwantes.
Namibia/South Africa (Little Namaqualand)

Conophytum burgeri L. Bol.
MESEMBRYANTHEMACEAE
Pale green to deep purple-red, globose bodies 1–2 cm in diameter, with base broader than apex and with persistent, whitish sheath; pink flowers.
Namibia/South Africa (Little Namaqualand)

Conophytum astylum L. Bol.
MESEMBRYANTHEMACEAE
Green to brownish-green bodies 10–15 mm long, with numerous small dots; whitish-pink flowers.
South Africa (Cape Province)

Conophytum catervum N.E. Br.
MESEMBRYANTHEMACEAE
Obconical bodies 2 cm high and 1 cm in diameter forming dense mats; bodies light green with reddish lower part and spotted top; yellow flowers. Hammer ascribes this species to *C. viridicatum* N.E. Br.
South Africa (Cape Province)

Conophytum concavum L. Bol.
MESEMBRYANTHEMACEAE
Up to 8 subconical bodies in clump; soft, velvety bodies 2–3 cm in diameter and 1.5 cm high; white flowers.
South Africa (Cape Province)

Conophytum ectypum N.E. Br.
MESEMBRYANTHEMACEAE
Pale green bodies to 1 cm in diameter forming flat clusters with age; white flowers.
South Africa (Cape Province)

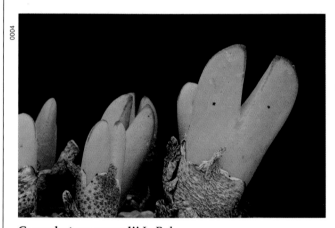

Conophytum conradii L. Bol.
MESEMBRYANTHEMACEAE
Compact plants with elongated bodies to 3.5 cm long and 9 mm wide; yellow flowers. Hammer ascribes this species to *C. bilobum* (Marloth) N.E. Br.
South Africa (Cape Province)

Conophytum elishae
(N.E. Br.) N.E. Br.
MESEMBRYANTHEMACEAE
Compressed, pale green bodies less than 1 cm in diameter, free only at tips; yellow flowers. Possibly a variety of *C. bilobum* N.E. Br.
South Africa (Cape Province)

Conophytum dispar N.E. Br.
MESEMBRYANTHEMACEAE
Obconical bodies to 1 cm in diameter, green with dark green dots; white flowers.
South Africa (Cape Province)

Conophytum extractum Tisch.
MESEMBRYANTHEMACEAE
Heart-shaped, dark, glaucous green bodies 2–3 cm long and 1–1.5 cm wide, covered with dots; yellow flowers. According to Hammer this species may be distinguished from *C. laetum* L. Bol. only by the abundant dots.
South Africa (Cape Province)

Conophytum flavum N.E. Br.
MESEMBRYANTHEMACEAE
Bodies to 2.5 cm in diameter and truncate or concave at top, whitish-green with many green spots, fissure 2–6 mm long; yellow flowers.
Namibia/South Africa (Little Namaqualand)

Conophytum giftbergense Tisch.
MESEMBRYANTHEMACEAE
Green to grey-green bodies to 1 cm long and 1 cm in diameter; white flowers. Considered by Hammer to be a form of *C. obcordellum*.
South Africa (Cape Province)

Conophytum fragile Tisch.
MESEMBRYANTHEMACEAE
Caespitose plant; grey-green bodies 1 cm in diameter with numerous dark spots; pink to mauve flowers.
Namibia/South Africa (Little Namaqualand)

Conophytum globuliforme Schick & Tisch.
MESEMBRYANTHEMACEAE
Light green bodies to 1 cm long and less than 1 cm in diameter with minute papillae; yellow flowers.
Namibia/South Africa (Little Namaqualand)

Conophytum frutescens Schwantes
MESEMBRYANTHEMACEAE
Small shrub to 20 cm high; stems with ascending branches; green bodies 1.5–2.5 cm in diameter with lighter dots; orange flowers.
Namibia/South Africa (Little Namaqualand)

Conophytum gratum (N.E. Br.) N.E. Br.
MESEMBRYANTHEMACEAE
Variable bodies (whitish-green, glaucous green, yellow-green or pink) 2.5 cm long and 2 cm wide with grey dots; magenta flowers.
South Africa (Cape Province)

Conophytum hirtum Schwantes
MESEMBRYANTHEMACEAE
Light green bodies to 1.5 cm long and to 3 mm thick with short lobes; yellow flowers.
South Africa (Cape Province)

Conophytum koubergense L. Bol.
MESEMBRYANTHEMACEAE
Rusty brown to yellow-green bodies 1 cm in diameter with top surface sometimes divided into 2 lobes, forming mats of from 4 to more than 20 bodies; pink to magenta flowers. Similar to *C. lithopoides* L. Bol.
South Africa (Cape Province)

Conophytum johannis-winkleri (Dinter & Schwantes) N.E. Br.
MESEMBRYANTHEMACEAE
Flat, pale blue to pale green, caespitose bodies to 2 cm high and 2 cm in diameter; yellow flowers. It is a northern form of *C. subrisum* (N.E. Br.) N.E. Br.
Namibia

Conophytum lavisianum L. Bol.
MESEMBRYANTHEMACEAE
Bodies to 4 cm long and 15 mm wide with lighter spots; yellow flowers.
South Africa (Cape Province)

Conophytum karamoepense L. Bol.
MESEMBRYANTHEMACEAE
Whitish-green to pale green bodies to 1.5 cm long and 7 mm in diameter; yellow flowers.
Namibia (Bushmanland)

Conophytum lithopoides L. Bol.
MESEMBRYANTHEMACEAE
Rusty brown to yellow-green bodies to 15 mm long and 8 mm wide with fine hairs and windows; flowers purple.
Namibia (Bushmanland)

Conophytum longitubum L. Bol.
MESEMBRYANTHEMACEAE
Considered to be a variant of *C. viridicatum*, from which it is usually distinguished only by its 'greener' colour.
South Africa (Cape Province)

Conophytum meridianum L. Bol.
MESEMBRYANTHEMACEAE
Elongated bodies less than 1 cm in diameter with remains of old leaves persistent towards base; pink flowers.
Namibia/South Africa (Little Namaqualand)

Conophytum luteum N.E. Br.
MESEMBRYANTHEMACEAE
Grey-green, pear-shaped bodies 15 mm in diameter with dark green spots; yellow flowers.
Namibia/South Africa (Little Namaqualand)

Conophytum meyeri N.E. Br.
MESEMBRYANTHEMACEAE
Caespitose plant; 2-lobed, keeled, green to whitish-green bodies 1.5 cm high and 2 cm in diameter covered with dots; white to yellow flowers.
South Africa (Cape Province)

Conophytum marginatum Lavis
MESEMBRYANTHEMACEAE
Light green bodies to 2.5 cm high and 6 mm in diameter, usually densely covered with darker spots; pink flowers.
Namibia (Bushmanland)

Conophytum microstoma L. Bol.
MESEMBRYANTHEMACEAE
A variant of *C. meyeri*, distinguished by small fissure and smaller size.
South Africa (Cape Province)

Conophytum minutum (Haw.) N.E. Br.
MESEMBRYANTHEMACEAE
Bluish-green bodies to 12 mm high and 1 cm wide covered with spots; pale pink to reddish-magenta, rarely pure white, flowers.
South Africa (Cape Province)

Conophytum obcordellum (Haw.) N.E. Br.
MESEMBRYANTHEMACEAE
Caespitose plant forming large clumps; round or elliptical, green to blue-green bodies to 2 cm in diameter with numerous black lines and dots; nocturnal, white flowers.
South Africa (Cape Province)

Conophytum misellum N.E. Br.
MESEMBRYANTHEMACEAE
Grey-green bodies 8 mm high and 6 mm in diameter with several dots; yellow flowers. Considered by Hammer to be a variety of *C. saxetanumi* (N.E. Br.) N.E. Br.
South Africa (Cape Province)

Conophytum pageae (N.E. Br.) N.E. Br.
MESEMBRYANTHEMACEAE
Bodies glaucous above, usually reddish on side to 1 cm high and 8 mm wide with flat apices; yellow flowers.
Namibia/South Africa (Little Namaqualand)

Conophytum mundum (N.E. Br.) N.E. Br.
MESEMBRYANTHEMACEAE
Grey-green bodies 12 mm high with translucent dots; yellow flowers.
South Africa (Cape Province)

Conophytum pardicolor Tisch.
MESEMBRYANTHEMACEAE
Green to brownish, cylindrical bodies to 1 cm in diameter with ochre markings; remains of old leaves persistent; white to pink flowers.
Namibia/South Africa (Little Namaqualand)

Conophytum pearsonii N.E. Br.
MESEMBRYANTHEMACEAE
Clump-forming, green to yellowish-green bodies to 16 mm high and 18 mm in diameter; violet-pink flowers.
South Africa (Cape Province)

Conophytum pubicalyx Lavis
MESEMBRYANTHEMACEAE
Small, green, papillate and pear-shaped bodies 5 mm long and 2–3 mm in diameter; reddish flowers.
South Africa (Cape Province)

Conophytum pictum (N.E. Br.) N.E. Br.
MESEMBRYANTHEMACEAE
Green, obconical bodies 15 mm long and 1 cm in diameter, often with red stripes and several dots; cream flowers. A variable species.
South Africa (Cape Province)

Conophytum pulchellum Tischer
MESEMBRYANTHEMACEAE
Caespitose plants; light green bodies 15 mm long and 7 mm in diameter with darker dots; white flowers.
South Africa (Cape Province)

Conophytum polyandrum Lavis
MESEMBRYANTHEMACEAE
Pale green bodies divided into 2 short lobes and covered with darker dots; pink to white flowers.
South Africa (Cape Province)

Conophytum rarum N.E. Br.
MESEMBRYANTHEMACEAE
Caespitose, subglobose, pale green to bluish-green bodies 1–2 cm in diameter; white flowers.
South Africa (Cape Province)

Conophytum recisum
N.E. Br.

MESEMBRYANTHEMACEAE

Pale green to yellowish-green bodies 10–15 mm in diameter and 5 cm high, with tips of lobes to 2 cm long; yellow flowers. Considered by Hammer to be a variant of *C. bilobum* (Marloth) N.E. Br.

South Africa (Cape Province)

Conophytum ruschii Schwantes

MESEMBRYANTHEMACEAE

A small form of *C. wettsteinii* N.E. Br.

Namibia/South Africa (Little Namaqualand)

Conophytum reconditum A.R. Mitch.

MESEMBRYANTHEMACEAE

Short, cylindrical pale green bodies 2 cm in diameter and 1.5–2 cm high with densely tuberculate lobes; deep fissure between lobes; white flowers.

South Africa (Cape Province)

Conophytum stephanii Schwantes

MESEMBRYANTHEMACEAE

Grey-green bodies 4–8 mm long and 4–6 mm wide densely covered with 1 mm long hairs; white, nocturnal flowers.

South Africa (Cape Province)

Conophytum robustum Tischer

MESEMBRYANTHEMACEAE

Green bodies 2.5 cm high and 1.8 cm in diameter with darker green dots; pink flowers. A variant of *C. gratum* N.E. Br.

Namibia

Conophytum stipitatum L. Bol.

MESEMBRYANTHEMACEAE

Green bodies to 15 mm long and 1 cm in diameter with dark dots and lines; pink to magenta flowers. A form of *C. uviforme* (Haw.) N.E. Br.

South Africa (Cape Province)

Conophytum subglobosum Tischer

MESEMBRYANTHEMACEAE

Green bodies 2 cm long and to 15 mm in diameter with darker dots; white, nocturnal flowers.

South Africa (Cape Province)

Conophytum umdauense L. Bol.

MESEMBRYANTHEMACEAE

Velvety green bodies to 5 cm long with lobes to 15 mm long; flowers yellow.

South Africa (Cape Province)

Conophytum tetracarpum Lavis

MESEMBRYANTHEMACEAE

Pear-shaped, pale green bodies 2 cm long and 12 mm in diameter with darker dots; yellow flowers.

South Africa (Cape Province)

Conophytum ursprungianum Tischer

MESEMBRYANTHEMACEAE

Light green bodies to 2.5 cm high and 15 mm in diameter with prominent, dark green to purple dots; white flowers. Considered by Hammer to be an extremely beautiful form of *C. obcordellum* N.E. Br.

South Africa (Calvinia District)

Conophytum truncatum (Thunb.) N.E. Br.

MESEMBRYANTHEMACEAE

Clump-forming plant; grey-green or bluish-green bodies to 15 mm long and 15 mm in diameter; leaves variable in shape (truncate, flat, semi-bilobed or convex); white flowers.

South Africa (Cape Province)

Conophytum uviforme (Haw.) N.E. Br.

MESEMBRYANTHEMACEAE

Grey-green to reddish bodies 1 cm high and wide with dark green or reddish dots and stripes; whitish-yellow flowers.

South Africa (Cape Province)

Conophytum variabile L. Bol.

MESEMBRYANTHEMACEAE

Cylindrical, green to brownish-green bodies 2–3 cm long and to 16 mm in diameter with lobes 1–5 mm long; yellow flowers.

South Africa (Cape Province)

Cotyledon ladismithiensis Poelln.

CRASSULACEAE

Dwarf, branching shrub; fleshy, spreading leaves 3–5 cm long, covered with hairs and armed with 2–4 teeth near apex; orange-yellow flowers. The plant illustrated is a small, recently propagated cutting.

South Africa (Cape Province)

Conophytum viridicatum (N.E. Br.) N.E. Br.

MESEMBRYANTHEMACEAE

Green bodies 2.5 cm high and 15 mm wide with translucent dots and lines; white flowers.

South Africa (Cape Province)

Cotyledon macrantha L.

CRASSULACEAE

Shrub to 1 m high; branches with light brown bark; dark green, pruinose leaves 10 cm long; red flowers.

South Africa (Cape Province)

Corallocarpus sp.

CUCURBITACEAE

Tuberous rootstock 10–15 cm in diameter with climbing stems; hairy stems and leaves; leaves 2–5 cm long; small, green flowers.

Tropical Africa

Cotyledon orbiculata L.

CRASSULACEAE

Shrub to 1.5 m high; thick stems with erect branches bearing leaves at tips; leaves 4–12 cm long, to 6 cm wide and covered with pruinose wax; inflorescence to 70 cm tall with yellowish-red flowers.

Cotyledon elata Haw.; *C. oblonga* Haw.; *C. ramosa* Haw.

Angola, Namibia, South Africa (Cape Province)

79

Cotyledon undulata Haw.

CRASSULACEAE

Shrub to 50 cm high with thick stems and erect branches; pruinose leaves 12 cm long and 6 cm wide; inflorescence 30–40 cm tall; orange-yellow flowers.

South Africa (Cape Province)

Crassula ausiensis Hutchison

CRASSULACEAE

Dense rosettes to 10 cm high; leaves 10–15 cm long and 3–5 cm wide covered with white hairs; white flowers.

Namibia

Crassula arborescens (Mill.) Willd.

CRASSULACEAE

Shrub to 4 m high with cylindrical branches; grey-green leaves to 7 cm long with red margins; whitish-pink flowers.

Crassula cotyledon Jacq.

South Africa (Cape Province)

Crassula barbata Thunb.

CRASSULACEAE

Rosettes 3–4 cm in diameter; grey-green leaves 2–4 cm long with long, white hairs on margins; white flowers. The shoots die after flowering but the plants survive because new rosettes arise from base.

South Africa (Cape Province)

Crassula arta Schönland

CRASSULACEAE

Stems to 8 cm high; green leaves cover stems to form dense columns; inflorescence 4 cm tall with white flowers. Considered to be a synonym of *C. deceptor* Schönland & Baker.

Namibia/South Africa (Little Namaqualand), South Africa (Cape Province)

Crassula barklyi N.E. Br.

CRASSULACEAE

Stems to 9 cm long, branching from lower part of trunk; green, white-margined leaves to 1 cm long; creamy-white flowers. The invalid name *C. teres* Marloth is widely used.

South Africa (Cape Province)

Crassula brevifolia Harv.
CRASSULACEAE
Small shrubs with stems to 50 cm long arising from base; light green leaves 1 cm long and 5 mm wide with red margins; pink flowers.
Crassula flavovirens Pillans; *C. pearsonii* Schönland
South Africa (Cape Province)

Crassula corallina Thunb.
CRASSULACEAE
Numerous leafy branches forming small clumps 8 cm high; elliptical, pale green leaves 5 mm long and 4 mm wide; creamy-white flowers.
Namibia

Crassula columella Marloth & Schönland
CRASSULACEAE
Shrub to 15 cm high; stems 8–10 cm tall and covered with compressed, green to yellowish-green leaves, sometimes tinged with red, 1.5–3 cm long; greenish-white flowers.
South Africa (Cape Province)

Crassula cornuta Schönland & Baker
CRASSULACEAE
Densely leafy stems; grey-green, triangular leaves to 15 mm long; white to yellow flowers. Considered to be a synonym of *C. deceptor* Schönland & Baker.
Namibia, South Africa (Cape Province)

Crassula commutata Friedrich
CRASSULACEAE
Shrub to 50 cm high; fleshy, red-margined leaves 1 cm long and 4 mm wide; glaucous green flowers often tinged with red. Considered to be a variety of *C. rupestris* Thunb.
Namibia

Crassula corymbulosa Link & Otto
CRASSULACEAE
Little, branched plant; grey-green to light green, triangular leaves 3–4 cm long and 2 cm wide with darker spots; inflorescence to 30 cm tall with white flowers. Considered by Toelken (1985) to be a subspecies of *C. capitella* Thunb.
South Africa (Cape Province, Natal)

Crassula deceptor Schönland & Baker f.

CRASSULACEAE

Stems to 8 cm high covered with green, ovate leaves 6–15 mm long forming dense columns; leaves with green dots; inflorescence 4 cm tall with white flowers.

Namibia, South Africa (Cape Province)

Crassula hemisphaerica Thunb.

CRASSULACEAE

Plants to 15 cm high; leaves 1.5–2 cm long and 1.5–2.5 cm wide arranged in rosettes; leaf margins with white hairs; white flowers.
Crassula alooides Dryand.
Namibia, South Africa (Cape Province)

Crassula ernestii Schönland & Baker f.

CRASSULACEAE

Small plants with branches to 15 cm long; hairy, semi-cylindrical, green to grey-green leaves 1 cm long; white to cream flowers.
South Africa (Cape Province)

Crassula herrei Friedrich

CRASSULACEAE

Several rosettes with slightly woody branches; green or glaucous green to brown leaves to 7 cm long; cream (rarely white) flowers.
South Africa (Cape Province)

Crassula falcata J.C. Wendl.

CRASSULACEAE

Plants to 1 m high, rarely branched; grey-green leaves 10 cm long and 23 cm wide with recurved apices; red flowers.
Rochea falcata DC.
South Africa (Cape of Good Hope)

Crassula hispida Schönland & Baker f.

CRASSULACEAE

Shrublet to 40 cm high, with few branches and persistent leaves 1–2 cm long and 1–2 mm wide covered with hairs; cream flowers.
South Africa (Cape Province)

Crassula justus-corderoyi Jacobs & Poelln.
CRASSULACEAE
Clump-forming stems with numerous dark green leaves to 2 cm long and 1 cm wide and covered with white hairs; reddish flowers.
South Africa (Cape Province)

Crassula marnieriana H. Huber & Jacobs
CRASSULACEAE
Small, much branched shrubs with glaucous green to reddish-brown leaves; white flowers. Considered to be a variety of *C. rupestris* Thunb.
South Africa (Cape Province)

Crassula lactea Solms
CRASSULACEAE
Shrub 30–50 cm high; green leaves united at base 2–4 cm long and with white dots; white flowers.
South Africa (Natal, Transvaal)

Crassula mesembryanthemoides (Haw.) Dietr.
CRASSULACEAE
Branched plants to 30 cm high; leaves 1–2 cm long and covered with white, translucent hairs; whitish-yellow flowers.
Namibia

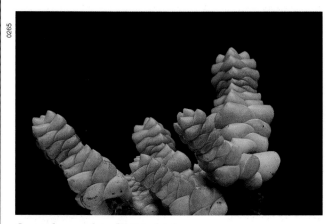

Crassula marchandii Friedrich
CRASSULACEAE
Stems 8–10 cm tall, covered with bright to olive-green, compressed leaves 1.5–3 cm long; greyish-green flowers.
South Africa (Cape Province)

Crassula mesembryanthemopsis Dinter
CRASSULACEAE
Thick, fleshy root; short stems with leaves arranged in rosettes of 4–8 leaf pairs; leaves whitish-grey-green with truncate tips; white flowers.
Namibia

Crassula 'Morgan's Beauty'
CRASSULACEAE
An attractive, compact cultivar (*C. falcata* x *C. mesembryanthemopsis*) with thick, grey-green leaves completely covering stem; salmon-pink flowers.

Crassula muscosa monstrose form
CRASSULACEAE
A fasciated form with leaves reflexed away from the stem.

Crassula multicava Lem.
CRASSULACEAE
Plants with erect branches to 40 cm high; leaves to 2 cm long and wide; pinkish-white flowers.
South Africa (Cape Province)

Crassula namaquensis subsp. comptonii
(Hutch. & Pillans) Toelken
CRASSULACEAE
Stems 10–20 cm high; grey- or blue-green, hairy leaves 3–4 cm long borne in clusters; white flowers. The leaves of this subspecies are triangular in section.
South Africa (Cape Province)

Crassula muscosa Thunb.
CRASSULACEAE
Slender, irregularly branched stems to 30 cm high; small leaves closely arranged in rows; small, yellowish-white flowers.
Crassula lycopodioides Lam.
Namibia, South Africa (Cape Province)

Crassula obliqua Solms
CRASSULACEAE
Freely branching shrub to 1 m high; grey-green leaves 3–4 cm long and 2–3 cm wide with small dark dots; pale pink flowers.
Namibia/South Africa (Little Namaqualand), South Africa (Natal)

Crassula obliqua Solms
CRASSULACEAE
A cultivated form with variegated leaves.

Crassula obvallata L.
CRASSULACEAE
Plant to 60 cm high with thick, densely leaved stems; grey-green leaves 4–6 cm long, flat on both sides; white flowers.
Namibia

Crassula perfoliata L.
CRASSULACEAE
Stems 1–1.5 m high; papillose, recurved leaves 10–15 cm long and 1–3 cm wide; red flowers.
South Africa (Cape Province)

Crassula perforata Thunb.
CRASSULACEAE
Small shrub with branches to 60 cm; greyish-green leaves, not caducous, to 2 cm long, constricted towards base and fused to the opposite one; whitish flowers.
Crassula anthurus E. Mey.;
C. conjuncta N.E. Br.;
C. nealeana L.C. Higgins;
C. perfilata Scop.; *C. petersoniae* Schönland
South Africa (Cape Province)

Crassula picturata Boom
CRASSULACEAE
Stemless plant; triangular, dark green leaves 10–12 mm long and 1 cm wide green with red spots; leaves arranged in spirals; pale pink to white flowers.
South Africa (Cape Province)

Crassula portulacea Lam.
CRASSULACEAE
Branched shrub to 1.5 m high; old leaves caducous; new leaves glossy green with red margins; white flowers.
South Africa (Cape Province)

Crassula pubescens Thunb.
CRASSULACEAE
Branched stems; green to brownish-green leaves 2 cm long and convex on both surfaces, with fine hairs; yellow to white flowers.
South Africa (Cape Province)

Crassula setulosa Harv.
CRASSULACEAE
Clump-forming stems 20–30 cm high; spirally arranged, hairy, red-tinged leaves in pairs, to 2 cm long and ending in acute tip; white flowers tinged with red.
South Africa (Natal, Orange Free State, Transvaal), Swaziland

Crassula pyramidalis Thunb.
CRASSULACEAE
Small shrub with branches to 15 cm long; triangular, green leaves, densely arranged to form cylindrical column; white flowers.
Crassula archeri Compton; *C. cylindrica* Schönland
South Africa (Cape Province)

Crassula socialis Schönland
CRASSULACEAE
Plants to 6 cm high with numerous rosettes; pale green, elliptical leaves to 1 cm long and 6 mm wide; white flowers.
South Africa (Cape Province)

Crassula rupestris Thunb.
CRASSULACEAE
Small, much branched shrubs to 50 cm high; fleshy leaves to 1.5 cm long, often with reddish margins; pinkish flowers.
South Africa (Cape Province)

Crassula susannae Rauh & Friedrich
CRASSULACEAE
Stems 1–4 cm long; truncate leaves 1 cm long, forming rosettes; white flowers.
South Africa (Cape Province)

Crassula tecta Thunb.
CRASSULACEAE

Much branched, clump-forming stems to 15 cm high; rounded, green leaves 2–4 cm long and covered with white warts; white flowers.

South Africa (Cape Province)

Cyanotis somalensis C.B. Clarke
COMMELINACEAE

Creeping stems to 30 cm long, rooting and forming new rosettes; densely hairy leaves 4–8 cm long; blue flowers.

Somalia

Crassula tetragona L.
CRASSULACEAE

Branches to 1 m high, with numerous carnose or woody stems; lanceolate, green leaves to 8 cm long; white flowers.

South Africa (Cape Province)

Cylindrophyllum comptonii L. Bol.
MESEMBRYANTHEMACEAE

Cylindrical leaves to 10 cm long and 1 cm in diameter, forming large clumps 25 cm and more in diameter; silvery-white flowers.

South Africa (Cape Province)

Crassula tomentosa Thunb.
CRASSULACEAE

Plant 50–80 cm high; densely hairy, grey-green leaves 1.5 cm long, arranged in rosettes; white to pale yellow flowers.

Crassula glabrifolia Harv.

Namibia

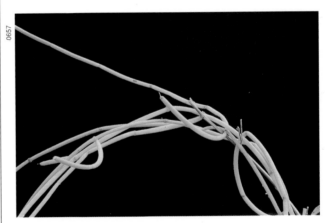

Cynanchum aphyllum (Thunb.) Schltr.
ASCLEPIADACEAE

Freely branching stems rooting at nodes; small leaves 3 mm long and 1 mm wide; green flowers with brown stripes.

Madagascar, Mozambique, South Africa (Natal)

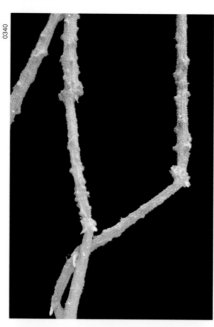

Cynanchum marnierianum Rauh

ASCLEPIADACEAE

Low bush with several dark green branches covered with tubercles and hairs; caducous leaves; greenish-brown flowers.

Madagascar

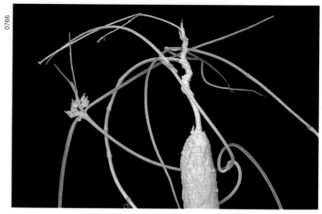

Cynanchum sp.

ASCLEPIADACEAE

An unidentified specimen with thick caudex and thin branches.

Cynanchum perrieri Choux

ASCLEPIADACEAE

Leafless shrub, branching from base; erect, grey-green stems over 1.5 m high; white flowers.

Madagascar

Cynanchum sp.

ASCLEPIADACEAE

An unidentified specimen with thick caudex, thin stems and small leaves.

Cynanchum sp.

ASCLEPIADACEAE

An unidentified specimen with rounded caudex 10–15 cm in diameter and long, thin branches; brown-green flowers.

Cyphostemma cirrhosa (Thunb.) Desc.

VITACEAE

Succulent main stem to 50 cm high with grey bark; climbing branches to 1.5 m long growing in different directions; leaves to 10 cm long; white flowers.

South Africa (Cape Province)

Cyphostemma currori
(Hook.f.) Desc.

VITACEAE

Freely branching stem over 4 m high with yellow, peeling bark; tripartite leaves; inconspicuous flowers 5 mm in diameter. Plant photographed in habitat.

Angola, Namibia

Cyphostemma juttae
(Dinter & Gilg) Desc.

VITACEAE

Stem to 2 m high, forming massive caudex with thick branches above; stem covered with yellow bark and papery skin, which peels off with age; green, acutely oval leaves to 20 cm long and 6 cm wide; inflorescence with red berries.

Namibia

Cyphostemma uter
(Exell & Mend.) Desc.

VITACEAE

Swollen trunk with peeling bark, branching repeatedly from apex and forming much branched low trees; green, triangular leaves 8 cm in diameter with undulate margins; greenish-yellow flowers.

Angola

Dactylopsis digitata (Aiton) N.E. Br.

MESEMBRYANTHEMACEAE

Stemless mats; cylindrical, grey-green leaves to 15 cm long and 2–3 cm thick; white flowers. The photograph shows the old leaves from which the new ones will emerge.

South Africa (Cape Province)

Dasylirion longissimum
Lem.

AGAVACEAE

Stem to 3 m tall; numerous green leaves 1–2 m long arranged in rosette; inflorescence 5 m tall; whitish flowers.

Mexico

Delosperma cooperi (Hook.f.) L. Bol.

MESEMBRYANTHEMACEAE

Low, freely branching shrub; leaves 5 cm long; purple flowers.
South Africa (Orange Free State)

Delosperma echinatum
(Aiton) Schawntes

MESEMBRYANTHEMACEAE

Bush to 30 cm high with dichotomously branched, light green stems; leaves 15 mm long and 7 mm thick and covered with bristly papillae; yellow flowers.

South Africa (Cape Province)

Delosperma pergamentaceum L. Bol.

MESEMBRYANTHEMACEAE

Shrub to 30 cm high; stems with 4–6 leaves 7 cm long and 10–15 mm thick; white flowers.

Namibia/South Africa (Little Namaqualand)

Delosperma nubigenum (Schltr.) L. Bol.

MESEMBRYANTHEMACEAE

Mat-forming plants; stems with branches to 20 cm long; leaves 3–5 cm long and narrowed towards base; yellow flowers. A hardy species.

South Africa (Cape Province)

Delosperma tradescantioides (A.Berger) L. Bol.

MESEMBRYANTHEMACEAE

Freely branching low shrub; branches rooting at nodes; light green leaves 2–3 cm long, 1 cm wide and 1–2 mm thick; flowers white.

South Africa (Cape Province)

Delosperma obtusum L. Bol.

MESEMBRYANTHEMACEAE

Shrub with prostrate branches; leaves 1–2 cm long and triangular in section; purple-red flowers.

South Africa (Orange Free State)

Deuterocohnia longipetala (Baker) Mez

BROMELIACEAE

Stems to 1 m long; rosette-forming leaves 40 cm long; yellow flowers with green apical spots.

Peru

Didierea madagascariensis Baill.
DIDIEREACEAE
Tree to 6 m high; branches with dense thorns 1–4 cm long and groups of leaves 2–3 cm long; small, inconspicuous flowers.
Madagascar   CITES App. II

Dinteranthus pole-evansii (N.E. Br.) Schwantes
MESEMBRYANTHEMACEAE
Greyish-white leaf pairs to 4.5 cm long and 4 cm wide with yellow or red dots; yellow flowers.
South Africa (Cape Province)

Didierea trollii Capuron & Rauh.
DIDIEREACEAE
Young stems grow horizontally, forming bush 50 cm high from which adult stems develop into trunks; leaves 1–2 cm long are grouped at centre of thorns; greenish-yellow flowers.
Madagascar   CITES App. II

Dinteranthus vanzjlii
(L. Bol.) Schwantes
MESEMBRYANTHEMACEAE
Several grey-green bodies to 4 cm high, similar to *Lithops* species; yellow flowers.
Lithops vanzjlii L. Bol.
South Africa (Cape Province)

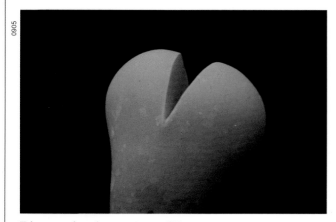

Dinteranthus inexpectatus Dinter
MESEMBRYANTHEMACEAE
Stemless, grey-green, roundish leaves to 3 cm long and 3 cm wide borne in pairs with translucent green dots; yellow flowers.
Namibia

Dinteranthus wilmotianus L. Bol.
MESEMBRYANTHEMACEAE
A single pair of smooth, grey-green leaves with dark dots, 5–6 cm long and united for half their length; yellow flowers.
South Africa (Cape Province)

Dioscorea elephantipes (L'Hér.) Engl.

DIOSCOREACEAE

Semi-globose caudex to 1 m in diameter; fissured bark; twining stems 1–2 m long with cordate to reniform, green leaves; greenish-yellow to yellow flowers 4 mm in diameter.

Testudinaria elephantipes (L'Hér.) Lindl.

Southern Africa

Dioscorea sylvatica var. paniculata Burch.

DIOSCOREACEAE

Flattened caudex; spreading stems; heart-shaped leaves 6 cm long and wide; greenish flowers 4 mm in diameter.

Testudinaria paniculata Dummer

Southern Africa

Dioscorea elephantipes (L'Hér.) Engl.

DIOSCOREACEAE

A young specimen.

Dischidia rafflesiana Wall.

ASCLEPIADACEAE

Thin, cylindrical, climbing stems 50–90 cm long; fleshy-green, opposite leaves; yellowish flowers.

Australia, Malaysia

Dioscorea elephantipes (L'Hér.) Engl.

DIOSCOREACEAE

A flowering stem.

Dolichos seineri Harms

LEGUMINOSAE

Giant subterranean caudex with 3–4 aerial stems forming bush; rounded leaves; violet flowers borne from leaf axils.

Namibia

Dorstenia bornimiana Schweinf.

MORACEAE

Tuber 3–7 cm in diameter from which short stems arise; roundish, green leaves 7 cm in diameter; greenish-yellow, disc-shaped inflorescence.

Central and southern Africa

Dorstenia crispa Engl.

MORACEAE

Cylindrical stems 30–40 cm high; oblong to narrowly lanceolate leaves 10–15 cm long, with slightly undulate to dentate margins, borne at growing apices; greenish-yellow, disc-shaped inflorescence 2 cm in diameter on 10 cm long stalk.

Kenya, Somalia

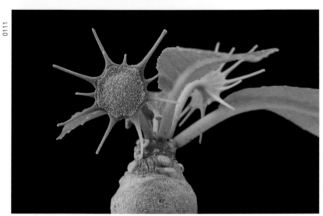

Dorstenia foetida (Forssk.) Schweinf.

MORACEAE

Stems to 15 cm high, developing small basal caudex 2–3 cm in diameter; leaves 5–10 cm long with dentate margins; greenish-yellow, disc-shaped inflorescence.

Kenya, Tanzania

Dorstenia hildebrandtii Engl.

MORACEAE

Fleshy, subglobose caudex, with succulent stems and few branches; leaves with undulate margins; greenish-yellow, disc-shaped inflorescence.

Kenya

Dorstenia radiata Lam.

MORACEAE

Greyish to brownish, branching, cylindrical stems 1–2 cm in diameter and to 30 cm high; thin, obovate leaves; greenish-yellow, disc-shaped inflorescence.

Southern Arabian peninsula

Dorstenia sp.

MORACEAE

Thick, succulent stems; green leaves with dentate margins; greenish-yellow, disc-shaped inflorescence. A vigorous plant.

Somalia (?)

Dracaena draco (L.) L.
AGAVACEAE

Tree to 10 m high; thick stem, unbranched until first inflorescence is produced, then with several spreading branches; leaves 30–60 cm long arranged in rosettes at ends of branches; white flowers tinged with green outside.

Canary Islands

Drosanthemum eburneum L. Bol.
MESEMBRYANTHEMACEAE

Elongated, hairy stems forming shrubs to 30 cm high; semi-cylindrical leaves, narrower towards apex, 1–2 cm long; white flowers.

South Africa (Cape Province)

Dracophilus delaetianus (Dinter) Dinter
MESEMBRYANTHEMACEAE

Branches bearing 4 light green (sometimes blue-tinged), rounded leaves with brown marks, 3–5 cm long and 15 mm in diameter, triangular in section; pink flowers.

Namibia, South Africa (Cape Province)

Dudleya albiflora Rose
CRASSULACEAE

Stems to 30 cm long and 2 cm in diameter, branching and forming dense clumps; rosettes 2–10 cm in diameter with 15–25 green leaves; white flowers.

Dudleya maranii D.A. Johans.

Mexico (Baja California)

Dracophilus proximus (L. Bol.) Walgate
MESEMBRYANTHEMACEAE

Branches 4–6 cm long bearing 4–8 smooth, grey-green leaves 4–5 cm long; pink flowers.

Juttadinteria proxima L. Bol.

Namibia, South Africa (Cape Province)

Dudleya brittonii D.A. Johans.
CRASSULACEAE

Unbranched stems with rosettes of 40–120 leaves; whitish-green, farinose leaves to 20 cm long and 8 cm wide; pale yellow flowers.

Mexico (Baja California)

Dudleya pauciflora Rose
CRASSULACEAE

Short stems 2 cm in diameter; rosettes to 7 cm in diameter, growing in clumps, with 15–20 deltoid to oblong leaves 3–7 cm long and to 1.5 cm wide; yellow flowers tinged with red.

Mexico (Baja California)

Duvalia polita N.E. Br.
ASCLEPIADACEAE

Dark green to brown, hexagonal, elongated stems to 10 cm long with tuberculate teeth; dark brownish-red flowers.

Angola, Mozambique

Duvalia angustiloba N.E. Br.
ASCLEPIADACEAE

Short, subspherical, 4- or 5-angled stems with tuberculate teeth; dark brown flowers.

South Africa

Duvalia reclinata (Masson) Haw.
ASCLEPIADACEAE

Green, 4- to 6-angled stems to 10 cm long with tuberculate teeth; green-brown flowers.

South Africa

Duvalia elegans (Masson) Haw.
ASCLEPIADACEAE

Stems 4- or 5-angled, 4–6 cm long and 1–1.5 cm in diameter with tuberculate teeth; red-brown to brown flowers with yellow-brown inner whorl.

South Africa

Dyckia brevifolia Baker
BROMELIACEAE

Stemless rosettes; leaves 10–20 cm long with marginal spines 2 mm long; yellow flowers.

Brazil

Dyckia ebdingii L.B. Sm.
BROMELIACEAE
Leaves arranged in rosettes 20–25 cm long with spiny margins; yellow flowers.
Brazil

Echeveria agavoides Lem.
CRASSULACEAE
Stemless, usually solitary rosette; few glossy green leaves to 8 cm long and 3 cm wide; inflorescence 20–25 cm tall; red or yellow flowers.
Echeveria obscura Poelln.; *Urbinia agavoides* Rose
Mexico (San Luis Potosí)

Eberlanzia disarticulata (L. Bol.) L. Bol.
MESEMBRYANTHEMACEAE
Shrub to 20 cm high; red-brown stems; grey-green, erect leaves; purple flowers.
Ruschia disarticulata L. Bol.
South Africa (Cape Province)

Echeveria amoena De Smet.
CRASSULACEAE
Stemless or short-stemmed rosettes; bluish-green, pruinose leaves 35 cm long borne in dense rosettes; red flowers.
Mexico

Eberlanzia spinosa (L.) Schwantes
MESEMBRYANTHEMACEAE
Shrub to 60 cm high with branched thorns; grey-green leaves 1–2 cm long with darker dots; pink flowers.
Namibia, South Africa (Cape Province)

Echeveria carnicolor E. Morren
CRASSULACEAE
Stemless rosettes; pruinose leaves tinged with pink to 7 cm long and 15 mm wide; inflorescence to 15 cm tall; pink flowers.
Mexico (Veracruz)

Echeveria desmetiana De Smet.
CRASSULACEAE
Stemless or short-stemmed rosettes; bluish-white, pruinose leaves with reddish margins 5–7 cm long and 2–4 cm wide; red flowers.
Mexico

Echeveria gibbiflora var. metallica E. Morren
CRASSULACEAE
Stems 30–50 cm tall; solitary rosettes with 15 leaves to 15 cm long. This variety is considered by E. Walther to be a cultivar.
Mexico

Echeveria elegans Rose
CRASSULACEAE
Stemless, clump-forming rosettes; thick, pointed, pruinose, grey-green leaves 3–7 cm long; pink flowers.
Mexico

Echeveria lauii Moran & J. Meyrán
CRASSULACEAE
Rosettes to 25 cm in diameter; whitish-blue, tongue-shaped leaves; pinkish flowers.
Mexico (Oaxaca)

Echeveria gibbiflora var. carunculata Hort.
CRASSULACEAE
Rosettes of 15–20 leaves; grey-green leaves flushed with red 15–30 cm long; inflorescence to 1 m tall; pink flowers. This variety has protuberances on upper surface of leaves.
Mexico

Echeveria leucotricha J.A. Purpus
CRASSULACEAE
Shrublet to 15 cm high; stems and leaves covered with white hairs; leaves to 10 cm long and 2.5 cm wide; red flowers.
Mexico (Puebla)

Echeveria multicaulis Rose

CRASSULACEAE

Branching stems 10–20 cm high; rosettes at tips of branches; glossy green leaves 2–3 cm long, 1–2 cm wide and tinged with red towards apex; reddish flowers yellow on inner surface.

Mexico

Echeveria pumila var. glauca E. Walther

CRASSULACEAE

Rosettes with numerous green to dark green leaves to 5 cm long and 2 cm wide forming large clusters; inflorescence to 15 cm tall; flowers rose-pink with scarlet centres.

Echeveria glauca E. Morren

Garden origin

Echeveria nodulosa (Baker) Otto

CRASSULACEAE

Branching stem to 20 cm tall; green leaves 5 cm long and 5 mm wide narrowing towards base; inflorescence 30 cm tall; pinkish-white flowers.

Echeveria discolor De Smet.

Mexico (Oaxaca, Puebla)

Echeveria purpusorum A. Berger

CRASSULACEAE

Stemless rosettes; green, acuminate leaves 4 cm long and 2 cm wide with red-brown spots; yellow flowers.

Mexico (Oaxaca)

Echeveria 'Perle von Nurnberg'

CRASSULACEAE

Rosettes to 15 cm in diameter with pink-tinged leaves. A hybrid of *E. gibbiflora* var. *metallica* x *E. potosina*.

Echeveria 'Rundelli'

CRASSULACEAE

Large clumps of rosettes 4–6 cm in diameter; thick, blue leaves with tufts of hairs at tip.

Garden origin

Echeveria setosa Rose & J.A. Purpus

CRASSULACEAE

Stemless rosettes with numerous offsets in older plants; each rosette with to 100 green leaves 5 cm long, 2 cm wide and densely covered by fine white hairs to 3 mm long; yellowish-red flowers.

Mexico (Puebla)

Echeveria shaviana E. Walther

CRASSULACEAE

Short-stemmed rosettes with numerous glaucous green leaves 4–8 cm long with undulate margins and teeth near apex; pink flowers.

Mexico

Echeveria subrigida (Robinson & Seaton) Rose

CRASSULACEAE

Short-stemmed, solitary rosettes; silvery-white leaves to 25 cm long and 10 cm wide with red margins; inflorescence to 1 m tall; red flowers.

Echeveria sangusta Poelln.

Mexico

Echeveria x kirchneriana

CRASSULACEAE

Rosettes 10–15 cm in diameter; leaves 5–8 cm long; varicoloured flowers (pink, orange and yellow). Hybrid of *Echeveria carnicolor* E. Morren and *E. derenbergii* J.A. Purpus.

Garden origin

Echeveria x scheideckeri De Smet

CRASSULACEAE

Short-stemmed, grey-green, pruinose leaves 8 cm long and 2 cm wide; red flowers with yellow tips. This is a hybrid of *Pachyphyton bracteosum* Link, Klotzsch & Otto and *Echeveria secunda* Booth.

x *Pachyveria scheideckeri* E. Walther

Garden origin

Echidnopsis cereiformis Hook.f.

ASCLEPIADACEAE

Spreading stems to 30 cm long, often rooting; ribs on branches and stems covered in 4-angled tubercles; 2–4 yellow flowers borne together.

Somalia, Yemen

99

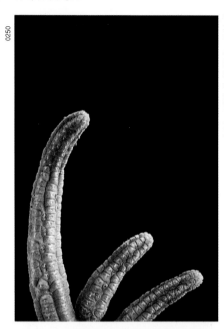

Echidnopsis dammaniana Sprenger
ASCLEPIADACEAE

Stems to 20 cm long, spreading, erect or curved and rooting when touching the soil; 2–5 green-brown flowers borne at end of stems.

Echidnopsis somalensis N.E. Br.

Ethiopia, Kenya, Somalia

Echidnopsis scutellata (Deflers) A. Berger
ASCLEPIADACEAE

Dark green, 8-angled stems to 10 cm long, with thick, dark green, caducous leaves and 6-angled tubercles; yellow flowers often mottled with purple-red.

Kenya

Echidnopsis nubica N.E. Br.
ASCLEPIADACEAE

Branched, 8-angled stems 20 cm long; tubercles separated by deep furrows; purple flowers. Considered by Bruyns to be a synonym of *E. cereiformis* Hook.f.

Sudan

Echidnopsis scutellata subsp. dhofarensis Bruyns
ASCLEPIADACEAE

Grey-green, 8-angled, tuberculate stems; thick, caducous leaves; yellow flowers.

Oman

Echidnopsis repens R.A. Dyer & I. Verd.
ASCLEPIADACEAE

Little-branched, creeping and rooting, 8- to 10-angled stems with thin, caducous leaves borne on tubercles of young stems; deep wine-red flowers. Considered by Bruyns to be a variety of *E. sharpei* A.C. White & B. Sloane.

Kenya, Tanzania

Echidnopsis scutellata subsp. planiflora (Bally) Bruyns
ASCLEPIADACEAE

Stems 8- to 15-angled; leaves longer than they are wide at the base, persisting as spines; bright yellow to brown campanulate flowers.

Echidnopsis chrysantha Lavranos

Somalia

Echidnopsis squamulata
(Decne.) P.R.O. Bally

ASCLEPIADACEAE

Green, 5- to 8-angled stems 50 cm long and rooting along their length; low, hexagonal tubercles with caducous leaves; red-brown flowers.

Yemen

Eriospermum dregei
Endl.

LILIACEAE

Tuber 5–10 cm wide with stolons; basal leaves reduced, 1 or more well developed, hairy and with parallel veins; leafless inflorescence; white to yellow flowers.

Southern Africa

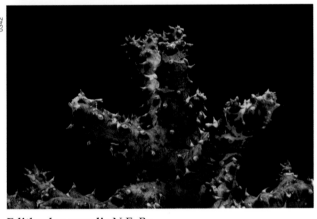

Edithcolea grandis N.E. Br.

ASCLEPIADACEAE

Stems 5-angled, to 30 cm high and with sharp thorny teeth; single, pale yellow flowers with red-brown spots borne at ends of shoots.

Kenya, Somalia, Tanzania

Euphorbia abdelkuri
Balf.

EUPHORBIACEAE

Grey stems to 2 m high with 5- to 8-angled branches and prominent tubercles; rudimentary, caducous leaves; yellow, poisonous latex; yellow-green, sessile inflorescence with several cyathia clustered at base of tubercles.

South Yemen (Socotra)

CITES App. II

Enarganthe octonaria (L. Bol.) L. Bol.

MESEMBRYANTHEMACEAE

Shrub 10–15 cm high; grey-green leaves 2–3 cm long and 6 mm in diameter; red flowers.

Namibia/South Africa (Little Namaqualand)

Euphorbia acrurensis
N.E. Br

EUPHORBIACEAE

Tree to 10 m high; thorny, 4-angled, dark green branches 30–40 cm long with callous veins towards leaf buds; caducous, green leaves 3–4 cm long; inflorescence borne at end of shoots.

Eritrea

CITES App. II

101

Euphorbia aeruginosa Schweick.
EUPHORBIACEAE

Small caudex with numerous branches from base; 4- to 5-angled branches 15 cm high with thorns to 7 mm long; yellow inflorescence borne at end of stems.

South Africa (Transvaal)   CITES App. II

Euphorbia albipollinifera L.C. Leach
EUPHORBIACEAE

Tuberous root continuing into the stem and forming caudex; tuberculate branches 5–10 cm long with small, caducous leaves; inflorescence borne on short peduncle from new growth.

South Africa (Cape Province)   CITES App. II

Euphorbia alcicornis Svent.
EUPHORBIACEAE

Main stem 1–5 m tall; secondary branches thick, thorny and 3-angled; rudimentary, caducous leaves; inflorescence borne on short peduncle from branch apices.

Madagascar   CITES App. II

Euphorbia alfredii Rauh
EUPHORBIACEAE

Stems 3–4 cm in diameter; dark green leaves 5–8 cm long and 2–3 cm wide borne in terminal rosettes; inflorescence borne on peduncle 2–4 cm long arising from stem apices; pink bracts.

Madagascar   CITES App. II

Euphorbia ambovombensis Rauh & Razaf.
EUPHORBIACEAE

Tuberous plant branching from base; branches 5–15 cm long; dark green (often purple) leaves 2–5 cm long with crinkled margins and upturned apices arranged in rosette; inflorescence borne on short peduncle near branch apices.

Madagascar   CITES App. I

Euphorbia aphylla
Brouss.
EUPHORBIACEAE

Spineless, leafless shrub 1 m high; grey-green cylindrical stems; yellow inflorescence borne on short peduncle from stem apices.

Canary Islands

CITES App. II

Euphorbia arida N.E. Br.
EUPHORBIACEAE

Main stem to 5 cm high and 5 cm thick with numerous spineless, tuberculate branches; caducous leaves 2–3 mm long; persistent peduncles; inflorescence borne at tips of branches; green bracts.

South Africa (Cape Province)

CITES App. II

Euphorbia avasmontana Dinter
EUPHORBIACEAE

Plant to 2 m tall; stem branching from base; yellowish-green, 5- to 8-angled branches 6–10 cm in diameter with spines in pairs; rudimentary, caducous leaves; inflorescence borne near stem apices.

Namibia, South Africa (Cape Province)

CITES App. II

Euphorbia avasmontana Dinter
EUPHORBIACEAE
A specimen in habitat.

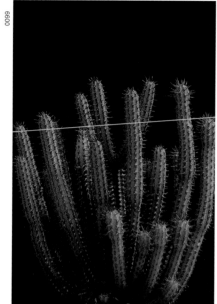

Euphorbia baioensis S. Carter
EUPHORBIACEAE

Plants branching from base; erect, cylindrical branches to 30 cm high and 2 cm in diameter with 8–10 ribs and red to black spines; yellow, almost sessile inflorescence borne along ribs.

Kenya

CITES App. II

Euphorbia balsamifera Aiton
EUPHORBIACEAE

Shrub to 2 m high; grey, spineless branches; leaves 2–5 cm long arranged in rosettes; yellow inflorescence borne at branch apices.

Canary Islands, Morocco, Somalia   CITES App. II

Euphorbia beharensis Leandri
EUPHORBIACEAE

Tuberous root with thin, spiny branches 30–50 cm long; green leaves 25 cm long; green inflorescence borne on short peduncle from branch apices.

Madagascar

CITES App. II

103

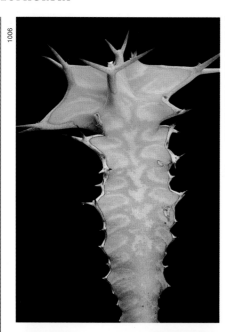

Euphorbia breviarticulata Pax
EUPHORBIACEAE

Shrub 4–5 m high; triangular, blue-green branches with yellow-green bands; spines 5–8 cm long; inflorescence borne on short peduncle from branch apices; yellow cyathia.

Ethiopia, Kenya, Somalia, Tanzania

CITES App. II

Euphorbia bubalina Boiss.
EUPHORBIACEAE

Spineless, cylindrical, solitary or branched stems 1–1.5 m high; lanceolate, light green leaves 10 cm long at apex of growing stems; inflorescence borne on peduncle to 15 cm long; green bracts with red margins.

South Africa (Cape Province)　　　　　　CITES App. II

Euphorbia brevitorta P.R.O. Bally
EUPHORBIACEAE

Tuberous root with several branches spreading and forming clumps to 1 m in diameter; small, triangular, caducous leaves; pairs of grey spines with brown tips; yellow, sessile inflorescence borne on new growth at branch apices.

Kenya　　　　　　CITES App. II

Euphorbia bupleurifolia Jacq.
EUPHORBIACEAE

Solitary stems, globose to elongate, 10–20 cm high; light green leaves 7 cm long borne at stem apex; inflorescence on peduncle to 5 cm long; green bracts.

South Africa (Cape Province, Natal)　　　　　　CITES App. II

Euphorbia brunellii Chiov.
EUPHORBIACEAE

Conical caudex 2–5 cm high and 1–3 cm in diameter with dark bark and several caducous, green leaves 3–6 cm long with reddish margins; inflorescence borne on peduncle 2–4 cm long.

Somalia　　　　　　CITES App. II

Euphorbia burmannii E. Mey.
EUPHORBIACEAE

Spineless shrub 80–180 cm high with small, green leaves; persistent reddish-brown leaf petioles; forked inflorescence to 5 cm long.

South Africa (Cape Province)

CITES App. II

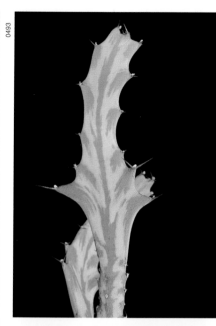

Euphorbia buruana Pax

EUPHORBIACEAE

Triangular, grey-green undulate branches with dark green stripes; rudimentary, caducous leaves; yellow inflorescence borne on short peduncle from newest growth.

Tanzania

CITES App. II

Euphorbia caput-medusae L.

EUPHORBIACEAE

Short caudex to 20 cm in diameter with several spreading branches to 60 cm long; leaves 2–3 cm long; yellowish-green inflorescence borne at stem apices.
Euphorbia fructus-pinii Mill.; *E. medusae* Thunb.; *E. tesselata* Haw.

South Africa (Cape Province)   CITES App. II

Euphorbia canariensis L.

EUPHORBIACEAE

Shrub with numerous 4- to 6-angled branches to 2–3 m high (12 m in habitat) arising from base; pairs of small spines; rudimentary, caducous leaves; greenish-red inflorescence borne on short peduncle.

Canary Islands

CITES App. II

Euphorbia clava Jacq.

EUPHORBIACEAE

Spineless, cylindrical stem to 1.5 m high with hexagonal tubercles to 6 mm long and 1–1.5 cm wide at base; several light green leaves 10–15 cm long; inflorescence borne on peduncle to 20 cm long; green bracts. Similar to *E. bubalina* but tubercles are more prominent and stems stouter.

South Africa (Cape Province)

CITES App. II

Euphorbia cap-saintemariensis Rauh

EUPHORBIACEAE

Subterranean caudex 5–10 cm in diameter; branches tipped with rosette of green to reddish-green leaves to 2.5 cm long with undulate edges; pale yellow to olive-green inflorescence born on forked peduncle 5 cm long.

Madagascar   CITES App. II

Euphorbia clavigera N.E. Br

EUPHORBIACEAE

Tuberous root fused to main stem to form thick caudex; stems 10–15 cm long with tubercles; spines to 1 cm long in pairs; rudimentary leaf scales; inflorescence borne on short peduncle.

Swaziland   CITES App. II

Euphorbia coerulescens
Haw.

EUPHORBIACEAE

Shrub to 1.5 m high; numerous bluish-grey, 4- to 6-angled branches 5 cm thick; bluish-grey stems; white to dark brown spines to 1.5 cm long in pairs; yellow inflorescence borne near branch apices.

South Africa (Cape Province)

CITES App. II

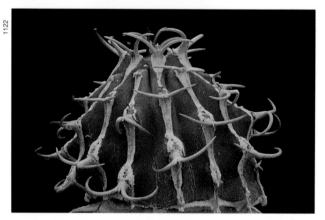

Euphorbia columnaris P.R.O. Bally

EUPHORBIACEAE

Plant 1–1.5 m high; solitary, 10- to 15-sided, dark green stem; pairs of recurved, whitish-grey spines 1–2 cm long; inflorescence on short peduncle with numerous cyathia borne near stem apex.

Somalia   CITES App. II

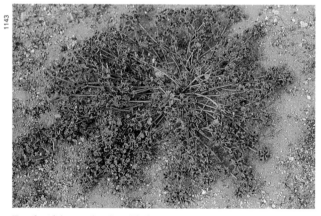

Euphorbia copiapina Phil.

EUPHORBIACEAE

Thick, tuberous grey-brown root 10 cm long and 1–4 cm in diameter; many branches 5–10 cm long with spirally arranged, greenish-grey leaves with reddish margins; red inflorescence borne on branched peduncle 5–10 cm long. Plant photographed in habitat.

Euphorbia calderensis Phil.; *E. subumbellata* Steud.

Chile   CITES App. II

Euphorbia cremersii
Rauh & Razaf.

EUPHORBIACEAE

Tuberous root 2–5 cm in diameter; thin stem, 10–15 cm long with few caducous leaves at apex; leaves 8 cm long with red margins; pale brown inflorescence borne on reddish peduncle 2–3 cm long.

Madagascar

CITES App. II

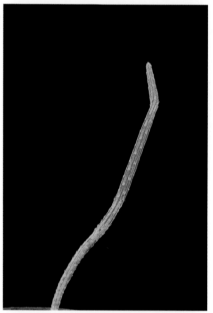

Euphorbia cryptospinosa
P.R.O. Bally

EUPHORBIACEAE

Tuberous root with erect stem 20–100 cm long with 5–10 ribs; spines forming longitudinal stripes; rudimentary, caducous leaves 3 mm long; ivory to pale red inflorescence.

Ethiopia, Kenya, Somalia

CITES App. II

Euphorbia cylindrica
A.C. White, R.A. Dyer, B. Sloane

EUPHORBIACEAE

Stem solitary or with few cylindrical branches 5 cm in diameter, covered with tubercles 5 mm long; light green leaves 4–6 cm long at top of growing apices; inflorescence borne on short peduncle from axil of tubercles.

South Africa (Cape Province)

CITES App. II

Euphorbia cylindrifolia Marn.-Lap. & Rauh
EUPHORBIACEAE
Plant with whitish subterranean branches; stems 10–15 cm long covered with leaf scars; cylindrical dark green leaves 2–3 cm long and 3 mm wide; brownish-pink inflorescence on peduncle 5–8 mm long. The illustration shows a form with a thick root forming a caudex.
Madagascar   CITES App. I

Euphorbia decidua P.R.O. Bally & L.C. Leach
EUPHORBIACEAE
Thick, subterranean stem bearing leaves 12 mm long in juvenile stage. At maturity the plant produces caducous branches to 12 cm long and 6 mm thick, with small, green, caducous leaves. Plant photographed in habitat.
Angola, Malawi, Zambia, northern Zimbabwe   CITES App. II

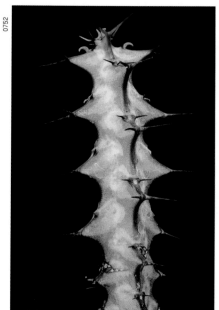

Euphorbia dauana S. Carter
EUPHORBIACEAE
Dark green to brown stem and branches with paler markings and prominent tubercles bearing spines in pairs; yellow inflorescence on short peduncle borne from tubercles.
Kenya

CITES App. II

Euphorbia didiereoides Denis
EUPHORBIACEAE
Thorny stems to 2 m high; rosettes of green, often red-margined leaves 5–10 cm long at apex; yellowish-green or orange inflorescence borne on branched peduncle.
Madagascar

CITES App. II

Euphorbia decaryi Guill.
EUPHORBIACEAE
Stoloniferous stems to 12 cm high with tubercles; silvery-green leaves 3–4 cm long and 2 cm wide with undulate margins borne at ends of stems; yellowish-green inflorescence on peduncle to 2 cm long.
Madagascar   CITES App. I

Euphorbia echinus Hook.f. & Coss.
EUPHORBIACEAE
Shrub to 1.5 m high; hexagonal, multi-branched stems; grey spines 1.5 mm long; rudimentary, caducous leaves; inflorescence borne on short peduncle near stem apices.
Morocco   CITES App. II

0101

Euphorbia enopla Boiss.
EUPHORBIACEAE

Leafless shrub to 1 m high freely branching from base; branches blue- or grey-green with red spines to 6 cm long; inflorescence borne on peduncle to 3 cm long; dark red bracts.

South Africa (Cape Province)   CITES App. II

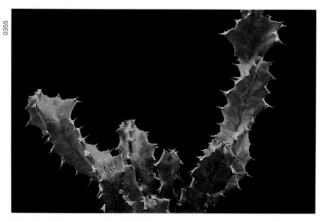

0355

Euphorbia enormis N.E. Br.
EUPHORBIACEAE

Thick, tuberous root with spiralling stems to 20 cm long and 2–3 cm thick, tubercles 6 mm long with spines in pairs; rudimentary, caducous leaves to 1 mm long; yellowish-green inflorescence borne on short peduncle.

South Africa (Transvaal)   CITES App. II

0190

Euphorbia enterophora
Drake
EUPHORBIACEAE

Arborescent plant with trunk to 2 m high; 2-angled, flat branches; green leaves growing only at apices; inflorescence borne at stem apices. Similar to *E. xylophylloides* from which it is distinguished by reddish fuzz on new growth.

Madagascar

CITES App. II

1123

Euphorbia espinosa Pax
EUPHORBIACEAE

Shrub to 3 m high; cylindrical stems with brown bark; rudimentary, caducous leaves; sessile inflorescence borne from leaf scars.

Euphorbia gynophora Pax
Tanzania, Zimbabwe

CITES App. II

0322

Euphorbia fasciculata
Thunb.
EUPHORBIACEAE

Clavate stems to 50 cm high with spine-like leaf clumps; rudimentary, caducous leaves; inflorescence borne on persistent peduncle 10–15 cm long from stem apex.

South Africa (Cape Province)

CITES App. II

0155

Euphorbia ferox Marloth
EUPHORBIACEAE

Spiny clumps to 60 cm in diameter with branches 8–25 cm long, partly hidden in soil; numerous brown spines (modified peduncles) greying with age; rudimentary, caducous leaves; inflorescence borne on peduncle 4–6 mm long at end of branches; brown bracts.

Euphorbia caespitosa N.E. Br.
South Africa (Cape Province)   CITES App. II

Euphorbia fimbriata
Scop.
EUPHORBIACEAE

Main stem cylindrical 30 cm or more high; 7–12 light green, ribbed, tuberculate, rebranching branches; spines to 4 cm long; rudimentary, caducous, green leaves with red tips; inflorescence borne on short peduncle from axils of tubercles.

South Africa (Cape Province)

CITES App. II

Euphorbia fractiflexa
S. Carter & J.R.I. Wood
EUPHORBIACEAE

Sharply 3-angled, green stems to 2.5 m high and 3 cm thick; stem angles are arranged in zigzag line; rudimentary, caducous leaves; yellow inflorescence with 2–8 cyathia on short peduncles.

Saudi Arabia, Yemen

CITES App. II

Euphorbia fluminis
S. Carter
EUPHORBIACEAE

Green 4-angled stems with green variegations to 2 m high; solitary spines 15 mm long and forked apically; green, caducous leaves 5–8 mm long; reddish inflorescence.

Kenya

CITES App. II

Euphorbia francoisii Leandri
EUPHORBIACEAE

Stoloniferous plants; variegated green leaves 5–7 cm long with red mid-rib and undulate margins arranged in rosettes; yellowish-green inflorescence on peduncle to 1 cm long.

Madagascar   CITES App. I

Euphorbia fortuita A.C. White, Dyer & B. Sloane
EUPHORBIACEAE

Tuberous root continuing into stem to form caudex 8–16 cm thick; branches 5–10 cm long; rudimentary, caducous leaves; cyathia clustered at end of branches; short peduncles.

South Africa (Cape Province)   CITES App. II

Euphorbia friedrichiae
Dinter
EUPHORBIACEAE

Caudex 15–20 cm high with several blue-green, spineless, tuberculate branches; milky-blue, waxy leaves 4 cm long; cyathia borne at tips of new growth on persistent peduncles.

Namibia

CITES App. II

Euphorbia fruticosa Forssk.
EUPHORBIACEAE

Spiny shrub 50 cm high; green-grey stems branching from base and forming clumps to 50 cm in diameter; black spines in pairs; bright yellow inflorescence born on ribs of new growth.

Yemen

CITES App. II

Euphorbia fusiformis A. Ham. ex Don
EUPHORBIACEAE

Cylindrical root with stems 1–2 cm long; lanceolate, green leaves with red margins and mid-vein 4–5 cm long; pink to reddish inflorescence with several cyathia arising from apex of cylindrical stems. The photograph shows a young seedling.

India

CITES App. II

Euphorbia globosa (Haw.) Sims
EUPHORBIACEAE

Tuberous root with numerous dark green, later grey, globose branches 13 cm long; green to reddish, caducous leaves 1–2 mm long; inflorescence borne on persistent, much-branched peduncle 10 cm long.

Euphorbia glomerata Marloth
South Africa (Cape Province)

CITES App. II

Euphorbia gorgonis A. Berger
EUPHORBIACEAE

Globose, subterranean stem producing small, dull green, tuberculate branches often tinged with red and 1–2.5 cm long (to 5 cm in cultivation) from stem apex; rudimentary, caducous leaves; inflorescence borne at ends of main stem and branches on peduncle to 1 cm long.

South Africa (Cape Province)

CITES App. II

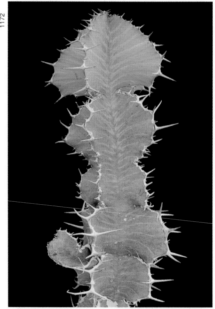

Euphorbia grandialata R.A. Dyer
EUPHORBIACEAE

Plant to 3 m high, branching from base; stems 10–15 cm in diameter divided into segments 10–15 cm long; spines in pairs; rudimentary, caducous leaves; inflorescence borne from stem apices on short peduncle.

South Africa (Transvaal)

CITES App. II

Euphorbia grandidens Haw.
EUPHORBIACEAE

Main trunk 6–10 m high, branching freely to form several stem-like, green branches ending in slender terminal branchlets; rudimentary, caducous leaves; inflorescence born on short peduncle from ends of branches.

South Africa (Transvaal)

CITES App. II

Euphorbia greenwayi
P.R.O. Bally & S. Carter
EUPHORBIACEAE

Branched, blue-green stems with whitish stripes; spines 1 cm long; rudimentary, caducous leaves; inflorescence borne on forked peduncle near branch apices; cyathia whitish outside and yellow inside with protruding red stamens.

Tanzania

CITES App. II

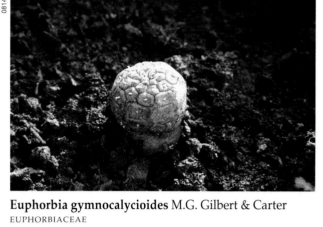

Euphorbia gymnocalycioides M.G. Gilbert & Carter
EUPHORBIACEAE

Short, cylindrical, tuberculate, bluish-green stem to 10 cm high and 8 cm in diameter; rudimentary, caducous leaves; inflorescence borne on previous year's growth; cyathia white outside, reddish-brown inside.

Ethiopia
CITES App. II

Euphorbia groenewaldii R.A. Dyer
EUPHORBIACEAE

Tuberous root 5–10 cm thick and to 20 cm high, continuing into main stem from which small, spirally twisted branches arise; rudimentary, caducous leaves; inflorescence borne on short peduncle from new and old branches.

South Africa (Transvaal)
CITES App. II

Euphorbia hadramautica Baker aff.
EUPHORBIACEAE

Brown stem, green when young; green leaves 10–15 cm long and to 4 cm wide with reddish veins; inflorescence borne amid leaves on peduncle 12 mm long from stem apices.

Arabian peninsula
CITES App. II

Euphorbia guillemetii Ursch & Leandri
EUPHORBIACEAE

Spiny shrub similar to *E. milii* but with smaller leaves.

Madagascar
CITES App. II

Euphorbia hamata
(Haw.) Sweet
EUPHORBIACEAE

Shrub to 40 cm high with short caudex and tuberous root; stems branching from base; branches and stems tuberculate; caducous, green leaves 1–2 cm long of variable shape; sessile inflorescence borne at branch apices; yellowish bracts.

South Africa (Cape Province)

CITES App. II

Euphorbia handiensis Burchard
EUPHORBIACEAE

Shrub to 80 cm high branching from base; branches with 8–14 ribs; spines 3 cm long in pairs; rudimentary, caducous leaves; reddish inflorescence borne from stem apices.

Canary Islands (Fuerteventura)

CITES App. II

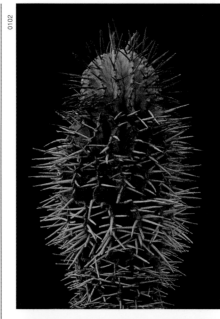

Euphorbia horrida Boiss.
EUPHORBIACEAE

Densely spined stems to 15 cm thick with 10–20 prominent angles (to 5 cm); rudimentary, caducous leaves; inflorescence borne near base of spines; peduncle to 1 cm long. Variable species growing in clumps to 1 m high. At least 6 varieties have been described.

South Africa (Cape Province)

CITES App. II

Euphorbia heptagona L.
EUPHORBIACEAE

Shrub to 1 m high branched at base and towards apices; grey-green branches; inflorescence borne on persistent, reddish-brown peduncle to 3 cm long at branch apices.

Euphorbia morinii A. Berger
South Africa (Cape Province)

CITES App. II

Euphorbia horrida var. striata A.C. White, Dyer & B. Sloane
EUPHORBIACEAE

Grey-green branches with wavy angles and often with white stripes; otherwise similar to the type species.

South Africa (Cape Province)

CITES App. II

Euphorbia horombensis Ursch & Leandri
EUPHORBIACEAE

Thorny, branched stems to 1 m high; green leaves 5–10 cm long with red margins crowded at stem apices; reddish-brown inflorescence borne on branched peduncle 8–10 cm long.

Madagascar

CITES App. II

Euphorbia horwoodii S. Carter & Lavranos
EUPHORBIACEAE

In the juvenile stage spherical, but when the plant's body increases in size 5–7 lateral branches develop and grow to 15 cm long; yellow inflorescence borne on forked penduncle 1 cm long.

Somalia

CITES App. II

Euphorbia hypogaea
Marloth

EUPHORBIACEAE

Caudex and branches grow underground with secondary branches 2–5 cm long appearing above soil level; branches covered with conical tubercles bearing rudimentary, caducous, glabrous leaves; inflorescence borne near apex of secondary branches on peduncle 1–1.5 cm long.

South Africa (Cape Province)

CITES App. II

Euphorbia infausta N.E. Br.

EUPHORBIACEAE

This is a variant of *E. meloformis* Aiton but is more caespitose and has taller stems. It should be regarded as synonym but is still found in many collections and trade catalogues under this name.

South Africa (Cape Province)

CITES App. II

Euphorbia inermis Mill.

EUPHORBIACEAE

Tuberous root with thick caudex to 15 cm in diameter from which several branches to 30 cm long arise; rudimentary, caducous leaves are arranged in spiral row; inflorescence clustered at branch ends on peduncle 3–4 mm long; wholly white bracteoles on male flowers.

South Africa (Cape Province)

CITES App. II

Euphorbia jansenvillensis Nel

EUPHORBIACEAE

Spineless, erect 5-angled, glaucous green stems to 15 cm long, branched and suckering from base; rudimentary, caducous leaves; inflorescence borne on short peduncle at upper ends of stems.

South Africa (Cape Province)

CITES App. II

Euphorbia inermis var. huttonae A.C. White & Dyer

EUPHORBIACEAE

Similar to *E. inermis* from which it is mainly distinguished by lack of bracteoles on male flowers.

Euphorbia huttonae N.E. Br.

South Africa (Cape Province)

CITES App. II

Euphorbia juttae Dinter

EUPHORBIACEAE

Spineless, bluish-green shrub 10–15 cm high, freely branching from base; grey-green leaves 2–3 cm long; inflorescence borne on short peduncle at apex of new branches.

Namibia

CITES App. II

Euphorbia knobelii Letty
EUPHORBIACEAE

Subterranean trunk with numerous erect, spiny, pale green, 5-angled stems to 1 m high and with dark green markings; spines 1 cm long in pairs; rudimentary caducous leaves; inflorescence borne on short peduncle at upper ends of stems.

South Africa (Transvaal)   CITES App. II

Euphorbia knuthii Pax
EUPHORBIACEAE

Tuberous plant with subterranean rizhomes; tuberculate, light green, aerial branches 5–15 cm long with grey-green stripes; pairs of spines 4–8 mm long; rudimentary, caducous leaves; inflorescence borne on short peduncle from stem apices; green bracts.

South Africa (Cape Province)   CITES App. II

Euphorbia kondoi Rauh & Razaf.
EUPHORBIACEAE

Plants to 70 cm high with thick root and several thin, spiny branches; green leaves 3 cm long and 3.5 mm wide with prominent mid-vein beneath; lemon yellow inflorescence borne just below branch apices on peduncle 2–4 mm long.

Madagascar

CITES App. II

Euphorbia lactea Haw.
EUPHORBIACEAE

Shrub to 2 m tall with 3- or 4-angled dark green branches with paler band; rudimentary, caducous leaves; yellow inflorescence borne on short peduncle from new stem growth.

India   CITES App. II

Euphorbia laikipiensis S. Carter
EUPHORBIACEAE

Stems branching from base; cylindrical, toothed branches 5–10 cm long; single white spines to 1 cm long; rudimentary, caducous leaves; yellow inflorescence borne on short peduncle.

Kenya   CITES App. II

Euphorbia lavranii Leach
EUPHORBIACEAE

Dwarf shrub to 20 cm high with numerous branches 5 mm thick; tubercles arranged in pairs; rudimentary, caducous leaves; inflorescence with numerous cyathia borne on short peduncle at branch apices.

Namibia   CITES App. II

Euphorbia ledienii A. Berger
EUPHORBIACEAE
Shrub to 2 m high with 5-angled stems arising from base; spines to 2 cm long in pairs; rudimentary, caducous leaves; sessile, yellow inflorescence borne near branch apices.
South Africa (Cape Province)   CITES App. II

Euphorbia lignosa
Marloth
EUPHORBIACEAE
Stems to 30 cm high, branching and rebranching from apex to form hemispherical mass to 1 m in diameter; branches hard and spiny; small, green leaves; sessile inflorescence borne near branch apices.
Namibia

CITES App. II

Euphorbia lophogona Lam.
EUPHORBIACEAE
Shrubs to 50 cm with spiny, 5-angled branches; showy, bright green leaves 15–20 cm long; flamboyant pink, cream or white inflorescence borne on peduncle 2–3 cm long.
Madagascar   CITES App. II

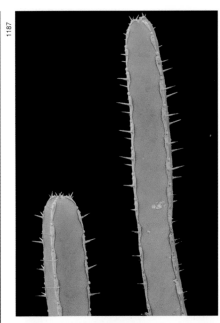

Euphorbia lyndenburgensis
Schweick & Letty
EUPHORBIACEAE
Trunk 60–100 cm high, branching from base and near apex; 4-angled, green or pale greenish-yellow stems; pairs of brown spines 5–8 mm long borne on ridges of stems; rudimentary, caducous leaves; sessile inflorescence with scale-like bracts.
South Africa (Transvaal)

CITES App. II

Euphorbia maleolensis E. Phillips
EUPHORBIACEAE
Short caudex to 10 cm thick developing from thick root; several tuberculate branches to 20 cm long; green leaves to 1 cm long in branch apices; inflorescence on peduncle 1 cm long borne among leaves in upper one-third of branches.
South Africa (Transvaal)   CITES App. II

Euphorbia mammillaris
L.
EUPHORBIACEAE
Small plants to 18 cm high; green branches 6 cm in diameter with hexagonal tubercles; solitary grey spines 1 cm long; rudimentary, caducous leaves; inflorescence with cyathia in clusters covering branch apices on peduncle 1–2 mm long.
South Africa (Cape Province)

CITES App. II

Euphorbia meloformis Aiton
EUPHORBIACEAE
Solitary, globose stems, rarely branched from base, to 10 cm in diameter; green stems with 8–12 ribs and lighter bands; rudimentary, caducous leaves; inflorescence with several cyathia borne on centre of stem apex; persistent, dichotomously forked peduncles.
South Africa (Cape Province)   CITES App. II

Euphorbia milii 'Lutea' Rauh
EUPHORBIACEAE
A cultivar with white bracts.
Madagascar

Euphorbia memoralis R.A. Dyer
EUPHORBIACEAE
Shrub to 2 m high; 5- to 7-angled, segmented, pale green stems with horny margins and brown spines 6 mm long; pale green, caducous leaves to 2 cm long; inflorescence borne on short peduncle near stem apices. Plant photographed in habitat.
Zimbabwe   CITES App. II

Euphorbia milii var. tananarivae Leandri
EUPHORBIACEAE
A little-branched variety with yellow bracts; stems 2–3 cm in diameter; green leaves with reddish margins 7–10 cm long.
Madagascar   CITES App. II

Euphorbia milii Des Moul.
EUPHORBIACEAE
Shrub to 1.5 m high in cultivation; large, caducous, green leaves with reddish margins at ends of thorny branches; cyathia are on long peduncles with red bracts; several varieties have been described.
Euphorbia splendens Bojer
Madagascar   CITES App. II

Euphorbia millotii Ursch & Leandri
EUPHORBIACEAE
Shrub to 20 cm high, branched from base; green-red leaves to 4 cm long at growing apices; reddish inflorescence with pendent cyathia borne on peduncle to 1 cm long.
Madagascar   CITES App. II

Euphorbia morattii Rauh
EUPHORBIACEAE

Subterranean caudex to 4 cm in diameter; 10–20 caducous leaves aranged in rosette; dark green leaves to 9 cm long and 2 cm wide with whitish spots, red mid-vein and crisped margins; brownish-red inflorescence borne from apex among leaves on peduncle 2–3 cm long.

Madagascar   CITES App. I

Euphorbia multiceps A. Berger
EUPHORBIACEAE

Plant to 30 cm high and to 20 cm in diameter at base with many tuberculate, horizontally spreading branches; green leaves 12 mm long; inflorescence borne at ends of branches on peduncle 4–6 mm long.

South Africa (Cape Province)   CITES App. II

Euphorbia mosaica P.R.O. Bally & S. Carter
EUPHORBIACEAE

Stems 3–5 cm high and 1–2 cm thick with many short branches; stems and branches 6- to 9-angled with tubercles; spines 1.5 mm long in pairs; rudimentary, caducous leaves; sessile, whitish inflorescence borne near stem and branch apices.

Somalia   CITES App. II

Euphorbia namuskluftensis L.C. Leach
EUPHORBIACEAE

Tuberous, rhizomatose root with several tuberculate branches 6 cm long and 5 mm thick; green, caducous leaves 2–3 mm long; purplish-green inflorescence borne at branch apices.

Namibia   CITES App. II

Euphorbia muirii N.E. Br.
EUPHORBIACEAE

Spineless stems to 20 cm long and 15 mm thick arising from base of caudex; erect leaves to 2 cm long and 1 mm wide; inflorescence near tips of branches on peduncle 2 cm long.

Southern Africa   CITES App. II

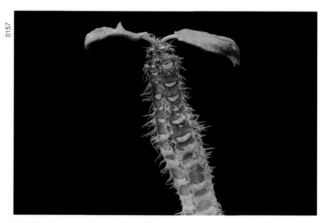

Euphorbia neohumbertii Boiteau
EUPHORBIACEAE

Shrub to 40 cm high; 5-angled, green stems with prominent greyish leaf scars and spines 8 mm long; green leaves to 10 cm long; red inflorescence borne at stem apices.

Madagascar   CITES App. II

Euphorbia neriifolia L.
EUPHORBIACEAE
Cylindrical or 5-angled, light green stems with black spines; light green leaves 8–15 cm long at apex of stems; yellow-green inflorescence borne on short peduncle on upper leaf axil.
India   CITES App. II

Euphorbia nivulia Buch.-Ham.
EUPHORBIACEAE
Shrub freely branching to 1.5 m high; green leaves 10 cm long; inflorescence borne on short peduncle.
India

CITES App. II

Euphorbia obesa Hook.f.
EUPHORBIACEAE
Spineless, grey-green, dwarf, spherical plants with transverse red-brown or purplish bands; rudimentary, caducous leaves; small inflorescence borne on short peduncle from stem apices; female and male flowers are borne on different plants.
South Africa (Cape Province)   CITES App. II

Euphorbia officinarum L.
EUPHORBIACEAE
Shrub 90–120 cm high; stem branched; branches 8- or 15-sided with horny margins; whitish-grey spines in pairs; rudimentary, caducous leaves; yellow inflorescence borne from apex of stems.
Morocco   CITES App. II

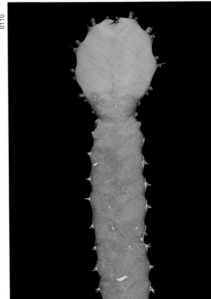

Euphorbia opuntioides N.E. Br.
EUPHORBIACEAE
Low shrub with characteristic, flattened, 2-angled branches 10–30 cm long; rudimentary, caducous leaves; red inflorescence borne near branch apices.
Angola

CITES App. II

Euphorbia opuntioides N.E. Br.
EUPHORBIACEAE
The flowering stem.

Euphorbia ornithopus Jacq.
EUPHORBIACEAE

Branches 4–10 cm long arising from thick main stem and forming mats; rudimentary, caducous leaves; inflorescence produced from branch apices on simple or branched peduncle to 10 cm long.

South Africa (Cape Province)　　　　CITES App. II

Euphorbia pauliana Ursch & Leandri
EUPHORBIACEAE

Solitary stems 30–50 cm high with thorns on tubercles arranged in spiral rows; leaves 15–25 cm long with undulate margins and, sometimes, red veins; long-stalked inflorescence with pendent, yellow cyathia. Each plant may have to 300 flowers.

Madagascar　　　　CITES App. II

Euphorbia pachypodioides Boiteau
EUPHORBIACEAE

Stems 30–50 cm high covered with old leaf scars arranged in spiral; bluish-green leaves 10–15 cm long and to 3.5 cm wide borne at ends of stems; several reddish-purple cyathia borne on peduncles to 15 cm long arising from stem apices.

Euphorbia antankara Leandri

Madagascar　　　　CITES App. II

Euphorbia pedilanthoides Denis
EUPHORBIACEAE

Subterranean caudex with several branches to 1 m high; spines 1 cm long in pairs; green leaves 2–4 cm long; yellowish-green to orange-red inflorescence borne near branch apices on peduncle 5 mm long.

Madagascar

CITES App. II

Euphorbia parciramulosa Schweinf.
EUPHORBIACEAE

Short-stemmed shrub to 2 m high with grey spines 4–5 cm long; caducous leaves 3–5 mm long; yellowish inflorescence borne from tips of branches.

Yemen

CITES App. II

Euphorbia persistens R.A. Dyer
EUPHORBIACEAE

Subterranean stems with many glaucous green, 3- to 5-angled branches 15–20 cm long with darker stripes; brown spines 15 mm long; inflorescence borne near branch apices on short peduncle.

South Africa　　　　CITES App. II

Euphorbia phosphorea Mart.

EUPHORBIACEAE

Shrub with many stems 5 mm thick; tiny green leaves at growing apices; small inflorescence borne near stem apices.

Brazil

CITES App. II

Euphorbia pillansii N.E. Br.

EUPHORBIACEAE

Plants with 7- to 10-angled, green branches to 30 cm long with pale and dark green bands; robust, grey spines 1–5 cm long; rudimentary, green, caducous leaves; inflorescence borne at branch apices on peducle to 12 mm long.

South Africa (Cape Province)

CITES App. II

Euphorbia piscidermis M.G. Gilbert

EUPHORBIACEAE

Globular to cylindrical stem to 5 cm in diameter and 5–8 cm high; stem covered in greyish-white or yellowish, pine-cone shaped tubercles arranged in spiral and covered with scale-like growths; inflorescence borne on short peduncle; cyathia green outside, yellow inside.

Ethiopia, Somalia

CITES App. II

Euphorbia platyclada
Rauh

EUPHORBIACEAE

Tuberous root with erect, rebranching, grey-green, spineless branches to 50 cm long with black and red markings; caducous leaves leaving evident leaf scar; red-brown inflorescence borne on short peduncles.

Madagascar

CITES App. II

Euphorbia poissonii Pax

EUPHORBIACEAE

Plant 1–1.5 m high; stems with cylindrical branches 4 cm in diameter; single spines; green leaves 10–15 cm long and 7 cm wide at apex; almost sessile, yellowish-green inflorescence.

Ghana, Nigeria

CITES App. II

Euphorbia polyacantha
Boiss.

EUPHORBIACEAE

Shrub 1–1.5 m high; 4- to 5-angled branches 4 cm in diameter; spines 6 mm long; small, grey, caducous leaves; almost sessile, yellow inflorescence borne at stems apices.

Ethiopia

CITES App. II

Euphorbia pseudocactus
A. Berger
EUPHORBIACEAE

Shrub to 1 m high and 2 m in diameter with numerous, spreading, 4- or 5-angled, green, segmented stems with V-shaped yellow lines; spines in pairs 1 cm long; rudimentary, caducous leaves; yellow, sessile inflorescence arising from new stems.
South Africa (Natal)

CITES App. II

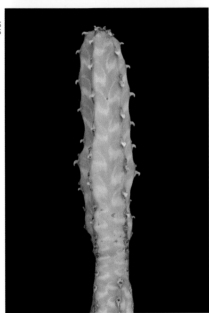

Euphorbia pseudocactus
var. lyttoniana Frick
EUPHORBIACEAE
A spineless variety.
South Africa

CITES App. II

Euphorbia pteroneura
A. Berger
EUPHORBIACEAE

Shrub 40–70 cm long; 4- to 6-angled, spineless branches; green, caducous leaves 4 cm long; yellow-green inflorescence borne at branch apices.
Mexico

CITES App. II

Euphorbia pugniformis Boiss.
EUPHORBIACEAE

Main stem arises from root forming subglobose body 5–8 cm thick crowned with cylindrical, tuberculate branches 5–10 cm high; lanceolate, caducous, green leaves 4–6 mm long; inflorescence with numerous cyathia and short peduncle arising from central part of body, less often from tips of branches.
South Africa (Cape Province)   CITES App. II

Euphorbia pulvinata Marloth
EUPHORBIACEAE

Green, 7- to 10-angled branches 15–30 cm long arising from base to form dense clumps to 1.5 m in diameter; persistent red peduncles to 15 cm long form spines, greying with age; rudimentary, caducous leaves; sessile inflorescence clustered at branch apices.
Lesotho, South Africa (Cape Province, Natal, Transvaal)   CITES App. II

Euphorbia quadrispina
S. Carter
EUPHORBIACEAE

Dark green, cylindrical branches to 20 cm long with lighter green markings; dark spines 1–2 cm long; rudimentary, caducous leaves; pinkish-orange inflorescence borne along stems.
Kenya

CITES App. II

Euphorbia ramiglans
N.E. Br.

EUPHORBIACEAE

Caudex with spineless, tuberculate branches 2–4 cm long; caducous leaves to 1 cm long; inflorescence borne on short peduncle at ends of branches.

South Africa (Cape Province)

CITES App. II

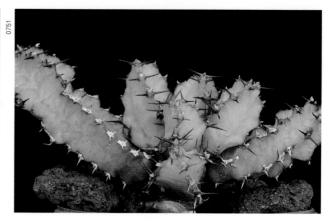

Euphorbia restricta R.A. Dyer

EUPHORBIACEAE

Stems 8 cm in diameter with numerous, 4- to 6-angled branches 10–15 cm long with horny margins; grey, black-tipped spines 1 cm long; yellow inflorescence borne near stem apices.

South Africa (Transvaal)   CITES App. II

Euphorbia ramipressa Croizat

EUPHORBIACEAE

Shrub with many 2-angled stems; rudimentary, caducous leaves; grey spines to 6 mm long; greenish inflorescence borne from branch apices. Known only in cultivation.

Distribution unknown   CITES App. II

Euphorbia richardsiae L.C. Leach

EUPHORBIACEAE

Plant to 15 cm high; thin, 4- to 5-angled stems with rudimentary, caducous leaves; inflorescence borne on short peduncle from stem apices.

Malawi   CITES App. II

Euphorbia resinifera
A. Berger

EUPHORBIACEAE

Shrub freely branching from base; 4-angled stems to 40 cm high; grey-green spines 5–8 mm long in pairs; yellow inflorescence borne on short peduncle from stem apices.

Euphorbia moquadarensis Hort.; *E. san-salvador* Hort.

Morocco

CITES App. II

Euphorbia samburuensis
P.R.O. Bally & S. Carter

EUPHORBIACEAE

Grey-green stems 2 cm in diameter; red to pale grey spines 2–5 cm long; small leaves; yellow inflorescence borne on short peduncle near stem apices.

Kenya

CITES App. II

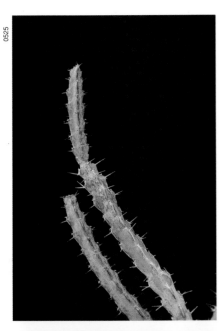

Euphorbia saxorum
P.R.O. Bally & S. Carter
EUPHORBIACEAE

Branching stems; main stem 50–60 cm long and decumbent; secondary, 4-angled branches erect, 10–20 cm high and 8 mm in diameter; stems and branches green; reddish-brown spines to 1 cm with continuous shields; rudimentary, caducous leaves; red inflorescence borne near branch apices.

Kenya

CITES App. II

Euphorbia sepulta P.R.O. Bally & S. Carter
EUPHORBIACEAE

Tuberous root with truncate, grey-green stems forming clumps to 30 cm in diameter; rudimentary, caducous leaves; grey spines 2–3 mm long; inflorescence borne from stem apices.

Somalia

CITES App. II

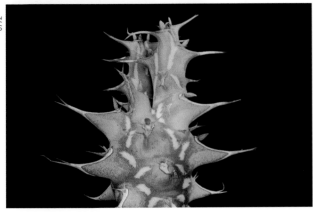

Euphorbia schizacantha Pax
EUPHORBIACEAE

Mature plants to 1.5 m high and 5 cm thick, with numerous green branches 8–10 cm long and 5 cm thick with pale green, longitudinal stripes; grey spines to 3 cm long; rudimentary, caducous leaves; red inflorescence borne from upper part of branches.

Ethiopia, Somalia

CITES App. II

Euphorbia sp. Lavranos & Newton 13176
EUPHORBIACEAE

There are 2 forms of this plant; 1 is compact and densely branched; the other (illustrated here) has longer branches; grey spines 2–3 cm long; rudimentary, caducous leaves; yellowish inflorescence on new growth.

Southern Africa

CITES App. II

Euphorbia schoenlandii Pax
EUPHORBIACEAE

Solitary plant to 1 m high; stems 20 cm in diameter with spiny tubercles; pale brown spines to 5 cm long, becoming whitish with age; rudimentary, caducous leaves; inflorescence borne on peduncle 1–3 cm long.

South Africa (Cape Province)

CITES App. II

Euphorbia squarrosa Haw.
EUPHORBIACEAE

Thick, subterranean caudex with numerous prostrate or erect stems 4–15 cm long with pairs of thorns 1–5 cm long on margins; rudimentary, caducous leaves; inflorescence borne on short peduncle with numerous cyathia.

Euphorbia mammillosa Lem.

South Africa (Cape Province)

CITES App. II

Euphorbia stellaespina Haw.
EUPHORBIACEAE

Massive clumps with several green stems (brown with age) to 50 cm high and 8 cm in diameter branching from base; brown, star-like spines 1 cm or more long; rudimentary, caducous leaves; inflorescence borne from branch apices on short peduncle.

South Africa (Cape Province)   CITES App. II

Euphorbia stellata Willd.
EUPHORBIACEAE

Dwarf plants with taproot to 15 cm long; leafless, tuberculate, prostrate stems to 15 cm long with spines at apices of tubercles; stems green or purplish-brown with white variegation on upper surface; inflorescence borne on short peduncle with small bracts.

South Africa (Cape Province)   CITES App. II

Euphorbia stenoclada Baill.
EUPHORBIACEAE

Shrub to 1 m high with flat, leafless branches with brown spines; yellow inflorescence borne from branch apices.

Madagascar   CITES App. II

Euphorbia suzannae Marloth
EUPHORBIACEAE

Spineless, green stems to 10 cm high with taproot; stems with several ribs each bearing prominent tubercles; small, caducous leaves borne at tips of tubercles; inflorescence at apex of main stem and branches.

South Africa (Cape Province)   CITES App. I

Euphorbia symmetrica A.C. White, Dyer & Sloane
EUPHORBIACEAE

Similar to *E. obesa* but with long taproot.

South Africa (Cape Province)   CITES App. I

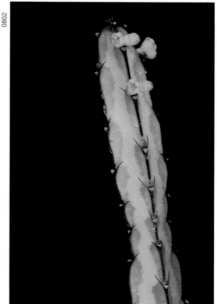

Euphorbia taruensis S. Carter
EUPHORBIACEAE

Rhizomatous stems to 20 cm high (to 45 cm in cultivation) branching from base; 4-angled green variegated branches; green, deltoid leaves 12 mm long; inconspicuous spines; almost sessile, yellow-brown inflorescence.

Kenya

CITES App. II

Euphorbia tenuispinosa
Gilli

EUPHORBIACEAE

Tuberous root with branching stems to 1 m high; 4-angled, olive-green variegated branches with prominent teeth; rudimentary, caducous leaves; blackish spines 3–6 mm long; yellowish-brown inflorescence borne on short penduncle.

Kenya

CITES App. II

Euphorbia trichadenia Pax

EUPHORBIACEAE

Tuberous root with herbaceous stems to 10 cm long; spineless; green leaves 5–8 cm long; inflorescence on short peduncle arising from forks of stems.

South Africa (Cape Province, Transvaal) CITES App. II

Euphorbia tirucalli L.

EUPHORBIACEAE

Spineless shrub to 4 m tall or tree to 12 m tall; light green branches 7–15 mm thick; few small, glaucous green leaves present only at tips of growing branches; sessile inflorescence clustered at branch apices.

Euphorbia rhipsaloides Welw.; *E. viminalis* Mill.

Tropical East Africa, southern Africa CITES App. II

Euphorbia tridentata Lam.

EUPHORBIACEAE

Short branches arising from thick stem to form mats; tuberous root; cylindrical, dull green, spineless branches with hexagonal tubercles; dark green, caducous leaves 4–6 mm long; inflorescence borne on short peduncle from branch apices.

South Africa (Cape Province) CITES App. II

Euphorbia tortirama R.A. Dyer

EUPHORBIACEAE

Body 30 cm high and 15 cm thick buried in soil with taproot; up to 50 branches 30 cm long arise from caudex; branches with tubercles bearing pairs of greyish spines to 2 cm long; rudimentary, caducous leaves; inflorescence on short peduncle at stem apices.

South Africa (Transvaal) CITES App. II

Euphorbia trigona Haw.

EUPHORBIACEAE

Shrub or small tree with 3- or 4-angled stems; green or pinkish-red leaves to 2 cm long; spines 3 mm long in pairs.

Euphorbia hermetiana Lem.

Namibia

CITES App. II

Euphorbia tubiglans
Marloth

EUPHORBIACEAE

Caudex with taproot 8–10 cm long and 4–5 cm thick; 5-angled, bluish-green, spineless branches to 15 cm long; rudimentary, caducous leaves; inflorescence borne on short peduncle near branch apices.

South Africa (Cape Province)

CITES App. II

Euphorbia vigueri Denis

EUPHORBIACEAE

Shrub to 1.5 m high; 6-angled stems with triangular leaf cushions bearing spine; green leaves 10 cm long and 3 cm wide at ends of branches; red inflorescence borne on 2–3 cm long peduncle arising from stem apices.

Madagascar

CITES App. II

Euphorbia uhligiana Pax

EUPHORBIACEAE

Stems 4-angled, 30–100 cm long branching from base with prominent teeth; grey spines to 15 mm long with black tips; rudimentary, caducous leaves; yellowish inflorescence borne near stem apices.

Kenya, Tanzania

CITES App. II

Euphorbia virosa Willd.

EUPHORBIACEAE

Large clumps to 2 m high; 5- to 8-angled, grey-green branches 5 cm in diameter; grey spines 1 cm long; rudimentary, caducous leaves; inflorescence borne on short peduncle at branch apices.

Angola, Namibia, South Africa

CITES App. II

Euphorbia valida N.E. Br.

EUPHORBIACEAE

Solitary, globose to elongated green stems to 13 cm in diameter and to 30 cm high with markings in lower part; spineless; persistent, yellowish-brown inflorescence 5–10 cm tall on branched, grey, persistent peduncle 10–20 cm long.

South Africa (Cape Province)   CITES App. II

Euphorbia wildii Leach

EUPHORBIACEAE

Cylindrical, spineless, tuberculate stems to 2 m high; bluish-green leaves (red in dry, sunny conditions) 10–12 cm long near apex; green inflorescence borne on 10 cm long peduncle arising near stem apices. Plant photographed in habitat at Great Dyke, Zimbabwe.

Zimbabwe

CITES App. II

Euphorbia xylophylloides Brongn. ex Lem.
EUPHORBIACEAE
Branching stems to 1.5 m high; 2-angled, flat, pale green branches; spineless; rudimentary, caducous leaves; inflorescence borne at branch apices.
Madagascar   CITES App. II

Faucaria longifolia L. Bol.
MESEMBRYANTHEMACEAE
Green leaves to 5 cm long, keeled towards apex and with several teeth; yellow flowers.
South Africa (Cape Province)

Faucaria bosscheana (A. Berger) Schwantes
MESEMBRYANTHEMACEAE
Glossy green, rhomboidal leaves 3 cm long in groups of 6–8; yellow flowers.
South Africa (Cape Province)

Faucaria peersii L. Bol.
MESEMBRYANTHEMACEAE
Rhomboidal, green leaves 2–4 cm long with whitish margins and 3–8 marginal teeth; yellow flowers.
South Africa (Cape Province)

Faucaria britteniae L. Bol.
MESEMBRYANTHEMACEAE
Grey-green leaves to 2.5 cm long with cartilaginous border and 3–4 or more teeth; yellow flowers.
South Africa (Cape Province)

Faucaria speciosa L. Bol.
MESEMBRYANTHEMACEAE
Green leaves 2–3 cm long and to 3 cm wide with dentate margins; large teeth 4 mm wide at base and tipped with bristles; yellow flowers.
South Africa (Cape Province)

Faucaria tigrina (Haw.) Schwantes
MESEMBRYANTHEMACEAE
Grey-green leaves 3–5 cm long with rounded lower surface; leaf margins bear 8–10 teeth, tapering to become hair-fine; yellow flowers.
South Africa (Cape Province)

Faucaria tuberculosa (Rolfe) Schwantes
MESEMBRYANTHEMACEAE
Dark green leaves to 2 cm long with several teeth-like tubercles on upper surface and several marginal teeth; yellow flowers.
South Africa (Cape Province)

Fenestraria aurantiaca N.E. Br.
MESEMBRYANTHEMACEAE
Clavate, light green leaves 2–3 cm long with translucent tips, forming clumps to 10 cm in diameter; yellow flowers.
Namibia

Fenestraria rhopalophylla (Schltr. & Diels) N.E. Br.
MESEMBRYANTHEMACEAE
Light green leaves to 3 cm long with transparent tips and forming clumps 10 cm and more in diameter; white flowers.
Namibia

Ficus petiolaris Kunth
MORACEAE
Small tree with yellow bark and long roots; pale green leaves 6 cm long and 4–5 cm wide with mid-vein often pink or scarlet; cultivated for its caudiciform appearance.
Mexico

Fockea edulis (Thunb.) K. Schum.
ASCLEPIADACEAE
Caudex to 30 cm in diameter; climbing or trailing stems 80 cm and more long; green, oblong leaves; whitish flowers. It may attain huge dimensions in habitat.
Southern Africa

Fockea edulis (Thunb.) K. Schum.
ASCLEPIADACEAE
A seedling showing the small caudex.

Fockea multiflora K. Schum.
ASCLEPIADACEAE
A thick, succulent caudex with climbing stems. In habitat a large part of the caudex grows under ground and the succulent stems may climb for several metres. Plant photographed in habitat.
Zimbabwe

Fockea multiflora K. Schum.
ASCLEPIADACEAE
A mature specimen that has fallen down because of the death of the 'companion' tree. Plant photographed in habitat.

Fockea sp.
ASCLEPIADACEAE
In recent years the interest in caudiciform plants has increased, and several unidentified specimens are being imported from the wild. Leaves are usually green, and greenish to whitish flowers are borne in leaf axils.
Southern Africa

Fockea sp.
ASCLEPIADACEAE
An unidentified specimen, but probably *F. tugelensis*.
Southern Africa

Fouquieria columnaris (Kellogg) Kellogg
FOUQUIERIACEAE
A large, elongated caudex with numerous spiny stems to 15 m high; smaller branches are arranged in spirals; greyish leaves 2–4 cm long; yellow flowers.
Idria columnaris Kellogg
Mexico, USA (southwest California)

CITES App. II

129

Fouquieria diguetii
I.M. Johnst.
FOUQUIERIACEAE
Shrub to 4 m tall; trunk branching from base; leaves 4–5 cm long; red flowers. The photograph shows a seedling.
Mexico, USA (southwest California)

Furcraea selloa K. Koch
AGAVACEAE
Stemless or short-stemmed rosettes 60–110 cm in diameter; bright green leaves to 1.2 m long and 10 cm wide; inflorescence 1.5 m tall; greenish-white flowers.
Guatemala, Mexico

Fouquieria diguetii I.M. Johnst.
FOUQUIERIACEAE
A large specimen with several branches from a well-developed caudex.

Gasteria armstrongii Schönland
LILIACEAE
Stemless, with opposite leaves to 5 cm long and 3 cm wide, covered with white tubercles. Leaves are distichous in young plants, forming rosettes 6–10 cm in diameter in adult plants; red flowers.
South Africa (Cape Province)

Frerea indica Dalzell
ASCLEPIADACEAE
Grey-green to green stems 5–10 cm long and 2 cm thick; persistent leaves 6 cm long; brown flowers with yellow central spot.
India   CITES App. II

Gasteria biformis Poelln.
LILIACEAE
Stem becomes elongated to 14 cm; green, distichous leaves 20–25 cm long with white spots; red flowers. Van Jaarsveld considers this to be a synonym of *G. bicolor* Haw.
South Africa (Cape Province)

0386

Gasteria brevifolia Haw.
LILIACEAE

Stemless plants with 10–14 dark green leaves to 15 cm long and 5 cm wide with spots arranged in transverse bands; leaves distichous in young plants, forming rosettes in adult plants; red flowers. Van Jaarsveld considers this a doubtful species.

South Africa (Cape Province)

0422

Gasteria gracilis Baker
LILIACEAE

Rosettes 15–20 cm in diameter; stemless, green leaves 5–10 cm long and 2–3 cm wide with white dots; red flowers. Van Jaarsveld considers this a doubtful species.

South Africa (Natal)

0366

Gasteria ernesti-ruschi Dinter
LILIACEAE

Stoloniferous plants forming dense clumps; up to 12 leaves 7 cm long and 3 cm wide with several white spots; inflorescence 50 cm tall; large, red flowers. Van Jaarsveld considers this to be a variety of *G. pillansi*.

Namibia/South Africa (Little Namaqualand)

0384

Gasteria liliputana Poelln.
LILIACEAE

Short-stemmed rosettes forming clumps; dark green, spotted leaves to 6 cm long; inflorescence 10 cm long; red flowers. Van Jaarsveld considers this to be a variety of *G. bicolor* Haw.

South Africa (Cape Province)

1229

Gasteria fuscopunctata Baker
LILIACEAE

Rosettes to 50 cm in diameter and 30–40 cm high; leaves 20–30 cm long and 7–8 cm wide with grooved upper surface and keel-shaped lower surface; red flowers.

Gasteria excelsa Baker
South Africa (Cape Province)

0126

Gasteria verrucosa (Mill.) C.-J. Duval
LILIACEAE

Rosettes of 10 grey-green, distichous leaves 15 cm long and 2 cm wide with numerous white tubercles and tuberculate margins; red flowers. Van Jaarsveld considers this to be a variety of *G. carinata* C.-J. Duval.

South Africa (Cape Province)

131

Gerrardanthus macrorhizus Harv.
CUCURBITACEAE

Spherical caudex to 50 cm in diameter; thin climbing branches; large, lanceolate leaves, dark green above, pale yellow, often purple, below; small, yellowish-brown flowers.

Kenya, Tanzania

Gibbaeum fissoides (Haw.) Nel
MESEMBRYANTHEMACEAE

Unequal sized, clump-forming, grey-green, sometimes red-tinged leaves about 3 cm long and 6–8 mm wide; red flowers.

Antegibbaeum fissoides (Haw.) Schwantes

South Africa (Cape Province)

Gibbaeum cryptopodium L. Bol.
MESEMBRYANTHEMACEAE

Stemless rootstock, branched, with subglobose (elongate in cultivation), pale green bodies 1.5–3 cm high; pink flowers.

South Africa (Cape Province)

Gibbaeum geminum N.E. Br.
MESEMBRYANTHEMACEAE

Short branches with 2–3 pairs of grey-green leaves to 1.5 cm long and covered with microscopic hairs; red flowers.

South Africa (Cape Province)

Gibbaeum dispar N.E. Br.
MESEMBRYANTHEMACEAE

Clump-forming pairs of unequal sized leaves separated by deep fissure; grey-green leaves covered with fine hairs; reddish-violet flowers.

South Africa (Cape Province)

Gibbaeum gibbosum (Haw.) N.E. Br.
MESEMBRYANTHEMACEAE

Woody rootstock, forming clumps 6–15 cm in diameter; unequal sized, green leaves 2–6 cm long; pale pink flowers.

Gibbaeum perviride (Haw.) N.E. Br.

South Africa (Cape Province)

Gibbaeum heathii (N.E. Br.) L. Bol.
MESEMBRYANTHEMACEAE
Plant with long rootstock growing in clumps; whitish-grey to grey-green leaves forming more or less spherical body 2–6 cm in diameter; white or pink flowers.
South Africa (Cape Province)

Gibbaeum petrense (N.E. Br.) Tisch.
MESEMBRYANTHEMACEAE
Stemless, clump-forming plant with fleshy roots; pale green leaves 1 cm long united for one-third of their length; red flowers.
South Africa (Cape Province)

Gibbaeum nebrowni Tisch.
MESEMBRYANTHEMACEAE
Stemless, clump-forming plants of 2–8 whitish-green to grey-green bodies 1–1.5 cm high and 1–2 cm wide covered with microscopic hairs; pink flowers.
Imitaria muririi N.E. Br.
South Africa (Cape Province)

Gibbaeum pubescens (Haw.) N.E. Br.
MESEMBRYANTHEMACEAE
Short, woody stems with remains of old leaves; whitish-grey leaves of unequal size, the longer 3 cm long, the smaller to 1 cm; purplish-red flowers.
South Africa (Cape Province)

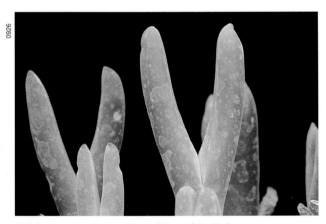

Gibbaeum pachypodium (Kensit) L. Bol.
MESEMBRYANTHEMACEAE
Plants forming clumps 20–40 cm in diameter; greenish or grey-green leaves 6–10 cm long and united at base; pink to pinkish-red flowers.
South Africa (Cape Province)

Gibbaeum pubescens var. shandii (N.E. Br.) Glen
MESEMBRYANTHEMACEAE
Variety with hairy, yellow-green or greyish leaves.
Gibbaeum shandii (N.E. Br.) Schwantes
South Africa (Cape Province)

Gibbaeum schwantesii Tisch.
MESEMBRYANTHEMACEAE
Similar to *G. velutinum* but with longer, dark green to green-brown or grey leaves; white flowers.
South Africa (Cape Province)

Gibbaeum velutinum (L. Bol.) Schwantes
MESEMBRYANTHEMACEAE
Clump-forming, branched plant; divaricate leaves of unequal size, the longer 5–6 cm, the shorter 4 cm long and united at base; pink flowers.
South Africa (Cape Province)

Glottiphyllum davisii L. Bol.
MESEMBRYANTHEMACEAE
Distichous, grey- to yellow-green leaves 3–4 cm long; yellow flowers.
South Africa (Cape Province)

Glottiphyllum fragans (Salm-Dyck) Schwantes
MESEMBRYANTHEMACEAE
Forked stems; densely arranged, whitish-green, more or less distichous leaves 6–8 cm long and 2–3 cm wide, 4 or more on each shoot; fragrant, yellow flowers.
South Africa (Cape Province)

Glottiphyllum jordaanianum Schwantes
MESEMBRYANTHEMACEAE
Distichous leaves, diverse in shape and size; the end of the longer leaf has roundish-keeled lower surface; yellow flowers.
South Africa (Cape Province)

Glottiphyllum latifolium N.E. Br.
MESEMBRYANTHEMACEAE
Soft, fleshy, light green leaves of unequal size to 8 cm long with translucent dots; yellow flowers.
South Africa (Cape Province)

Glottiphyllum linguiforme (L.) N.E. Br.
MESEMBRYANTHEMACEAE

Distichous, linguiform, upwardly curving, green leaves to 6 cm long; yellow flowers.

South Africa (Cape Province)

Glottiphyllum parvifolium L. Bol.
MESEMBRYANTHEMACEAE

Semi-cylindrical, more or less erect, acute, green leaves 3–4 cm long; yellow flowers.

South Africa (Cape Province)

Glottiphyllum nelii Schwantes
MESEMBRYANTHEMACEAE

Light green, distichous leaves, 12 cm long and 3–5 cm wide, more or less erect with rounded and hooked tips; yellow flowers.

South Africa (Cape Province)

Glottiphyllum regium N.E. Br.
MESEMBRYANTHEMACEAE

Erect shoots, each with 2 pairs of unequal sized, light green leaves, the longer 1 to 10 cm long; yellow flowers.

South Africa (Cape Province)

Glottiphyllum oligocarpum L. Bol.
MESEMBRYANTHEMACEAE

Several creeping stems with unequal sized, greenish leaves, often red-tinged at tips, 4–5 cm long and arranged in rows; yellow flowers.

South Africa (Cape Province)

Glottiphyllum surrectum (Haw.) L. Bol.
MESEMBRYANTHEMACEAE

Erect, semi-cylindrical, green leaves with triangular tips; yellow flowers.

South Africa (Cape Province)

135

Graptopetalum bellum (Moran & J. Meyrán) D.R. Hunt
CRASSULACEAE
Compact, almost flat rosettes; grey-green leaves 1–2 cm long; 5–15 vivid magenta-pink flowers over 2.5 cm in diameter.
Tacitus bellus Moran & J. Meyrán
Mexico

Graptopetalum filiferum (S. Watson) Whitehead
CRASSULACEAE
Stemless rosettes to 6 cm in diameter with up to 100 light greyish-green leaves 3 cm long and 12 mm wide, ending in filiform brown bristle 12 mm long; inflorescence 8 cm high; whitish flowers with red spots.
Mexico

Graptopetalum macdougallii Alexander
CRASSULACEAE
Stemless; bluish leaves 3–4 cm long and 15 mm wide arranged in dense rosettes; several inflorescences with whitish-yellow flowers.
Mexico

Graptopetalum paraguayense (N.E. Br.) E. Walther
CRASSULACEAE
Decumbent stems to 30 cm long; grey-green leaves 3–5 cm long and 1–2 cm wide; branched inflorescence; spotted red flowers.
Mexico

Greenovia aurea (Chr. P. Sm.) Webb & Berth.
CRASSULACEAE
Low shrub forming clumps of rosettes; blue-green, pruinose leaves 5–10 cm long with undulate margins; yellow flowers. During dry season rosettes close up, protecting the apical meristem.
Canary Islands

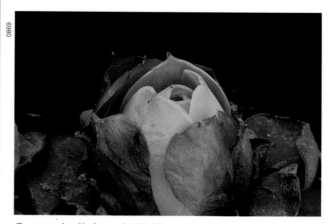

Greenovia diplocycla Webb
CRASSULACEAE
Similar to *G. aurea* but not offsetting.
Canary Islands

Greenovia dodrantalis (Willd.) Webb & Berth.
CRASSULACEAE
Procumbent plants forming clumps of small rosettes; roundish, blue-green leaves with waxy surface; bright yellow flowers.
Canary Islands

Haworthia aranea (A. Berger) M.B. Bayer
LILIACEAE
A variant of *H. bolusii* but with larger, recurved leaves.
South Africa (Cape Province)

Haworthia angustifolia var. liliputana Uitewaal
LILIACEAE
Stemless rosettes 6 cm in diameter; 15–20 yellowish-green leaves to 5 cm long with small, marginal teeth; inflorescence 20 cm high; pinkish-white flowers with brownish-pink veins.
South Africa (Cape Province)

Haworthia attenuata Haw.
LILIACEAE
Short-stemmed rosettes; 30–40 dark green leaves 8 cm long with white tubercles; inflorescence 40 cm tall; white flowers with green veins.
South Africa (Cape Province)

Haworthia arachnoidea (L.) C.-J. Duval
LILIACEAE
Stemless rosettes to 6 cm in diameter with several leaves 15 mm long with white marginal hairs; inflorescence 30 cm tall; white flowers with green veins.
Haworthia gigas Poelln.; *H. setata* Haw.
South Africa (Cape Province)

Haworthia attenuata variegated form
LILIACEAE
A cultivated form with variegated leaves.
South Africa (Cape Province)

Haworthia batesiana Uitewaal
LILIACEAE
Dense clumps of small rosettes 4–5 cm in diameter; light green leaves 2-3 cm long with reticulate pattern; inflorescence 30 cm tall; white flowers with brownish-green veins.
South Africa (Cape Province)

Haworthia coarctata Haw.
LILIACEAE
Elongated stem 20 cm high; rosettes of dark green leaves 4–6 cm long with white dots; inflorescence 30 cm tall; white flowers with green veins.
Haworthia chalwinii Marloth & A. Berger; *H. fallax* Poelln.; *H. fulva* G.G. Sm.; *H. musculina* G.G. Sm.
South Africa (Cape Province)

Haworthia bolusii Baker
LILIACEAE
Stemless rosettes 8–15 cm in diameter; 30–50 incurved, pale green leaves to 8 cm long with numerous bristles; inflorescence 50 cm tall; white flowers with green veins.
South Africa (Cape Province)

Haworthia comptoniana G.G. Sm.
LILIACEAE
Stemless rosettes 5–9 cm in diameter; dark green, triangular leaves 4–5 cm long, 2 cm wide at base with spots and lines; inflorescence 20 cm tall; white flowers with greenish-brown veins.
South Africa (Cape Province)

Haworthia chloracantha Haw.
LILIACEAE
Stemless rosettes 3–8 cm in diameter; 10–40 yellow-green leaves 6–8 cm long; inflorescence 20 cm tall; white flowers with green veins.
South Africa (Cape Province)

Haworthia cooperi Baker
LILIACEAE
Caespitose rosettes 4 cm in diameter; pale green leaves 3 cm long with 6 mm long terminal bristle; inflorescence 40 cm tall; pinkish-white flowers with green veins.
South Africa (Cape Province)

Haworthia cymbiformis (Haw.) C.-J. Duval
LILIACEAE

Stemless rosettes 10 cm in diameter; numerous pale green, translucent leaves 3–5 cm long with dark stripes; inflorescence 20 cm tall; white flowers with brownish-green veins. A variable species; several varieties have been described.

Haworthia lepida G.G. Sm.; *H. planifolia* Haw.

South Africa (Cape Province)

Haworthia emelyae Poelln.
LILIACEAE

Stemless rosettes 6–9 cm in diameter; up to 20 recurved, grey-green leaves 3–4 cm long and 1–3 cm broad with flat, translucent area and numerous tubercles; inflorescence 30 cm tall; white flowers with green veins.

Haworthia picta Poelln.

South Africa (Cape Province)

Haworthia emelyae var. multifolia M.B. Bayer
LILIACEAE

A variety with slender leaves; up to 50 in each rosette in large specimens.
South Africa (Cape Province)

Haworthia fasciata (Willd.) Haw.
LILIACEAE

Stemless rosettes 7 cm in diameter; numerous green leaves 4 cm long and 13 mm wide with white tubercles; inflorescence 40 cm tall; reddish-white flowers with brown veins.

South Africa (Cape Province)

Haworthia fasciata var. concolor Salm-Dyck
LILIACEAE

Variety with white tubercles arranged in bands; flowers as in the type species.
South Africa (Cape Province)

Haworthia glauca Baker
LILIACEAE

Stem to 20 cm high branching from base; spirally arranged, tuberculate, grey-green (bluish-green in mature plants), triangular leaves 5 cm long; inflorescence 30 cm tall; greenish-white flowers with brown veins.

South Africa (Cape Province, Orange Free State)

Haworthia herbacea (Mill.) Stearn
LILIACEAE

Stemless, caespitose rosettes 5 cm in diameter; numerous green leaves 2 cm long and 8 mm wide with darker lines and transparent marginal teeth; inflorescence 30 cm tall; white flowers with green veins.

Haworthia aegrota Poelln.; *H. luteorosea* Uitewaal; *H. paynei* Poelln.

South Africa (Cape Province)

Haworthia koelmaniorum Oberm. & D.S. Hardy
LILIACEAE

Solitary rosettes; brown, tuberculate leaves 7 cm long and 2 cm wide at base; inflorescence 35 cm tall; flowers greenish-white with grey-green veins. Leaves may be recurved in cultivation.

South Africa (Transvaal)

Haworthia limifolia Marloth
LILIACEAE

Offsetting, caespitose rosettes 8–10 cm in diameter; up to 20 dark green leaves 5–10 cm long with several tubercles arranged in transverse rows; inflorescence 35 cm tall; white flowers with grey-green veins. Several varieties and forms have been described, but only *H. limifoia* var. *gigantea* and var. *ubombensis* are recognized by M.B. Bayer (1982).

South Africa (Transvaal)

Haworthia magnifica var. notabilis (Poelln.) M.B. Bayer
LILIACEAE

Stemless rosettes; brownish-green leaves 3–5 cm long with whitish marginal teeth. This variety has erect leaves.

South Africa (Cape Province)

Haworthia maughanii Poelln.
LILIACEAE

Plant 4–8 cm in diameter; greyish-green leaves 2–3 cm long and 1.5 cm wide at base; inflorescence 20 cm tall; white flowers with brown veins.

South Africa (Cape Province)

Haworthia mirabilis subsp. mundula (Smith) M.B. Bayer
LILIACEAE

Rosette 5 cm in diameter of 15–20 light green leaves 3–5 cm long with pale yellow markings and small marginal teeth; inflorescence 50 cm tall; white flowers with greenish veins. A proliferous variety.

South Africa (Cape Province)

Haworthia obtusa var. pilifera (Baker) Uitewaal
LILIACEAE
Rosettes 4 cm in diameter; green, almost translucent leaves 2–3 cm long and 13 mm wide, convex on both sides, with darker lines and transparent teeth ending in fine bristle; inflorescence 35 cm tall; white flowers with green veins.
South Africa (Cape Province)

Haworthia pumila (L.) C.-J. Duval
LILIACEAE
Solitary, stemless rosette to 20 cm in diameter and 15–25 cm tall; up to 50 erect, dark green leaves covered with white tubercles; inflorescence 40 cm tall; yellow flowers with green veins. Probably the largest species within the genus.
Haworthia margaritifera (L.) Haw.
South Africa (Cape Province)

Haworthia papillosa Haw.
LILIACEAE
Stemless rosettes 10 cm in diameter; few, erect, dark green or reddish leaves to 8 cm long and 8 mm wide with white tubercles; inflorescence 40 cm tall; yellow flowers with green veins. M.B. Bayer regards this species as a synonym of *H. pumila*.
South Africa (Cape Province)

Haworthia pygmaea Poelln.
LILIACEAE
Solitary rosette 5 cm in diameter; 10 truncate, green leaves 3 cm long with longitudinal, whitish lines and translucent area; inflorescence 40 cm tall; greyish-white flowers with broad, brownish-green veins.
South Africa (Cape Province)

Haworthia parksiana Poelln.
LILIACEAE
Rosettes 2–3 cm in diameter; numerous dark green, recurving leaves 1–2 cm long with thin tubercles; inflorescence 25 cm tall; white flowers with green veins.
South Africa (Cape Province)

Haworthia radula (Jacq.) Haw.
LILIACEAE
Caespitose, stemless rosettes; green leaves 8 cm long and 2 cm wide at base with white spots; inflorescence 30 cm tall; white flowers with reddish-brown veins.
South Africa (Cape Province)

Haworthia reinwardtii (Salm-Dyck) Haw.

LILIACEAE

Elongated rosettes to 15 cm high and 5 cm in diameter; numerous green leaves 1–2 cm long arranged in spirals and with whitish tubercles; inflorescence 40 cm tall; pinkish-white flowers with greyish-brown veins. A variable species.

South Africa (Cape Province)

Haworthia tessellata Haw.

LILIACEAE

Stemless rosettes 10 cm in diameter; 10–15 dark green, translucent, recurved leaves 3–5 cm long and 2–3 cm wide at base arranged in spirals and with longitudinal lines; inflorescence 50 cm tall; greenish-white flowers with green veins. M.B. Bayer (1982) considers this to be a variety of *H. venosa* Haw.

Namibia, South Africa (Cape Province)

Haworthia sordida Haw.

LILIACEAE

Stemless rosettes with few, rigid, finely tuberculate, grey-green leaves to 10 cm long; inflorescence 45 cm tall; greyish-white flowers with brownish-green veins.

South Africa (Cape Province)

Haworthia truncata Schönland

LILIACEAE

Erect, truncate, green leaves 2–3 cm long with translucent window; inflorescence 25 cm tall; white flowers with green veins.

South Africa (Cape Province)

Haworthia starkiana Poelln.

LILIACEAE

Stemless rosettes to 15 cm in diameter; up to 30 green leaves 7 cm long and 2 cm wide; inflorescence 35 cm tall; white flowers with brownish veins.

South Africa (Cape Province)

Haworthia turgida Haw.

LILIACEAE

Rosettes 5–8 cm in diameter; pale green leaves 1–3 cm long with light green longitudinal lines; inflorescence 70 cm tall; white flowers with green veins.

South Africa (Cape Province)

Haworthia viscosa (L.) Haw.
LILIACEAE

Elongated rosettes to 15 cm high; long, broadly triangular, brownish-green to olive-green leaves 3–4 cm long; white flowers with grey to green veins.

South Africa (Cape Province)

Hereroa dyeri L. Bol.
MESEMBRYANTHEMACEAE

Plants to 10 cm in diameter with tuberous root; branches covered with remains of old leaves; leaves 5–8 cm long bilobial at apex; yellow flowers.

South Africa (Cape Province)

Hechtia epigyna Harms
BROMELIACEAE

Densely scaly, green to red-brown leaves 40 cm long with spines 3 mm long; cylindrical inflorescence; white flowers.

Mexico

Hereroa incurva L. Bol.
MESEMBRYANTHEMACEAE

Plant 3–5 cm high; grey-green, incurved leaves 3–4 cm long; yellow flowers.

South Africa (Cape Province)

Hereroa carinans (Haw.) L. Bol.
MESEMBRYANTHEMACEAE

Plant 3–5 cm high; short branches and stems; unequal sized, grey-green leaves 2–4 cm long; yellow flowers.

South Africa (Cape Province)

Hereroa muirii L. Bol.
MESEMBRYANTHEMACEAE

Plants 6–10 cm high; branches with 4–6 semi-cylindrical leaves 4–7 cm long; yellow flowers.

South Africa (Cape Province)

143

Hereroa puttkameriana (A. Berger & Dinter) Dinter

MESEMBRYANTHEMACEAE

Grey-green leaves 6–8 cm long with dark dots and curved outwards towards apex; yellow flowers.

Namibia

Hoodia bainii R.A. Dyer

ASCLEPIADACEAE

Bush with branches to 20 cm high and 3 cm thick, with 15 tuberculate angles; tubercles with pale brown spine; dull yellow flowers 6–7 cm in diameter.

Namibia, South Africa (Cape Province)

Hoodia currori (Hook.) Decne.

ASCLEPIADACEAE

Stems with 15–25 angles, 30–60 cm high and 3–4 cm in diameter and branching from base to form large clumps; green or pink flowers. Plant photographed in habitat.

Angola, Namibia

Hoodia husabensis Nel

ASCLEPIADACEAE

Tuberculate stems with 16–20 angles, to 70 cm high and 4 cm in diameter; pinkish-violet to grey-violet flowers.

Namibia

Hoya bella Hook.

ASCLEPIADACEAE

Shrubby species with straight stems to 1 m long and short branches; thick, dark green leaves to 5 cm long; white flowers with purple centre borne in umbels.

Hoya paxtonii Hort.

India, Malaysia

Hoya imperialis Lindl.

ASCLEPIADACEAE

Trailing shrub; stems over 6 m long; green, elliptical leaves 15–20 cm long, recurved at tip and rounded at base; dark purple flowers 5–7 mm in diameter borne in pendent umbels.

Eastern India

Hoya kerrii Craib
ASCLEPIADACEAE

Climbing stems to 3 m long; dark green leaves 10–15 cm long; up to 20 creamy-white flowers with hairy interiors in each umbel.

Laos, Thailand

Huernia boleana M.G. Gilbert
ASCLEPIADACEAE

Tuberculate, 4- to 5-angled stems, grey-green to green mottled with purple, 6–10 cm long and branching from base; cream flowers with red spots.

Ethiopia

Hoya longifolia Wall.
ASCLEPIADACEAE

Climbing stems 1–2 m long; dark green, fleshy leaves 10–15 cm long; 15–20 white to pink flowers with rose-pink or red centres, 1–2 cm in diameter, in each umbel.

Himalayas, Malaysia, Thailand

Huernia keniensis R.E. Fr.
ASCLEPIADACEAE

Light green, 4- to 5-angled stems 5–10 cm high; white flowers with dark purple interiors.

Kenya

Huernia aspera N.E. Br.
ASCLEPIADACEAE

Light green, 4- to 5-angled stems 10–15 cm high; teeth 4–8 mm long; red-brown flowers.

Tanzania

Huernia leachii Lavranos
ASCLEPIADACEAE

Stem to 1.5 m long and 5–9 mm thick; caducous green leaves 2 mm long; light brownish-green or yellowish flowers with concentric purple lines.

Malawi, Mozambique

0807

Huernia levyi Oberm.
ASCLEPIADACEAE
Green to pinkish-brown, 4- to 5-angled stems to 7 cm high, branching from base; red-brown flowers.
Zambia, Zimbabwe

0450

Huernia macrocarpa var. schweinfurthii A.C. White & B. Sloane
ASCLEPIADACEAE
Light green, 4- to 5-angled stems 7–12 cm high with teeth to 1 cm long; red-brown flowers.
Saudi Arabia, Yemen

0501

Huernia pendula E.A. Bruce
ASCLEPIADACEAE
Cylindrical to 4-angled, pendulous stems to 1 m long and branching at right angles to main trunk; light green to pinkish tubercles in pairs; dark brown flowers.
South Africa (Cape Province)

0330

Huernia pillansii N.E. Br.
ASCLEPIADACEAE
Erect stems 3–4 cm high and densely covered with recurved bristles; green tubercles 5 mm long; 1–3 pale yellow flowers with small, reddish spots borne at base of young stems.
South Africa (Cape Province)

0844

Huernia recondita M.G. Gilbert
ASCLEPIADACEAE
Prostrate, 4- to 6-angled stems 20–50 cm long; flowers with red and yellow bands.
Ethiopia

0325

Huernia schneideriana A. Berger
ASCLEPIADACEAE
Numerous, slender, 5- to 7-angled, light green stems 10–20 cm long; brown flowers, velvety black inside. Possibly a hybrid of *H. verekeri* Stent x *H. aspera* N.E. Br.
Malawi, Mozambique

Huernia verekeri Stent

ASCLEPIADACEAE

Green to reddish, 5- to 7-angled stems 4–8 cm high; teeth to 8 mm long; reddish flowers.

South Africa (Transvaal), Swaziland

Huernia zebrina N.E. Br.

ASCLEPIADACEAE

Stems 4- to 5-angled, 6–8 cm high; teeth 4–5 mm long; yellowish flowers with numerous transverse, purple-brown bands.

Botswana, Namibia, South Africa (Transvaal)

Ibervillea sonorae (S. Watson) Greene

CUCURBITACEAE

Large, more or less globose caudex with several climbing branches over 3 m long; caducous green leaves; green-yellow flowers.

Mexico

Ipomoea bolusiana Schinz

CONVOLVULACEAE

Caudex to 20 cm in diameter; thin stems with simple or lobed green leaves; purple flowers borne near base of stem.

Madagascar

Ipomoea holubii Baker

CONVOLVULACEAE

Caudex to 20 cm in diameter with several thin stems and filiform, green leaves; deep pink to purple flowers.

Botswana, Namibia

Ipomoea marmorata Britten & Rendle

CONVOLVULACEAE

Tuberous root; stems 20–30 cm high; large, silver-green, palmate leaves; red to pink flowers.

Central Africa

Ipomoea sp.
CONVOLVULACEAE

The genus *Ipomoea* includes species of interest to caudiciform enthusiasts, and several fine specimens have been imported from the wild. Identification is difficult, and unidentified specimens are shown here and in the following two photographs.
Central Africa

Jatropha berlandieri
Torr.

EUPHORBIACEAE

Tuberous base from which stems to 50 cm long arise; green leaves; red flowers.
Mexico, USA (Texas)

Ipomoea sp.
CONVOLVULACEAE

An unidentified specimen.
Central Africa

Jatropha gossypiifolia L.
EUPHORBIACEAE

Shrub or small tree 2–4 m tall; 3-lobed leaves with red veins and margins covered with short hairs; younger leaves are deep bronze-red; red flowers.
Tropical America

Ipomoea sp.
CONVOLVULACEAE

An unidentified specimen.
Central Africa

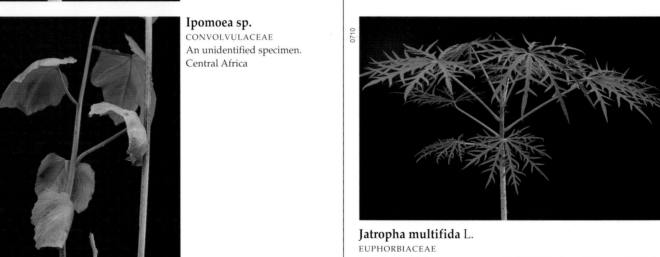

Jatropha multifida L.
EUPHORBIACEAE

Tree to 7 m high; green leaves with 10–15 finely cut lobes, white below; inflorescence with scarlet flowers. Young plants are cultivated for their caudiciform aspect.
Central America

Jatropha podagrica Hook.

EUPHORBIACEAE

Dichotomously branching shrub with caudex 50 cm high; 3-lobed, green leaves, glaucous white below, about 18 cm long and wide, borne at branch apices; dichotomously branched inflorescence; scarlet flowers.

Guatemala, Panama

Jatropha urens L.

EUPHORBIACEAE

Succulent stem 30–50 cm high covered with long hairs; large green leaves with paler veins also covered with hairs; white flowers.

Cnidoscolus urens (L.) Arthur

West Indies

Jatropha variabilis Radcl.-Sm.

EUPHORBIACEAE

Tuberous root; stems to 40 cm high; green, hairy leaves 5–10 cm long and variable in shape; red flowers.

Somalia

Jordaniella clavifolia (L. Bol.) H.E.K. Hartmann

MESEMBRYANTHEMACEAE

Low shrub; stems forming mats; dull grey-green leaves to 22 mm long and acuminate at apex; yellow flowers.

Cephalophyllum clavifolium (L. Bol.) L. Bol.

South Africa (Cape Province)

Jovibarba allionii (Jord. & Fourr.) Webb

CRASSULACEAE

Rosettes 2–3 cm in diameter; hairy, yellowish-green leaves with reddish flush on apex; flower stems 10–15 cm high with greenish-white flowers. Plant photographed in habitat.

France, Italy (southern Alps)

Jovibarba allionii (Jord. & Fourr.) Webb

CRASSULACEAE

A close-up of the flowers.

Jovibarba arenaria (C. Koch) Opiz
CRASSULACEAE
Globular rosettes to 2 cm in diameter; bright green leaves flushed with red at apex; offsets on horizontal stems close to parent rosette; pale yellow flowers.
Austria (Carinthia, southern Tyrol, Styria), Italy (Carnia)

Jovibarba sobolifera (Sims) Opiz
CRASSULACEAE
Rosettes 2–3 cm in diameter; pointed, bright green leaves with red lower surface and ciliate margins; yellow-green flowers.
Central and eastern Europe to eastern Carpathians

Jovibarba heuffelii (Schott) Á. & D. Löve
CRASSULACEAE
Rosettes 5–8 cm in diameter; green, grey, brown or red leaves; some forms may have 3 different colours in the same rosette; yellowish-white flowers. This species is not stoloniferous.
Europe (Balkans, eastern Carpathians)

Juttadinteria albata L. Bol.
MESEMBRYANTHEMACEAE
Erect stems; grey-green leaves 2–3 cm long and triangular towards apex with transparent dots and reddish edges; white flowers.
South Africa (Cape Province)

Jovibarba hirta (L.) Opiz
CRASSULACEAE
Rosettes 3–7 cm in diameter with leaves glabrous on both sides and ciliate on edges; several small offsets arise from axils of middle leaves of parent rosette.
Austria/Italy (eastern Alps), Carpathians, Hungary, Balkans (northwest)

Juttadinteria deserticola (Marloth) Schwantes
MESEMBRYANTHEMACEAE
Erect, densely leaved stems; roundish, grey-green leaves 1.5–2 cm long with transparent dots; white flowers.
Namibia

Juttadinteria insolita (L. Bol.) L. Bol.
MESEMBRYANTHEMACEAE
Stems 8–10 cm long with 4–6 leaves; bluish-green, papillose leaves 2–3 cm long; white flowers.
South Africa (Cape Province)

Juttadinteria suavissima (Dinter) Schwantes
MESEMBRYANTHEMACEAE
Stems to 20 cm long; 3-angled, grey-green leaves with recurved tips, 2–4 cm long and with indistinct dots; fragrant white flowers.
Namibia

Kalanchoe beauverdii Raym.-Hamet
CRASSULACEAE
Thin, climbing stems to 6 m long; leaves 5–10 cm long and 5–20 mm wide; plantlets formed near leaf apex; black-violet flowers.
Madagascar

Kalanchoe beharensis Drake
CRASSULACEAE
Stem to 3 m high; green leaves to 20 cm long and 10 cm wide with dense covering of fine hairs on both surfaces; inflorescence 60 cm tall; green-yellow flowers.
Madagascar

Kalanchoe cv
CRASSULACEAE
An interesting cultivar about 20 cm tall; grey-green leaves with reddish margins and horny lower surface. Probably related to *K. beharensis*.

Kalanchoe fedtschenkoi Raym.-Hamet & E.P. Perrier
CRASSULACEAE
Bush with several branches 30–40 cm long; bluish-green leaves 1–2 cm long and 2 cm wide with brown margins; inflorescence 30 cm tall; brownish-pink flowers.
Madagascar

Kalanchoe gastonis-bonnieri Raym.-Hamet & E.P. Perrier
CRASSULACEAE
Shrub to 60 cm high; pruinose leaves 16 cm long and 4 cm wide; inflorescence 30 cm high; pale green flowers.
Madagascar

Kalanchoe mangini Raym.-Hamet & E.P. Perrier
CRASSULACEAE
Several woody branches to 30 cm long; succulent leaves with red margins; red flowers.
Madagascar

Kalanchoe integra Kuntze
CRASSULACEAE
Erect, branching stems 1–2 m high; green leaves 5–8 cm long; yellowish or pale orange flowers.
Kalanchoe laciniata (L.) DC.
Eastern Africa, India, Thailand

Kalanchoe marmorata Baker
CRASSULACEAE
Stems branching from base; green leaves 10 cm long with large brown spots; inflorescence 8 cm long; white flowers.
Kalanchoe grandiflora A. Rich.
Eritrea

Kalanchoe x kewensis Dyer
CRASSULACEAE
Decumbent stem; glaucous green leaves to 30 cm long and 5–10 mm thick; whitish flowers. A hybrid of *K. flamonea* Stapf x *K. bentii* C.H. Wright ex Hook.f.
Garden origin

Kalanchoe millotii Raym.-Hamet & E.P. Perrier
CRASSULACEAE
Branched, hairy shrub 30 cm high; leaves 3–6 cm long and 2–4 cm wide covered with hairs; pink or yellow flowers.
Madagascar

Kalanchoe orgyalis Baker

CRASSULACEAE

Hairy shrub 50 cm high; bronze-coloured, hairy leaves 5–7 cm long; yellow flowers.

Madagascar

Kalanchoe somaliensis Hook.f.

CRASSULACEAE

Shrub 20–30 cm high, branching from base; pruinose leaves 8–13 cm long with irregularly dentate margins; white flowers.

Ethiopia, Kenya, Somalia, Tanzania, Uganda

Kalanchoe rhombopilosa Mannoni & Boiteau

CRASSULACEAE

Small, little-branched shrub; convex, grey-green leaves 2 cm long and wide narrowing towards stem, with red spots; green-yellow flowers with red lines.

Madagascar

Kalanchoe synsepala Baker

CRASSULACEAE

Erect stems 20–30 cm high; reddish leaves to 15 cm long with dentate margins; yellow-green flowers.

Madagascar

Kalanchoe scapigera Welw.

CRASSULACEAE

Shrub to 40 cm high; pruinose leaves 4–5 cm long; red flowers.
Kalanchoe farinacea Balf.f.

Angola, South Yemen (Socotra)

Kalanchoe thyrsifolia Harv.

CRASSULACEAE

Densely leafy stems to 1 m high; pruinose leaves 10–15 cm long and 4–6 cm wide with reddish margins; yellow flowers.

South Africa (Cape Province), Transvaal

Kalanchoe tomentosa
Baker
CRASSULACEAE
Densely leafy shrub to 50 cm high branching from base; leaves and stems velvety; leaves 7 cm long and 2 cm wide with blotches on margins and at tips; yellow-green flowers.

Madagascar

Kedrostis africana (L.) Cogn.
CUCURBITACEAE
Caudiciform base; climing stems to 6 m long; palmate leaves 10 cm in diameter; small, white to yellow-green flowers.

Central and southern Africa

Kalanchoe tubiflora (Harv.) Raym.-Hamet
CRASSULACEAE
Erect stems to 1 m high; subcylindrical leaves grooved on upper surface and with several reddish-brown spots and adventitious buds near apex; red to violet flowers.

Bryophyllum verticillatum Scott-Elliot
Madagascar

Kedrostis hirtella (Naudin) Cogn.
CUCURBITACEAE
Thick caudex with climbing branches; sagittate, green leaves 5–10 cm long; greenish-yellow flowers.
Central Africa

Kalanchoe zimbabwensis Rendle
CRASSULACEAE
Erect stems 40–50 cm high; hairy leaves 5 cm long and 4 cm wide with sinuate margins and rounded at apex; yellow flowers.
Zimbabwe

Lampranthus primivernus (L. Bol.) L. Bol.
MESEMBRYANTHEMACEAE
Small plant 15–20 cm high; blue-grey leaves 2–3 cm long and 9 mm thick with reddish edges and acuminate apex; pink flowers.
South Africa (Cape Province)

Lapidaria margarethae (Schwantes) Dinter
MESEMBRYANTHEMACEAE
Short stems growing in clumps of up to 8 green to whitish or reddish-white leaves together; leaves 1.5 cm long and 1 cm wide; yellow flowers.
Argyroderma margarethae Schwantes
Namibia

Leipoldtia plana (L. Bol.) L. Bol.
MESEMBRYANTHEMACEAE
Shrub with branches 10–15 cm long and 2 mm thick; grey-green, roundish leaves 12 mm long; pink flowers.
South Africa (Cape Province)

Leipoldtia compacta L. Bol.
MESEMBRYANTHEMACEAE
Small shrub 7–10 cm high; 2- to 4-leaved branches offsetting from axils; bluish-green to yellowish-green leaves 1–2 cm long; pink flowers.
South Africa (Cape Province)

Lewisia sp.
PORTULACACEAE
Fleshy rootstock, often caudex-like; dark green leaves in rosettes; pinkish to purple flowers. This is one of several hybrids of *L. cotyledon* B.L. Rob.
North America

Leipoldtia pauciflora L. Bol.
MESEMBRYANTHEMACEAE
Shrub to 35 cm high; spreading branches; leaves 2–3 cm long and 3–4 mm wide and thick; purplish flowers.
South Africa (Cape Province)

Lithops aucampiae L. Bol.
MESEMBRYANTHEMACEAE
Body 2–3 cm in diameter; unequal sized leaves variable brown in colour (sandy to ochre) with green to brown dots; yellow flowers.
South Africa (Cape Province)

Lithops aucampiae 'Kuruman'
MESEMBRYANTHEMACEAE
A cultivar with larger opaque area in the centre.
South Africa (Cape Province)

Lithops aucampiae var. euniceae (de Boer) D.T. Cole
MESEMBRYANTHEMACEAE
A variety with different shades of yellow, pink or grey.
South Africa (Cape Province)

Lithops aucampiae var. fluminalis D.T. Cole
MESEMBRYANTHEMACEAE
A variety with pale grey margins.
South Africa (Cape Province)

Lithops aucampiae var. koelemanii (de Boer) D.T. Cole
MESEMBRYANTHEMACEAE
A rust to grey-brown variety with dark lines.
South Africa (Cape Province)

Lithops bromfieldii L. Bol.
MESEMBRYANTHEMACEAE
Body 1.5–3 cm in diameter; unequal sized, grey to brown leaves with grey-green margins; yellow flowers. A variable species.
South Africa (Cape Province)

Lithops bromfieldii var. insularis (L. Bol.) B. Fearn
MESEMBRYANTHEMACEAE
This variety differs from the type species in having concave upper surface with larger dots.
Lithops insularis L. Bol.
South Africa (Cape Province)

Lithops bromfieldii var. insularis 'Sulphurea'
MESEMBRYANTHEMACEAE
A yellowish-green cultivar.

Lithops dinteri Schwantes
MESEMBRYANTHEMACEAE
Body 2–3 cm in diameter; unequal sized, green to brown leaves with blood-red dots in the windows; yellow flowers.
Namibia

Lithops bromfieldii var. mennellii (L. Bol.) Fearn
MESEMBRYANTHEMACEAE
A variety with yellow-brown to pink bodies and brown fissures.
Lithops mennellii L. Bol.
South Africa (Cape Province)

Lithops divergens L. Bol.
MESEMBRYANTHEMACEAE
Body 1.5–2 cm in diameter; divergent, grey leaves with deep fissure and small dots; yellow flowers.
South Africa (Cape Province)

Lithops comptonii L. Bol.
MESEMBRYANTHEMACEAE
Body 2–3 cm in diameter; unequal sized, blue-green to pinkish leaves with opaque margins; yellow flowers. A variable species.
South Africa (Cape Province)

Lithops divergens var. amethystina de Boer
MESEMBRYANTHEMACEAE
This variety is distinguished by its broader and deeper fissure and darker colour.
South Africa (Cape Province)

Lithops dorotheae Nel
MESEMBRYANTHEMACEAE

Dark beige body 2–3 cm in diameter; translucent, grey-green windows with red dots and lines; yellow flowers.

South Africa (Cape Province)

Lithops gesinae de Boer
MESEMBRYANTHEMACEAE

Unequal sized, opaque leaves with pink or yellow spots; greyish-green windows; yellow flowers.

Namibia

Lithops fulviceps (N.E. Br.) N.E. Br.
MESEMBRYANTHEMACEAE

Grey, rose-tinged body 2.5–3 cm in diameter and covered with grey-green spots; shallow fissure; yellow flowers.

Namibia

Lithops gracilidelineata Dinter
MESEMBRYANTHEMACEAE

Body 1.5–3 cm in diameter; deep fissure; pale grey leaves almost equal in size with pattern of dark lines; yellow flowers.

Namibia

Lithops fulviceps var. lactinea D.T. Cole
MESEMBRYANTHEMACEAE

Lilac-lined upper surface; many blue-green spots and blood-red rugae.

Namibia

Lithops hallii de Boer
MESEMBRYANTHEMACEAE

Body 1.5–2 cm in diameter; deep fissure; unequal sized, grey to pale brown leaves with translucent windows and red dots; white flowers.

South Africa (Cape Province)

Lithops hallii 'Brown'
MESEMBRYANTHEMACEAE
A cultivar with brown leaves.

Lithops herrei L. Bol.
MESEMBRYANTHEMACEAE
Body 2–3 cm in diameter; deep fissure; divergent, grey to pale grey leaves with dark lines; yellow flowers.
Lithops translucens L. Bol.
Namibia, South Africa (Cape Province)

Lithops hallii 'Green Soapstone'
MESEMBRYANTHEMACEAE
A cultivar with greenish-yellow leaves.

Lithops hookeri (A. Berger) Schawntes
MESEMBRYANTHEMACEAE
Body 2–2.5 cm in diameter; conjunct, pale brown leaves with brown lines and markings forming vermiculate pattern; flowers yellow.
South Africa (Cape Province)

Lithops hallii 'White'
MESEMBRYANTHEMACEAE
A cultivar with whitish-grey leaves.

Lithops hookeri 'Vermiculate'
MESEMBRYANTHEMACEAE
A cultivar similar to var. *dabneri*.

159

Lithops hookeri var. dabneri (L. Bol.) D.T. Cole
MESEMBRYANTHEMACEAE
Grey variety with close vermiculate pattern.
Lithops dabneri L. Bol.
South Africa (Cape Province)

Lithops hookeri var. susannae (D.T. Cole) D.T. Cole
MESEMBRYANTHEMACEAE
A pale grey variety with darker markings.
Lithops susannae D.T. Cole
South Africa (Cape Province)

Lithops hookeri var. elephina (D.T. Cole) D.T. Cole
MESEMBRYANTHEMACEAE
Differs from the type species in having leaves in various shades of grey, some-times tinged with pale pink.
South Africa (Cape Province)

Lithops julii (Dinter & Schawnt.) N.E. Br.
MESEMBRYANTHEMACEAE
Body 2–3 cm in diameter; deep fissure; divergent, dark green leaves with brown to olive-green windows; white flowers.
Namibia

Lithops hookeri var. marginata (Nel) D.T. Cole
MESEMBRYANTHEMACEAE
A pink to ochre variety with dark green or red patterns.
Lithops marginata Nel
South Africa (Cape Province)

Lithops julii 'Chrysocephala'
MESEMBRYANTHEMACEAE
A pale, milky-grey cultivar with darker markings.

Lithops julii subsp. fulleri (N.E. Br.) Fearn
MESEMBRYANTHEMACEAE
Smaller than the type species with convex upper surface.
Lithops fulleri N.E. Br.
South Africa (Cape Province)

Lithops karasmontana 'Mickbergensis'
MESEMBRYANTHEMACEAE
A variable form with fewer marks than the type species and more uniform in colour.
Namibia

Lithops julii subsp. fulleri var. rouxii (L. Bol.) D.T. Cole
MESEMBRYANTHEMACEAE
Leaves more conjunct than the type species and pale grey with pink dots and lines. A variable form.
Namibia

Lithops karasmontana subsp. bella (N.E. Br.) D.T. Cole
MESEMBRYANTHEMACEAE
Body 2–3 cm in diameter; divergent, grey-green leaves with convex upper surface and olive-green dots.
Lithops bella N.E. Br.
Namibia

Lithops karasmontana (Dinter & Schwantes) N.E. Br.
MESEMBRYANTHEMACEAE
Green or brownish to ochre body 1.5–3 cm in diameter with rugose upper surface; white flowers. A variable species.
Namibia

Lithops karasmontana subsp. eberlanzii 'Witputzensis'
MESEMBRYANTHEMACEAE
Body 2.5–3 cm in diameter; grey-green upper surface with paler colours and larger markings and with red dots; white flowers.
Namibia

Lithops karasmontana 'Summitatum'
MESEMBRYANTHEMACEAE
A cultivar with dark red or brown rugae.

Lithops lesliei 'Albiflora'
MESEMBRYANTHEMACEAE
Upper surface has olive-green markings; white flowers.

Lithops karasmontana var. aiaisensis (de Boer) D.T. Cole
MESEMBRYANTHEMACEAE
Body 2–3 cm in diameter; upper surface less rugose than the type species; opaque grey with shades of green, brown, pink or cream; white flowers.
Namibia

Lithops lesliei 'Albinica'
MESEMBRYANTHEMACEAE
A cultivar with yellowish-green patterning; white flowers.

Lithops karasmontana var. lericheana (Dinter & Schwantes) D.T. Cole
MESEMBRYANTHEMACEAE
Body 1.5–2 cm in diameter; equal sized, pale olive-green to pinkish-grey or yellowish leaves with rugose upper surface and dull green dots; white flowers.
Lithops lericheana (Dinter & Schwantes) Dinter & Schwantes
Namibia

Lithops lesliei 'Storm's Albinigold'
MESEMBRYANTHEMACEAE
Similar to 'Albinica' but with yellow flowers.

Lithops lesliei var. mariae D.T. Cole
MESEMBRYANTHEMACEAE
Body 2–3 cm in diameter; sandy-gold, densely marked leaves; yellow flowers.
South Africa (Cape Province)

Lithops marmorata (N.E. Br.) N.E. Br.
MESEMBRYANTHEMACEAE
Bodies 3 cm in diameter; opaque grey-green with pale green, cream or pink dots and lines; yellow flowers.
South Africa (Cape Province)

Lithops lesliei var. minor de Boer
MESEMBRYANTHEMACEAE
A smaller, brown variety with dark green markings.
South Africa (Cape Province)

Lithops marmorata 'Framesii'
MESEMBRYANTHEMACEAE
Body 2.5–3 cm in diameter; divergent, pale grey leaves with darker grey markings; deep fissure; white flowers.
South Africa (Cape Province)

Lithops lesliei var. venteri (Nel) de Boer & Boom
MESEMBRYANTHEMACEAE
A pale grey variety with fine markings.
Lithops venteri Nel
South Africa (Cape Province)

Lithops meyeri L. Bol.
MESEMBRYANTHEMACEAE
Body 2–3 cm in diameter; deep fissure; divergent, pale grey leaves tinged with yellow, pink or green; yellow flowers.
South Africa (Cape Province)

163

Lithops olivacea L. Bol.
MESEMBRYANTHEMACEAE

Body 18–24 mm in diameter; pale grey-green or beige with translucent panels; yellow flowers.

South Africa (Cape Province)

Lithops optica 'Rubra'
MESEMBRYANTHEMACEAE

Body 2–3 cm in diameter; deep fissure; unequal sized, divergent, grey-green leaves with translucent windows; white flowers. This cultivar has purplish-red, unmarked leaves.

Namibia

Lithops olivacea var. nebrownii D.T. Cole
MESEMBRYANTHEMACEAE

Differs from the type species in its yellowish- or pinkish-beige colour.

South Africa (Cape Province)

Lithops otzeniana Nel
MESEMBRYANTHEMACEAE

Body 2.5–3 cm in diameter; deep fissure; various shades of grey-green, sometimes tinged with pale pink; windows translucent bluish- or greyish-green; yellow flowers.

South Africa (Cape Province)

Lithops optica 'Maculate'
MESEMBRYANTHEMACEAE

Body 2–3 cm in diameter; deep fissure; unequal sized, divergent, grey-green leaves with translucent windows; white flowers. The windows of this cultivar are irregularly shaped.

Namibia

Lithops pseudotruncatella subsp. dendrita (Nel) D.T. Cole
MESEMBRYANTHEMACEAE

This subspecies has more regular network of fine, dark brown markings; yellow flowers.

Lithops dendritica Nel

Namibia

Lithops pseudotruncatella var. elisabethiae (Dinter) de Boer & Boom
MESEMBRYANTHEMACEAE
Body 2–2.5 cm in diameter; grey tinted with lilac-blue with dark grey markings; yellow flowers.
Lithops elisabethiae Dinter
Namibia

Lithops pseudotruncatella var. groendrayensis (Jacobs.) D.T. Cole
MESEMBRYANTHEMACEAE
Grey-white or grey-green bodies 2–4 cm in diameter; yellow flowers.
Namibia

Lithops ruschiorum (Dinter & Schwantes) N.E. Br.
MESEMBRYANTHEMACEAE
Body 2–3.5 cm in diameter; round end, upper surface convex, grey or cream with dots or with network of lines; yellow flowers.
Namibia

Lithops salicola L. Bol.
MESEMBRYANTHEMACEAE
Body 2–2.5 cm in diameter; grey with translucent windows and red-dotted tips; white flowers.
South Africa (Cape Province)

Lithops schwantesii Dinter
MESEMBRYANTHEMACEAE
Body 2.5 cm in diameter; opaque greyish, pinkish-grey or reddish-brown with dark green or red dots; yellow flowers. A variable species.
Namibia

Lithops schwantesii 'Triebneri'
MESEMBRYANTHEMACEAE
Body 3–4 cm in diameter; shallow fissure; upper surface flat, grey or pale brown with broken network of cinnamon lines; yellow flowers.
Namibia

Lithops schwantesii var. marthae (Loesch & Tisch.) D.T. Cole
MESEMBRYANTHEMACEAE

Grey to greenish-pink bodies, 2–3 cm in diameter, with some vein-like ochre markings; yellow flowers.

Lithops marthae Loesch & Tisch.

Namibia

Lithops schwantesii var. rugosa (Dinter) de Boer & Boom
MESEMBRYANTHEMACEAE

Body 1.5–2 cm in diameter; grey to pale lilac with network of deeply impressed brown lines, appearing rugose; yellow flowers.

Lithops rugosa Dinter

Namibia

Lithops terricolor N.E. Br.
MESEMBRYANTHEMACEAE

Body 1.5 cm in diameter; pink, grey or red with violet or greenish dots covering the top; yellow flowers.

Lithops localis Schwantes

Namibia, South Africa (Cape Province)

Lithops turbiniformis (Haw.) N.E. Br.
MESEMBRYANTHEMACEAE

Although now considered a synonym of *L. hookeri*, this is still found in cultivation under this name.

South Africa (Cape Province)

Lithops vallis-mariae (Dinter & Schwantes) N.E. Br.
MESEMBRYANTHEMACEAE

Body 2–4 cm in diameter; shallow fissure; grey with network of obscure, translucent lines; yellow flowers. A variable species.

Namibia

Lithops verruculosa Nel
MESEMBRYANTHEMACEAE

Body 2–3 cm in diameter; deep fissure; grey with finely fissured darker window covered with brown dots; yellow flowers. A variable species.

South Africa (Cape Province)

Lithops villetii L. Bol.
MESEMBRYANTHEMACEAE
Body 2–3 cm in diameter; greenish-grey with windows in various shades of greyish-green; white flowers.
South Africa (Cape Province)

Machairophyllum acuminatum L. Bol.
MESEMBRYANTHEMACEAE
Clumps to 1 m in diameter; short, branching stem with triangular, pale green leaves to 5 cm long and 1 cm wide; yellow flowers.
South Africa (Cape Province)

Lithops viridis Luck
MESEMBRYANTHEMACEAE
Body 17–20 mm in diameter; deep fissure; dull grey, divergent leaves with translucent grey-green windows; yellow flowers.
South Africa (Cape Province)

Malephora crassa (L. Bol.) Jacobs & Schwantes
MESEMBRYANTHEMACEAE
Prostrate stems, 10–20 cm long, branching from nodes; green leaves 2–4 cm long and reddish at apex when grown in strong sun; yellow flowers.
South Africa (Cape Province)

Lithops werneri Schwantes & Jacobs
MESEMBRYANTHEMACEAE
Body 10–18 mm in diameter; deep fissure; divergent, unequal sized, pale grey leaves with dark olive-green markings; yellow flowers.
Namibia

Malephora lutea (Haw.) Schwantes
MESEMBRYANTHEMACEAE
Branches with numerous shoots; acuminate, yellowish-green leaves 2–3 cm long and narrowed towards apex; yellow flowers.
South Africa (Cape Province)

Melothria punctata Cogn.
CUCURBITACEAE

Long stems arising from thick root; bright green, 3- or 5-lobed leaves; white flowers.

Central Africa

Mestoklema arboriforme (Burch.) N.E. Br.
MESEMBRYANTHEMACEAE

Tree-like shrub to 30 cm high, with distinct, much-branched trunk 2–3 cm thick; pale green, roundish, hairy leaves 1–1.5 cm long and triangular in section; yellow to orange flowers.

South Africa (Cape Province), Namibia

Merremia sp.
CONVOLVULACEAE

A large, unidentified specimen.

Tropical Africa

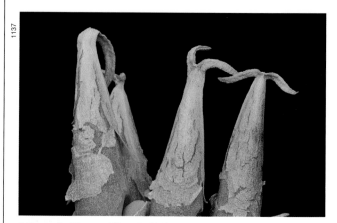

Mitrophyllum affine L. Bol.
MESEMBRYANTHEMACEAE

Branches 10–15 cm long; spreading, light grey-green leaves to 3 cm long and 1 cm in diameter at base, covered with remains of dry leaves; yellow flowers.

South Africa (Cape Province)

Merremia tuberosa Rendle
CONVOLVULACEAE

Tuberous root with numerous climbing stems 1–3 m long in cultivation (may reach 20 m in habitat); glabrous leaves 8–15 cm long; yellow flowers.

Tropical Africa

Mitrophyllum herrei L. Bol.
MESEMBRYANTHEMACEAE

Shrub to 70 cm high with 2 types of light green leaves: those 2.5 cm long are united for half their length; those 3 cm long are elongated; yellow flowers.

South Africa (Cape Province)

0873

Mitrophyllum pillansii
N.E. Br.

MESEMBRYANTHEMACEAE

Stems to 30 cm high; leaves united at base to form conical body 8–10 cm long, narrowed into short tip and covered with remain of dry leaves; white flowers.

South Africa (Cape Province)

0872

Mitrophyllum ripense L. Bol.

MESEMBRYANTHEMACEAE

Shrub 10–15 cm high; green to brownish-green leaves 4–8 cm long with free portion 2 cm long; yellow flowers.

South Africa (Cape Province)

0625

Momordica rostrata A. Zimm.

CUCURBITACEAE

Fleshy, caudiciform stem buried in the ground in habitat; thin, climbing stems to 7 m long; compound leaves 5 cm long; yellow flowers.

Eastern Africa

1008

Monadenium arborescens P.R.O. Bally

EUPHORBIACEAE

Succulent tree to 4 m high; main stem 10 cm thick and 5-angled, with few glaucous green, ascending branches; green leaves with red undersides 7–20 cm long and 4–11 cm wide; red inflorescence.

Kenya

0664

Monadenium coccineum
Pax

EUPHORBIACEAE

Stems 5-angled, 30–90 cm long and 10–15 mm thick; leaves 8 cm long with keeled mid-rib; scarlet to orange inflorescence.

Tanzania

0712

Monadenium echinulatum Stapf

EUPHORBIACEAE

Succulent stems 30–70 cm high and 1 cm in diameter with short prickles; alternate green leaves 3–12 cm long and 1–6 cm wide; green inflorescence flushed with pink.

Tanzania

Monadenium elegans
S. Carter
EUPHORBIACEAE

Shrub to 3 m high with exfoliating bark; branches become pendulous with age; spines in groups of 3; undulate leaves 4 cm long; whitish-red inflorescence.

Tanzania

Monadenium guentheri var. mammillare P.R.O. Bally
EUPHORBIACEAE

Tuberous root; many erect stems to 15 cm high and 2–3 cm thick, or decumbent to 30 cm long; large tubercles on stems; green leaves 4–5 cm long and 9 mm wide at tips of branches; pale green inflorescence.

Tanzania

Monadenium ellembeckii N.E. Br.
EUPHORBIACEAE

Shrub to 1 m high with several erect stems 12–25 mm thick branching from base; few caducous leaves 8–10 mm long; yellow-green inflorescence.

Ethiopia, Somalia

Monadenium heteropodum (Pax) N.E. Br.
EUPHORBIACEAE

Tuberous root; trailing stems to 35 cm long and 3 cm in diameter; tubercles with rhomboid base; green leaves to 3.5 cm long and 1.5 cm wide; whitish-green inflorescence.

Tanzania

Monadenium guentheri Pax
EUPHORBIACEAE

Tuberculate stems 15–20 cm or more high with 1–3 spines; green leaves 1–4 cm long crisped at apex; greenish-white inflorescence.
Kenya

Monadenium invenustum N.E. Br.
EUPHORBIACEAE

Tuberous root; fleshy, cylindrical stems to 80 cm long; dark green, succulent leaves 4 cm long with pale green veins; whitish-pink inflorescence.
Kenya

Monadenium magnificum E.A. Bruce
EUPHORBIACEAE

Shrub 4- to 5-angled, 1.5 m high and to 4 cm thick at base with spine clusters on margins; fleshy, green leaves with red undersides 15 cm long; bright scarlet inflorescence.

Tanzania

Monadenium ritchei subsp. nyambense S. Carter
EUPHORBIACEAE

Tuberculate stems 40 cm long and 3 cm in diameter with short spines; leaves 2–3 cm long, dark green above, paler below; yellow-green inflorescence. This subspecies has glabrous leaves.

Kenya

Monadenium reflexum Chiov.
EUPHORBIACEAE

Stems to 35 cm high and 6 cm in diameter, covered with tubercles 1–2 cm long; green or reddish leaves 2–3 cm long; yellow-green or reddish inflorescence.

Ethiopia, Kenya

Monadenium rubellum (P.R.O. Bally) S. Carter
EUPHORBIACEAE

Fleshy, decumbent, green stems 5–25 cm long with light green stripes; green leaves 4 cm long tinged with red and with acute apex; pink inflorescence.

Kenya

Monadenium rhizophorum P.R.O. Bally
EUPHORBIACEAE

Succulent stems 10 cm long borne at apices of rhizomes; yellow-green leaves 3–5 cm long, often purple near veins; greenish-yellow inflorescence. This species propagates easily by means of prolific rhizomes.

Kenya

Monadenium schubei (Pax) N.E. Br.
EUPHORBIACEAE

Erect, tuberculate, dark green stems 10–45 cm high and to 4 cm in diameter; red-brown spines 2 mm long; greenish leaves 5–7 cm long and 2 cm wide; green inflorescence.

Tanzania, Zimbabwe

Monadenium sp. Lavranos 23368

EUPHORBIACEAE

Stems 10–15 cm tall branching from nodes; new growth green, older stems grey; small, caducous, green leaves.

Somalia

Monadenium spinescens (Pax) P.R.O. Bally

EUPHORBIACEAE

Tree to 6 m high with yellowish-brown, peeling bark; tuberculate branches 2–3 cm in diameter with spines below leaf scales; dark green leaves 20–30 cm long with pale yellow veins above; bright red inflorescence.

Tanzania

Monadenium stapelioides Pax

EUPHORBIACEAE

Erect stems, which are decumbent when more than 15 cm long, with tubercles arranged in spirals; green leaves 3–5 cm long borne on growing parts of young stems; pink inflorescence.

Kenya, Tanzania

Monadenium torrei
Leach

EUPHORBIACEAE

Similar to *M. spinescens*, but to 3 m high and young branches are more tuberculate.

Mozambique, Tanzania

Monadenium yattanum
P.R.O. Bally

EUPHORBIACEAE

Tuberous root with erect, tuberculate stems 20 cm long and 1–1.5 cm thick; fleshy leaves 5–10 cm long dark green above and light green below; inflorescence green with brown stripes.

Kenya

Monanthes anagensis Praeger

CRASSULACEAE

Low, spreading shrub; glabrous green, alternate leaves 2.5 cm long with grooved upper surface; yellowish-green flowers.

Canary Islands (Tenerife)

Monanthes muralis (Webb & Bolle) H. Christ

CRASSULACEAE

Small, arborescent shrub with erect, grey-red stems; dark green, tuberculate leaves 5–10 mm long, spotted with grey and with grooved upper surface; pale yellow flowers, sometimes red-striped.

Canary Islands (Hierro, La Palma)

Monilaria globosa (L. Bol.) L. Bol.

MESEMBRYANTHEMACEAE

Stems 1.5 cm in diameter and covered with remains of old leaves; green secondary leaves globose to conical and 1–2 cm thick; white flowers.

South Africa (Cape Province)

Monanthes polyphylla Haw.

CRASSULACEAE

Filiform stems with many-leaved rosettes 1–2 cm in diameter forming soft, shiny, dense clumps; cylindrical, light green, papillate leaves; red flowers.

Canary Islands

Monilaria pisiformis (Haw.) Schwantes

MESEMBRYANTHEMACEAE

Low stems with several branches to 3 cm long; short, dark green leaves united to form globose bodies; secondary, more or less cylindrical leaves 5–6 cm long; reddish, white-margined flowers.

Mitrophyllum pisiforme Haw.

South Africa (Cape Province)

Monanthes subcrassicaulis (Kuntze) Praeger

CRASSULACEAE

Green stems 1–2 cm long; dense, semi-cylindrical leaves 1 cm long; hairy flowering stems; red flowers.

Canary Islands (Gomera, La Palma, Tenerife)

Myrmecodia echinata Miq.

RUBIACEAE

Tuberculate caudex 10 cm thick; stems 5–10 cm long with thick, green leaves; white flowers. The caudex has a series of cavities inhabited by ants.

Malaysia

Namaquanthus vanheerdei L. Bol.
MESEMBRYANTHEMACEAE
Shrub 15–20 cm high and 20 cm in diameter; grey-green leaves 3–7 cm long cover the stems; purplish flowers.
Namibia/South Africa (Little Namaqualand)

Namibia cinerea (Marloth) Dinter & Schwantes
MESEMBRYANTHEMACEAE
Low-growing plant; grey-green leaves 1.5 cm long and 1 mm wide with triangular upper surface and with whitish dots; violet flowers.
Namibia

Namibia ponderosa (Dinter) Dinter & Schwantes
MESEMBRYANTHEMACEAE
Grey-white leaves with dark dots 2 cm long and 15–18 mm wide form clumps to 20 cm in diameter and 10 cm high; white flowers.
Namibia

Nelia robusta Schwantes
MESEMBRYANTHEMACEAE
Short-stemmed plants forming clumps 5–10 cm in diameter; yellowish-green to green leaves 2–4 cm long, narrowed towards apex and with reddish spots; whitish-yellow flowers.
Namibia/South Africa (Little Namaqualand)

Neohenricia sibbettii L. Bol.
MESEMBRYANTHEMACEAE
Monotypic genus; several short stems bearing 4 leaves covered with white tubercles; white, nocturnal flowers.
South Africa (Orange Free State)

Nolina recurvata Lem.
AGAVACEAE
Globose caudex over 1 m in diameter with few stems to 6 m high; green leaves to 1 m long and 1–2 cm wide; tall, branched inflorescence; white flowers.
Beucarnea recurvata Lem.; *Nolina tuberculata* Hort.
Mexico

Notechidnopsis tessellata (Pillans) Lavranos & Bleck

ASCLEPIADACEAE

Leafless, 6- to 10-angled stems 10–20 cm high; tubercles tipped with soft, green, spine-like apex; flowers light yellow inside and brownish-yellow outside.

Caralluma tessellata Pillans

South Africa (Cape Province)

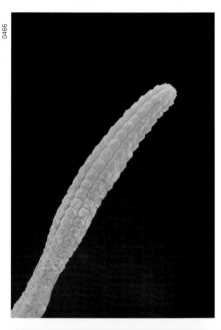

Ocimum tenuiflorum L.

LABIATAE

Branched stems, woody at base; elliptical leaves 2–3 cm long and 1–2 cm wide with dentate margins; stems and leaves covered with white hairs; pink or white flowers.

India, Malaysia

Nycteranthus sp.

MESEMBRYANTHEMACEAE

A well-grown specimen of an unidentified species.

South Africa (Cape Province)

Odontophorus marlothii N.E. Br.

MESEMBRYANTHEMACEAE

Dwarf shrub with prostrate branches; green to dark green leaves 2–3 cm long and keeled towards apex with 5–8 marginal teeth ending in curved tip; yellow flowers.

Namibia/South Africa (Little Namaqualand)

Nycteranthus viridiflorus (Aiton) Schwantes

MESEMBRYANTHEMACEAE

Roots woody; fleshy, branching stems to 40 cm long; recurved, green, hairy leaves 2–4 cm long, persisting as short spines after drying; pale green flowers.

Sphalmanthus viridiflorus (Aiton) N.E. Br.

South Africa (Cape Province)

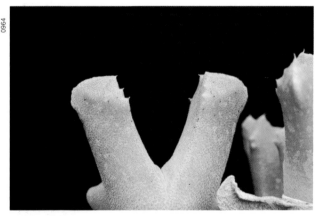

Odontophorus nanus L. Bol.

MESEMBRYANTHEMACEAE

Branches 1–2 cm long; grey to dark green leaves 1–2 cm long with dentate margins; white flowers.

Namibia/South Africa (Little Namaqualand)

Operculicarya decaryi H. Perrier
ANACARDIACEAE
Oblong caudex 30–40 cm high; branching and rebranching stems; small, green leaves shed during dry season.
Madagascar

Ophthalmophyllum friedrichiae (Dinter) Dinter
MESEMBRYANTHEMACEAE
Solitary, cylindrical bodies 2–3 cm long; greenish-white lobes tinged with red with translucent windows; white flowers.
Namibia

Ophthalmophyllum australe L. Bol.
MESEMBRYANTHEMACEAE
Solitary, papillose, green bodies, often purple towards apex, 1.5–3 cm long with short hairs; windowed lobes 3–5 mm long; pink flowers.
South Africa (Cape Province)

Ophthalmophyllum fulleri Lavis
MESEMBRYANTHEMACEAE
Obconical bodies 2 cm long and 3 cm in diameter, green to yellowish, translucent; lobes 1–2 cm long with translucent windows; purplish flowers.
South Africa (Cape Province)

Ophthalmophyllum dinteri Schwantes
MESEMBRYANTHEMACEAE
Solitary, subcylindrical bodies 2–3 cm long; greenish-white lobes tinged with red with translucent windows; pink flowers.
Namibia

Ophthalmophyllum latum Tisch.
MESEMBRYANTHEMACEAE
Cylindrical bodies to 2.5 cm high and 2 cm wide, light green with translucent windows; lobes 2–5 mm long; white flowers.
South Africa (Cape Province)

Ophthalmophyllum longum (N.E. Br.) Tisch.

MESEMBRYANTHEMACEAE

Solitary bodies 2–3 cm long and 2 cm wide; deep fissure; divergent, yellowish-green leaves with large translucent dots; pale pink flowers.

Namibia/South Africa (Little Namaqualand)

Ophthalmophyllum pubescens Tisch.

MESEMBRYANTHEMACEAE

Several light green bodies 3–5 cm high and 2 cm in diameter with large, translucent windows; lobes to 1 cm long; pink flowers.

South Africa (Cape Province)

Ophthalmophyllum lydiae Jacobs

MESEMBRYANTHEMACEAE

Olive-green bodies 2–2.5 cm long and 1.5 cm wide with minute papillae; transparent tips; white flowers.

Namibia/South Africa (Little Namaqualand)

Ophthalmophyllum schultdii Schwantes

MESEMBRYANTHEMACEAE

Dark purple, usually solitary bodies 2.5 cm high and 1.5 cm wide with translucent windows; lobes 3–5 mm long; white flowers.

Namibia

Ophthalmophyllum praesectum (N.E. Br.) Schwantes

MESEMBRYANTHEMACEAE

Green bodies to 3 cm long and 18 mm wide with translucent windows; forming small clumps; lobes 3–5 mm long; pinkish-violet flowers.

Conophytum praesectum N.E. Br.

South Africa (Cape Province)

Ophthalmophyllum verrucosum Lavis

MESEMBRYANTHEMACEAE

Bodies usually solitary, 3 cm high and 1 cm in diameter; fissure 3–5 mm deep; red-brown, papillose leaves with translucent dots; white flowers.

South Africa (Cape Province)

177

Orbea semota (N.E. Br.) Leach 'Lutea'

ASCLEPIADACEAE

Stems 10–15 cm high and branching from base; teeth to 1 cm long; flowers yellow with brown markings. This cultivar has pale green to yellow-green stems.

Kenya, Tanzania

Orbea variegata (L.) Haw.

ASCLEPIADACEAE

Erect, 4-angled stems 5–20 cm long, freely branching from base and with acute, green, purple-tipped teeth; 1–5 pale yellow flowers with purple-brown spots.

Stapelia variegata L.

South Africa (Cape Province)

Orbea variegata (L.) Haw.

ASCLEPIADACEAE

A close-up of the flower.

Orbea verrucosa (Masson) Leach

ASCLEPIADACEAE

Stems 8–15 cm long and 1–2 cm in diameter branching from base; erect, green branches; teeth 3–6 mm long with rudimentary, caducous leaves; pale yellow, brown-spotted flowers 4–6 cm in diameter.

Stapelia verrucosa Masson

South Africa (Cape Province)

Orbeanthus hardyi (R.A. Dyer) Leach

ASCLEPIADACEAE

Green stems 30 cm long and to 1 cm thick mottled with purple and growing horizontally, rooting and branching freely; disc-shaped, yellowish-cream flowers with red markings.

Stultitia hardyi R.A. Dyer

South Africa (Transvaal)

Orbeopsis caudata (N.E. Br.) Leach

ASCLEPIADACEAE

Erect, pale green stems 6–10 cm long; straight, spiny teeth more than 1 cm long; yellow flowers with numerous purple dots.

Caralluma caudata N.E. Br.; *C. praegracilis* Oberm.

Malawi, Namiba, Zimbabwe

Ornithogallum caudatum Aiton
LILIACEAE
Bulbs with many bulblets, forming clumps; flaccid, green leaves to 30 cm long and 2–3 cm wide; inflorescence 1 m tall; numerous white flowers with green stripes.
South Africa (Cape Province, Natal)

Orostachys furusei Ohwi
CRASSULACEAE
Clump-forming rosettes; glaucous blue-green, rounded leaves to 5 cm long; inflorescence 30 cm tall; white flowers.
China, Japan

Orostachys chanetii (Lév.) A. Berger
CRASSULACEAE
Rosettes 10–15 mm tall and 10–15 mm in diameter with grey-green leaves of different lengths; pyradmidal inflorescence 10–15 cm tall; numerous white flowers with red outside.
China

Orostachys minutus (Komarov) A. Berger
CRASSULACEAE
Rosettes 3–4 cm in diameter; leaves of 2 different lengths with red markings and short terminal spine; white-pink flowers.
Orostachys kanboensis Ohwi
China, South Korea

Orostachys erubescens A. Berger
CRASSULACEAE
Rosettes growing in clumps with green or grey-green leaves of 2 different lengths ending in soft white tip; white flowers.
China (north), Japan, Korea

Orostachys spinosus (L.) A. Berger
CRASSULACEAE
Rosettes 8–10 cm or more in diameter growing in clumps; green leaves of 2 different lengths with white terminal spine; yellow flowers.
Eastern CIS to north and central Asia

Orostachys thyrsiflorus Fisch.
CRASSULACEAE
Offsetting rosettes 4–5 cm in diameter; green to glaucous green leaves 6–8 mm long end in white spine; white flowers.
Mongolia

Othonna arborescens L.
COMPOSITAE
Shrub 50–80 cm high; branched, flexuous stems; oblong leaves 5 cm long and 2 cm wide; inflorescence with yellow flowers.
South Africa (Cape Province)

Othonna capensis L.H. Bailey
COMPOSITAE
Short, freely branching stems; trailing branches; pale to dark green, cylindrical leaves 2–3 cm long and 6 mm wide with cartilaginous apex; yellow flowers.
South Africa (Cape Province)

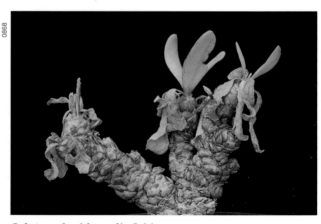

Othonna clavifolia Marloth
COMPOSITAE
Short-stemmed shrub; light green leaves (purple during dormancy) 2 cm long and 9 mm thick borne at ends of branches; yellow flowers.
Namibia

Othonna euphorbioides Hutch.
COMPOSITAE
Dwarf shrub to 10 cm high; brown branches 1–2 cm thick; light green, pruinose leaves 2 cm long, shed during dormancy; greyish spines as long as the leaves; yellowish flowers.
Namibia

Othonna lepidocaulis Schltr.
COMPOSITAE
Dwarf shrub to 25 cm tall; thick branches covered with cartilaginous leaf bases; green leaves 3–6 cm long; yellow flowers.
Namibia/South Africa (Little Namaqualand)

PACHYPHYTUM

Othonna litoralis Dinter
COMPOSITAE
Shrub 35 cm high; bluish-green leaves 3–4 cm long and 12 mm wide borne at ends of branches; yellowish flowers.
Namibia

Pachycormus discolor
(Benth.) Coville
ANACARDIACEAE
Tree 5–6 m tall with caudiciform base from which grow several green stems covered with exfoliating, white, papery bark; tiny green, pinnate leaves; red flowers.
Mexico (Baja California)

Othonna retrofracta Less.
COMPOSITAE
Stems 60 cm high, thickened at base; thin, brown branches; lobate, green leaves 8 cm long and 2–3 cm wide with tooth on each side, shed during dormancy; yellowish flowers.
Namibia, South Africa (Cape Province)

Pachycymbium keithii (R.A. Dyer) Leach
ASCLEPIADACEAE
Glaucous green, 4-angled stems 7–10 cm high, branching from base and often mottled red; deltoid teeth 1–2 cm long; dark brown flowers.
Mozambique, South Africa (Natal, Transvaal), Zimbabwe

Oxalis succulenta Barn.
OXALIDACEAE
Short-branched stems to 15 cm; green leaves with petiole 2.5 cm long; yellow flowers on long pedicels.
Chile

Pachyphytum bracteosum
Link, Klotzsch, Otto
CRASSULACEAE
Stem to 30 cm high; whitish-grey leaves 6–10 cm long and 2–3 cm wide; inflorescence 30 cm tall; red flowers.
Mexico

181

Pachyphytum compactum Rose
CRASSULACEAE
Stem 10 cm long; cylindrical, light green to grey-white, pruinose leaves 2–3 cm long; inflorescence 30 cm tall; reddish flowers.

Mexico

Pachyphytum viride E. Walther
CRASSULACEAE
Stems 10 cm high and 3 cm in diameter; semi-cylindrical, yellowish-green leaves 10–14 cm long, flattened towards apex and borne at tips of stems; reddish flowers.

Mexico

Pachyphytum hookeri (Salm-Dyck) A. Berger
CRASSULACEAE
Shrublet to 60 cm high; grey-green leaves 2–4 cm long and 1–2 cm thick; inflorescence 30 cm long; red flowers.

Pachyphytum roseum Baker

Mexico

Pachypodium baronii Const. & Bois
APOCYNACEAE
Large, poorly branched, flask-shaped stems 2–3 m high; grey-green branches with conical spines 1 cm long; green leaves to 15 cm long; red flowers.

Madagascar   CITES App. I

Pachyphytum oviferum J.A. Purpus
CRASSULACEAE
Prostrate, white stems 10–15 cm long; white leaves 2–4 cm long and 2–3 cm wide; red flowers.

Mexico

Pachypodium baronii var. windsorii Pichon
APOCYNACEAE
Globose stems to 10 cm in diameter; thick, cylindrical branches; short spines; leaves at ends of branches; red flowers.

Madagascar   CITES App. I

Pachypodium bispinosum (L.f.) DC.

APOCYNACEAE

Possibly a variant of *P. succulentum*; pink to dull purple flowers.
South Africa (Cape Province)   CITES App. II

Pachypodium densiflorum Baker

APOCYNACEAE

Caudex to 30 cm in diameter with cylindrical branches to 70 cm (giving lateral spread to 2 m); spines 5–6 mm long; dark green leaves 2–4 cm long with fine white hairs on lower surface; yellow flowers.
Madagascar   CITES App. II

Pachypodium brevicaule Baker

APOCYNACEAE

Flattened caudex to 60 cm in diameter with silvery-grey bark; sparse, hairy leaves 1–3 cm long and to 1.5 cm wide; white spines; lemon-yellow flowers.
Madagascar   CITES App. I

Pachypodium geayi Const. & Bois

APOCYNACEAE

Similar to *P. lamerei* but with thinner leaves to 30 cm long and covered with grey hairs; white flowers.
Madagascar   CITES App. II

Pachypodium decaryi Poiss.

APOCYNACEAE

Short, rounded, tuberous caudex to 40 cm high, suddenly branching in thin stems; leaves 5–6 cm long and 4–5 cm wide arranged in terminal rosettes and with soft marginal hairs; greenish-white flowers.
Madagascar   CITES App. I

Pachypodium lamerei Drake

APOCYNACEAE

Spiny tree to 8 m high; dark green leaves 15–20 cm long and crowded at stem apex; white flowers. After flowering 2–3 branches develop at apex of flowering stem.
Madagascar

CITES App. II

Pachypodium lamerei cristate form
APOCYNACEAE

An attractive cristate form.

Pachypodium rutenbergianum Vatke
APOCYNACEAE

Stems 4–8 m tall with swollen trunk to 60 cm in diameter at base; short branches with spines 1 cm long; green leaves 10–15 cm long and 4 cm wide; white flowers.

Madagascar   CITES App. II

Pachypodium lealii Welw.
APOCYNACEAE

Clavate, broad-based stems with numerous erect branches; green leaves 4–8 cm long; 3 spines 2–3 cm long; white flowers.

Namibia, South Africa (Cape Province)   CITES App. II

Pachypodium saundersii N.E. Br.
APOCYNACEAE

Similar to *P. lealii* but stems are longer and leaves less hairy; flowers have red stripes. It is considered by some authors to be a variety of *P. lealii.*

South Africa (Natal), Zimbabwe

CITES App. II

Pachypodium namaquanum Welw.
APOCYNACEAE

Rarely branched stems 1–3 m high and covered with brown spines to 5 cm long; hairy, green leaves 8–12 cm long and 2–6 cm wide clustered at stem apices; brownish-red flowers.

Namibia   CITES App. I

Pachypodium succulentum DC.
APOCYNACEAE

Caudex to 15 cm in diameter, growing underground in habitat; fleshy, branched stems 20–60 cm long; leaves 5–6 cm long and 1 cm wide borne along new shoots; spines 1–2 cm long usually in pairs; pink flowers.

South Africa (Cape Province)   CITES App. II

Pedilanthus macrocarpus Benth.
EUPHORBIACEAE
Shrub with erect, grey-green stems 1–1.5 m high; thin, caducous, grey-green leaves; red inflorescence.
Mexico

Pelargonium cortusifolium L'Hér.
GERANIACEAE
Shrub 30 cm high and 30 cm in diameter; short stems covered with remains of dry leaves; grey-green, hairy, roundish leaves 1–5 cm long and 1.5–4 cm wide with undulate margins; white flowers.
Namibia

Pedilanthus tithymaloides (L.) Poit.
EUPHORBIACEAE
Shrub 1–2 m tall; irregular stems; green leaves 6 cm long with prominent mid-rib; red inflorescence.
West Indies

Pelargonium cotyledonis (L.) L'Hér.
GERANIACEAE
Thick stems to 30 cm high; rounded, green leaves (turning red with age) 2–5 cm in diameter with evident veins above and grey hairs below; white flowers.
Saint Helena

Pelargonium ceratophyllum L'Hér.
GERANIACEAE
Low shrub to 20 cm high with small, heavily branched caudex 3–4 cm thick; short stems; greyish-green succulent leaves 15 cm long and pinnately divided; white flowers.
Namibia

Pelargonium crithmifolium G.G. Smith
GERANIACEAE
Succulent, branched stems to 50 cm high with irregular swellings; hairy, pale green leaves 5–12 cm long and pinnately divided; white flowers.
Namibia

Pelargonium dasyphyllum E. Mey.
GERANIACEAE
Shrub to 20 cm high; succulent, grey-green to greyish-brown stems; compound, green leaves 6 cm long and 3 cm wide with dentate margins; white flowers.
South Africa (Cape Province)

Pelargonium ferulaceum Willd.
GERANIACEAE
Thick, fleshy stems 30–70 cm high; young branches hairy; green leaves 5–15 cm long and 2–5 cm wide, usually with red-brown tips; variable white to greenish-yellow flowers with red streaks.
Namibia

Pelargonium gibbosum (L.) L'Hér.
GERANIACEAE
Succulent stems scrambling among bushes to 3 m long and with swollen nodes; semi-succulent, glaucous green leaves variable in size and shape; greenish-yellow flowers.
South Africa (Cape Province)

Pelargonium incrassatum (Andrews) Sims
GERANIACEAE
Shrub to 20 cm and more high with large underground tubers; green leaves 5–9 cm long and 3–6 cm wide; purple flowers.
Namibia

Pelargonium klinghardtense R. Knuth
GERANIACEAE
Stems to 80 cm high branching from base; light glaucous green leaves 3–6 cm long and 3 cm wide covered with microscopic hairs; white flowers.
Namibia

Pelargonium lobatum (Burm.f.) L'Hér.
GERANIACEAE
Plant 20–30 cm high; large tubers covered with brown bark; short stems; 3-lobed, hairy, green leaves to 30 cm in diameter; dark purple flowers.
South Africa (Cape Province)

Pelargonium mirabile Dinter

GERANIACEAE

Shrub 30 cm high and 40 cm in diameter; greyish-brown stems 1–2 cm in diameter; greyish-green leaves 3–5 cm long and 2–4 cm wide with undulate margins; white, pale yellow or pink flowers with red markings.

Namibia

Pelargonium pulchellum Sims

GERANIACEAE

Small shrub to 1 m high; stems distinctly jointed; green, ovate, 5-lobed leaves 3–5 cm long and covered with hairs; inflorescence 50 cm high; white flowers.

Namibia

Pelargonium rapaceum (L.) L'Hér.

GERANIACEAE

Stemless plant with subterranean tuber 5 cm in diameter; linear, green, hairy leaves to 40 cm long and 4–5 cm wide; pink flowers with red stripes.

South Africa (Cape Province)

Pelargonium tetragonum (L.f.) L'Hér.

GERANIACEAE

Bush to 20 cm high branching from base with distinctly jointed, thin stems; hairy, green leaves 2.5 cm long with reddish-brown margins; cream to pale pink flowers.

Southern Africa

Pelargonium xerophyton Schltr.

GERANIACEAE

Shrub forming clumps 30–60 cm high; green to grey stems; dull green leaves 1 cm long and 1 cm wide covered with microscopic hairs; white flowers.

Namibia

Peperomia asperula Hutchison & Rauh

PIPERACEAE

Succulent stems to 10 cm high with short internodes; leaves 1–8 cm long and 9 mm wide arranged in dense rows, translucent above, green-grey below; yellowish-grey flowers.

Peru

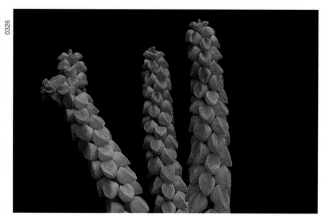

Peperomia columella Rauh & Hutchison
PIPERACEAE
Small shrub; freely branching stems 10 cm long and covered by leaves in whorls of 5; succulent leaves 1 cm long and 6 mm in diameter with translucent window above; yellowish-green flowers.
Peru

Peperomia dolabriformis R. Knuth
PIPERACEAE
Small shrub; stems 10 cm long with leaves at apex; leaves 5–6 cm long and 6 mm thick with translucent, lateral stripes; long inflorescence; yellowish-green flowers.
Peru

Phyllanthus mirabilis Muell.
EUPHORBIACEAE
Shrub or small tree with stems to 12 cm long; ovate, green leaves, paler below and 2–3 cm long; inflorescence borne from leaf axils; reddish bracts.
Burma, Cambodia, Laos, Malaysia

Piaranthus cornutus N.E. Br.
ASCLEPIADACEAE
Freely branching, green, globose to elongate stems 1.5–3.5 cm long and 1.5–2 cm in diameter; stems tuberculate with 3–5 tubercle-like teeth; pale yellow flowers with purple dots.
South Africa (Cape Province)

Piaranthus foetidus N.E. Br.
ASCLEPIADACEAE
Globose, tuberculate, green to grey-green, sometimes reddish, stems 4 cm in diameter with dentate margins; hairy yellow flowers with red lines and spots.
Namibia, South Africa (Cape Province)

Piaranthus framesii Pillans
ASCLEPIADACEAE
Bluish-green or reddish, 4- to 5-angled stems 4–7 cm long and 1–1.5 cm in diameter with tuberculate teeth; white flowers with red spots.
South Africa (Cape Province)

Piaranthus pallidus C.A. Lückh.

ASCLEPIADACEAE

Pale green, globose to oblong, obscurely angled stems 2–3 cm long; yellow flowers.

South Africa (Cape Province)

Plectranthus prostratus Gürke

LABIATAE

Low-growing species with many pendent, soft branches; thick, soft, green leaves about 1 cm long; purple flowers.

Tanzania

Piaranthus pillansii N.E. Br.

ASCLEPIADACEAE

Procumbent, clavate, obtusely angled stems 3–4 cm long and 1–1.5 cm in diameter; yellow flowers.

South Africa (Cape Province)

Pleiospilos bolusii (Hook.f.) N.E. Br.

MESEMBRYANTHEMACEAE

Solitary plants with 1 pair of light grey-green or brownish-green leaves 4–7 cm long and 3–4 cm thick with numerous dots; yellow flowers.

South Africa (Cape Province)

Plectranthus amboinicus (Lourteig) Spreng

LABIATAE

Many decumbent stems to 1 m long; green, ovate leaves 4–5 cm long and 4 cm wide with small hairs and aromatic glands on both sides; white flowers.

Tropical Africa

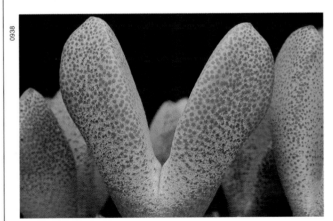

Pleiospilos compactus subsp. canus (Haw.) H.E.K. Hartmann & Liede

MESEMBRYANTHEMACEAE

Stemless, clump-forming rosettes of 4–8 grey-green, purple-tinged leaves to 9 cm long; yellow flowers.

Pleiospilos canus (Haw.) L. Bol.

South Africa (Cape Province)

Pleiospilos compactus subsp. minor (L. Bol.)
H.E.K. Hartmann & Liede
MESEMBRYANTHEMACEAE
Rounded, grey-green leaves 3–6 cm long and covered with dark green dots in pairs of 2–3 on each stem; yellow flowers.
Pleiospilos minor L. Bol.
South Africa (Cape Province)

Pleiospilos leipoldtii L. Bol.
MESEMBRYANTHEMACEAE
Divergent, grey-green or purple-tinged leaves to 8 cm long and 3 cm wide with flat upper surface; yellow flowers.
South Africa (Cape Province)

Pleiospilos magnipunctatus (Haw.) Schwantes
MESEMBRYANTHEMACEAE
Grey-green or brownish leaves 4–9 cm long, united at base for 1 cm and with flat upper surface, convex back and prominent dots; yellow flowers.
South Africa (Cape Province)

Pleiospilos nelii Schwantes
MESEMBRYANTHEMACEAE
Semi-cylindrical, grey-green leaves to 8 cm long, borne in pairs and with flat upper surface and numerous dots; yellow-pink to orange flowers.
Pleiospilos pedunculatus L. Bol.; *P. tricolor* N.E. Br.
South Africa (Cape Province)

Plumeria acuminata Aiton
APOCYNACEAE
Tree to 8 m high; green leaves 30–40 cm long; yellow and white, scented flowers. After flowering 2–3 branches develop at apex of flowering stem.
Mexico

Plumeria rubra L.
APOCYNACEAE
Tree to 7 m high; bright green leaves 40 cm long with paler mid-rib; dark pink, scented flowers. Branching pattern as in *P. acuminata*.
Mexico to Panama

Poellnitzia rubiflora
(L. Bol.) Uitewaal
LILIACEAE
Elongated stems 15–20 cm high, offsetting from base; tri-angular leaves 4 cm long and 2 cm wide ending in pungent, yellow-green tip; inflorescence 12 cm long; red flowers.
South Africa (Cape Province)

Portulacaria afra var. foliis-variegatis H. Jacobsen
PORTULACACEAE
Shrub to 3 m high with horizontally spreading, segmented branches; opposite leaves 1.2 cm long and 1 cm wide; pink flowers. The leaves of this form are mottled with yellow.
Mozambique, South Africa (Cape Province, Transvaal)

Polymita albiflora (L. Bol.) L. Bol.
MESEMBRYANTHEMACEAE
Shrub 10–15 cm high; acute leaves 5–10 mm long, united at base but tips spreading, margins hairy; white flowers.
Ruschia albiflora L. Bol.
South Africa (Cape Province)

Pseudolithos migiurtinus (Chiov.) P.R.O. Bally
ASCLEPIADACEAE
Fleshy, hemispherical, often elliptical in section, pale green or yellow-green to grey stems 12 cm in diameter; numerous tubercles around the stems; brown flowers.
Pseudolithos sphaericus P.R.O. Bally
Somalia

Portulaca pilosa L.
PORTULACACEAE
Thick roots with woody stems; cylindrical green leaves to 12 mm long with reddish margins. In the type species the flowers are yellow; this specimen is a cultivar, 'Shaggy Garden Purslane', which has purple flowers.
Mexico, USA (southeast)

Pterodiscus aurantiacus Welw.
PEDALIACEAE
Bottle-shaped caudex to 30 cm in diameter with several thick branches; lanceolate, bluish-green leaves 10–15 cm long with sinuate margins; yellow flowers.
Namibia

Pterodiscus luridus Hook.

PEDALIACEAE

Caudex to 10 cm in diameter and covered with grey bark; branches 10–15 cm long; leaves 7–8 cm long and 2 cm wide, dark green above, whitish below; yellow flowers.

Namibia, South Africa (Cape Province)

Quaqua mamillaris (L.) P.V. Bruyns

ASCLEPIADACEAE

Stems 5- to 6-angled, 15–25 cm high and 3 cm thick; teeth 1–2 cm long; dark red flowers.

Caralluma mamillaris (L.) N.E. Br.

Namibia, South Africa (Cape Province)

Puya mirabilis (Mez) L.B. Sm.

BROMELIACEAE

Rosette of 60–70 green leaves to 70 cm long with marginal teeth; inflorescence 50 cm tall; green flowers.

Argentina, Bolivia

Rabiea albipuncta (Haw.) N.E. Br.

MESEMBRYANTHEMACEAE

Rosettes of 3–4 pairs of green leaves 4 cm long and triangular in cross-section with numerous tuberculate dots; yellow flowers.

South Africa (Orange Free State)

Pyrenacantha malvifolia Engl.

ICACINACEAE

Swollen caudex to 1 m in diameter producing twining, leafy stems; green leaves; orange flowers.

Kenya, Tanzania

Raphionacme burkei N.E. Br.

ASCLEPIADACEAE

Grey caudex 8–15 cm in diameter; much-branched stems 15 cm long; grey-green leaves 3 cm long; purple flowers.

Botswana, Namibia, South Africa (Transvaal)

Raphionacme galpinii Schltr.
ASCLEPIADACEAE
Caudex 8–10 cm in diameter and 15 cm long; stems 7–10 cm tall; silvery-green leaves 4–6 cm long; greenish flowers.
South Africa (Transvaal)

Raphionacme procumbens Schltr.
ASCLEPIADACEAE
Large tuberous caudex; spreading stems 20–40 cm long; greyish-green leaves 3 cm long and covered with short hairs; greenish flowers.
Namibia

Raphionacme sp.
ASCLEPIADACEAE
Long, trailing stems 1–2 m long; leaves to 10 cm long. One of several unidentified specimens present in private collections.
Southern Africa

Rechesteineria leucotricha Hoehne
GESNERIACEAE
Caudex to 30 cm in diameter; shoots with 4–6 leaves; stems and leaves covered with silvery hairs; pink to orange flowers.
Brazil

Rhombophyllum dolabriforme (L.) Schwantes
MESEMBRYANTHEMACEAE
Freely branching shrub to 30 cm high; grey, erect branches; grass green leaves 2–3 cm long with transparent dots and tooth-like, projecting tip; yellow flowers.
South Africa (Cape Province)

Rhombophyllum neelii Schwantes
MESEMBRYANTHEMACEAE
Shrub 20–30 cm high; stems with short internodes; bilobial, pale bluish to grey-green leaves 1.5 cm long; yellow flowers.
South Africa (Cape Province)

Rhombophyllum romboideum (Salm-Dyck) Schwantes
MESEMBRYANTHEMACEAE
Stemless rosettes with 4–5 pairs of unequal sized, grey-green leaves 2.5–5 cm long and 1–2 cm wide; yellow flowers.
South Africa (Cape Province)

Rhytidocaulon sp.
ASCLEPIADACEAE
Fleshy, cylindrical, grey to brown stem 2 cm thick; caducous, green leaves 2 mm long; variable flowers.
Arabian peninsula; Ethiopia, Somalia (for the whole genus)

Rosularia chrysantha (Boiss.) Takht.
CRASSULACEAE
Rosettes 2.5 cm in diameter; green, hairy leaves 2–3 cm long with rounded apex; yellow flowers.
Turkey (south and southwest)

Rosularia pallida (Schott & Kotschy) Stapf
CRASSULACEAE
Small rosettes; densely hairy, green or blue-green leaves 12–18 mm long; whitish-yellow flowers.
Turkey (east and southeast)

Ruschia clavata L. Bol.
MESEMBRYANTHEMACEAE
Erect stems to 20 cm long; green to bluish-green, semiglobose leaves 3 mm in diameter; purplish flowers.
South Africa (Cape Province)

Ruschia crassa (L. Bol.) Schwantes
MESEMBRYANTHEMACEAE
Shrub with erect or prostrate stems; glaucous green leaves 1–2 cm long; white flowers.
South Africa (Cape Province)

Ruschia frutescens (L. Bol.) L. Bol.
MESEMBRYANTHEMACEAE

Shrub to 60 cm high; semi-cylindrical, spreading, greyish-green leaves 5–6 cm long and 1 cm in diameter; whitish flowers.

South Africa (Cape Province)

Ruschia macowanii (L. Bol.) Schwantes
MESEMBRYANTHEMACEAE

Shrub 15–20 cm high; elongated stems; grey-green leaves 2–3 cm long; pink flowers.

South Africa (Cape Province)

Ruschia multiflora (Haw.) Schwantes
MESEMBRYANTHEMACEAE

Shrub with freely branching, repeatedly forked stems; grey-green leaves 3 cm long with translucent dots; white flowers.

South Africa (Cape Province)

Ruschia sarmentosa (Haw.) Schwantes
MESEMBRYANTHEMACEAE

Shrub 60 cm high; branches spreading and rooting at nodes; light green, triangular leaves 3 cm long with translucent dots and ending with reddish tip; reddish flowers.

South Africa (Cape Province)

Ruschia stenophylla (L. Bol.) L. Bol.
MESEMBRYANTHEMACEAE

Shrub with fleshy, napiform (turnip-shaped) root; semi-cylindrical, spotted, green leaves 4–5 cm long; pink-purple flowers.

South Africa (Cape Province)

Ruschianthus falcatus L. Bol.
MESEMBRYANTHEMACEAE

Shrub with tuberous roots; stems covered with remains of dry leaves; unequal sized, pale blue-green leaves, the larger 3–5 cm long, borne in pairs; yellow flowers.

Namibia

Sansevieria cylindrica Bojer

AGAVACEAE

Dark green, cylindrical leaves 1 m long and 1–2 cm in diameter with lighter stripe; white flowers.

Angola

Sansevieria gracilis N.E. Br

AGAVACEAE

Stoloniferous stems; leaves 20–50 cm long and 1 cm in diameter, armed with brown apical spine; white flowers.

Eastern Africa

Sansevieria pearsonii N.E. Br.

AGAVACEAE

Erect green leaves 60–90 cm long with several longitudinal furrows and ending in sharp tip; white flowers.

Tropical Africa

Sansevieria raffilii var. glauca N.E. Br.

AGAVACEAE

Leaves 60 cm long and 7–10 cm wide; white flowers. The leaves of this variety are lighter in colour than the type species.

Tropical Africa

Sansevieria singularis Britton

AGAVACEAE

Cylindrical, grey, grey-brown or reddish leaves to 50 cm high (over 1 m in cultivation); flowers not known.

Tropical Africa

Sansevieria thyrsifolia Thunb.

AGAVACEAE

Light green leaves to 8 cm wide and 15–40 cm high with several whitish bands and spots; fragrant, greenish-white flowers.

Southern Africa

Sansevieria trifasciata 'Hahnii'

AGAVACEAE

A dwarf cultivar with broad leaves marked with yellow transverse bands.

Sansevieria trifasciata 'Laurentii'

AGAVACEAE

This is one of the oldest cultivars of *S. trifasciata* Prain. It has attractive leaves to 70 cm long with yellow margins.

Sansevieria trifasciata 'Moonshine'

AGAVACEAE

A cultivar with bluish-green (yellowish when young) leaves 10 cm wide and 30 cm high.

Sarcocaulon ciliatum Moffett

GERANIACEAE

Shrub to 20 cm high and 30 cm in diameter with freely branching stems; grey-brown branches with brown spines; green leaves covered with short hairs; yellow flowers.

South Africa (Cape Province)

Sarcocaulon crassicaule Rehm

GERANIACEAE

Small, spiny shrub to 25 cm high; recurved branches 10–15 cm long and 1–1.4 cm thick, with whitish-grey, recurved thorns; green to grey-green leaves about 1.5 cm long; white or pale yellow flowers.

Sarcocaulon burmannii (DC.) Sweet

Namibia/South Africa (Little Namaqualand), South Africa (Cape Province, Karoo)

Sarcocaulon herrei L. Bol.

GERANIACEAE

Shrub to 25 cm high and 40 cm in diameter; freely branching, greyish-yellow stems; yellowish-green leaves; dry leaf petioles have spiny appearance; pale yellow flowers.

Sarcocaulon lorrei Stiles

South Africa (Cape Province)

Sarcocaulon inerme Rehm
GERANIACEAE
Shrub to 30 cm high and 30 cm in diameter; stems branching above ground; grey-brown branches with 4 rows of bluish-green leaves covered with short hairs and with dentate margins; pink to purple flowers.
Namibia

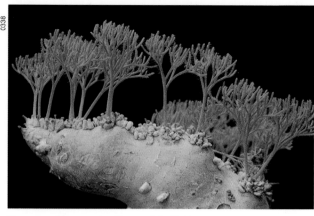

Sarcocaulon peniculinum Moffett
GERANIACEAE
Dwarf shrub to 8 cm high and 18 cm in diameter; stems branching at soil level or below; greyish-white branches; green leaves covered with small hairs; pale pink flowers.
Namibia

Sarcocaulon multifidum R. Knuth
GERANIACEAE
Horizontally growing branches 10–12 cm long and 1.5 cm thick; hairy, green, bifid leaves 7–10 cm long; pink flowers.
Namibia

Sarcocaulon vanderietiae L. Bol.
GERANIACEAE
Shrub 15 cm high and 25 cm in diameter; spiny stems 1 cm in diameter; green leaves 6–8 cm long; pale pink flowers.
South Africa (Cape Province)

Sarcocaulon patersonii (DC.) Don
GERANIACEAE
Light grey stems to 20 cm long with straight spines 1–3 cm long; hairy, green leaves 1 cm long; red flowers.
Namibia

Sarcostemma viminale R. Br.
ASCLEPIADACEAE
Erect, cylindrical, light green stems 4–5 mm thick and dichotomously branched; small, light green leaf scales; white flowers.
Namibia, South Africa (Cape Province)

Sceletium anatomicum (Haw.) L. Bol.

MESEMBRYANTHEMACEAE

Small shrub with prostrate branches; stems to 20 cm long; yellow-green leaves 2–3 cm long with translucent papillae; white flowers.

South Africa (Cape Province)

Schwantesia succumbens (Dinter) Dinter

MESEMBRYANTHEMACEAE

Whitish-green leaves 4–8 cm long, cylindrical at base and triangular in section towards apex; yellow flowers.

Namibia

Sceletium joubertii L. Bol.

MESEMBRYANTHEMACEAE

Short, prostrate branches; green leaves (often obscured by remains of old leaves) 3–4 cm long with numerous papillae; yellow flowers.

South Africa (Cape Province)

Scilla dimartinoi Brullo & Pavone

LILIACEAE

Brown bulbs 2–4 cm in diameter; up to 10 leaves 12–22 cm long and 1–2 cm wide with short, marginal cilia; inflorescence 10 cm tall; bluish-white flowers. Plant photographed in habitat.

Italy (Lampedusa Island)

Schwantesia ruedebuschii Dinter

MESEMBRYANTHEMACEAE

Clumps to 10 cm high; leaves 5 cm long and 1 cm wide, armed at ends with 3–7 thick, brown-tipped teeth to 4 mm long; yellow flowers.

Namibia

Scilla pauciflora Baker

LILIACEAE

Small bulbs, offsetting and forming large clumps; pale green leaves with dark green markings; greenish flowers.

Southern Africa

199

Scilla socialis Baker

LILIACEAE

Green to purple bulbs 2–4 cm in diameter; spreading, fleshy leaves 10–15 cm long and 2 cm wide with some dark green marks above, green or pink-purple below; purple flowers.

Ledebouria socialis Jessop

Southern Africa

Scilla violacea Hutch.

LILIACEAE

A form of *S. socialis*; leaves have green marks above and are deep pink-purple beneath; purple flowers.

Southern Africa

Sedum acre L.

CRASSULACEAE

Numerous stems from thin stolon forming low clumps; crowded, mid- to yellow-green leaves 1–2 mm long; yellow flowers.

Northern Africa, Europe

Sedum aizoon 'Euphorbioides'

CRASSULACEAE

Erect stems to 60 cm high; thick root; lanceolate leaves 5–8 cm long with toothed margins; yellow flowers. This cultivar is more robust and compact than the type species.

Sedum aizoides Salm-Dyck; *S. maximowiczii* Regel; *S. woodwardii* N.E. Br.

Asia; naturalized in Europe

Sedum album L.

CRASSULACEAE

Erect or creeping stems; green or reddish leaves 6–15 mm long; white flowers. A variable species; several varieties have been described.

Sedum athoum DC.; *S. balticum* H.E.K. Hartmann; *S. turgidum* d'Urv.

North Africa, western Asia, Europe

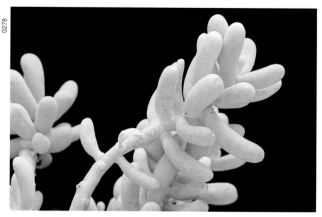

Sedum allantoides Rose

CRASSULACEAE

Small shrub to 40 cm high; white-grey leaves 2–3 cm long, at first in lax basal rosette, becoming crowded along the lengthening stem; greenish-white flowers.

Mexico

Sedum anacampseros L.
CRASSULACEAE

Stems creeping and rooting at nodes; grey-green leaves 1–2.5 cm long and 1–2 cm wide, loosely crowded towards stem apices; purple flowers.

Sedum rotundiflorum Lam.

Southern Europe (Spain to the Tyrol)

Sedum anopetalum DC.
CRASSULACEAE

Prostrate stems to 25 cm long; glaucous green, cylindrical leaves 1 cm long and pointed towards tips; whitish flowers.

Sedum verlotii Jord.

Southern and central Europe and into Asia Minor

Sedum dasyphyllum L.
CRASSULACEAE

Numerous horizontal branches forming low clumps; grey, opposite leaves; white flowers with pink vein. Several forms have been described, differentiated on the basis of the size of the leaves and of the whole plant.

Sedum burnatii Briquet; *S. glanduliferum* Guss.; *S. glaucum* Lam.

Mediterranean countries

Sedum ellacombianum Praeger
CRASSULACEAE

Several stems arising from lower part of older ones; green leaves crowded along stems, increasing in size towards stem base; inflorescence flat and branched; pale yellow flowers.

Japan

Sedum furfuraceum Moran
CRASSULACEAE

Creeping and rooting stems 8–10 cm long; erect branches; waxy, green leaves 1 cm long, round in section; white flowers tipped with pink ventrally and red dorsally.

Mexico

Sedum hintonii R.T. Clausen
CRASSULACEAE

Stems 8–10 cm long; sparse branches; densely hairy leaves 1.5–2 cm long arranged in rosettes; white flowers.

Mexico

Sedum hispanicum L.
CRASSULACEAE

Many stems 5–15 cm long arising from base; glaucous green leaves 1–2 cm long pointed at tips and sometimes tinged with red; white flowers with pinkish-tipped veins. A variable species.

Sedum glaucum Waldst. & Kitaibel; *S. sexifidum* Fisher & E. Mey.

Central Europe to Iran

Sedum lancerottense R.P. Murray
CRASSULACEAE

Similar to *S. nudum* but with larger leaves; yellow flowers.

Canary Islands (Lanzarote)

Sedum kamtschaticum Fisch.
CRASSULACEAE

Similar to *S. aizoon* but to 30 cm high; stems branching at base; leaves 2–4 cm long with toothed margins, entire towards base; orange-yellow flowers.

China, Japan, Korea, northeast Siberia

Sedum lineare Thunb.
CRASSULACEAE

Erect to prostrate stems; light green leaves 2–3 cm long and 3 cm wide at base; yellow flowers.

Sedum subtile Miq.; *S. zentaro-tashiroi* Makino

Japan

Sedum lanceolatum Torr.
CRASSULACEAE

Many freely offsetting stems to 12 cm high; green, alternate leaves increasing in size towards stem base; inflorescence consists of 3 short, forked branches with yellow flowers.

Sedum shastense Britton; *S. stenopetalum* var. *subalpinum* Fröd.; *S. subalpinum* Blank.

North America (west)

Sedum middendorffianum (Maxim.) A.G. Boriss.
CRASSULACEAE

Many stems arising from lower part of old stems; green leaves increasing in size towards stem base; inflorescence variable in size with 4 forked branches bearing yellow flowers.

Korea, Mongolia, Siberia

Sedum morganianum Walther
CRASSULACEAE

Many long, pendent stems arising from base; greenish-blue, pruinose leaves crowded along stems; inflorescence with 1–6 pink flowers. Suitable for growing in hanging-baskets.

Known in cultivation in Mexico

Sedum nicaeense All.
CRASSULACEAE

Woody stems 15–35 cm high and branching from base; pointed green leaves 1–2 cm long; white flowers with green vein.
Sedum rufescens Ten.; *S. sediforme* (Jacq.) Pau
Mediterranean countries

Sedum multiceps Coss. & Durieu
CRASSULACEAE

Small, much branched bush to 12 cm tall; stems covered with withered leaves; leaves, 6–8 mm long and papillose below, borne in clusters near tips of stems; yellow flowers.

Algeria

Sedum nudum Aiton
CRASSULACEAE

Small shrub to 10 cm high; stems branching from base, creeping and rooting; green or glaucous green, oblong leaves 1 cm long; yellowish-green flowers.
Madeira

Sedum nevii A. Gray
CRASSULACEAE

Much branched stems, bare at base, leafy above and rooting at nodes; glaucous green leaves 1–1.5 cm long and 4 mm wide arranged in rosettes; flowers white.

USA (Virginia to Alabama)

Sedum nussbaumerianum Bitter
CRASSULACEAE

Small shrub 10 cm tall; stems branching horizontally, yellowish-green leaves 4 cm long with red edges; white flowers.
Mexico

Sedum oaxacanum Rose
CRASSULACEAE
Stems 10–15 cm long, freely branching and rooting at nodes; grey-green leaves 4–6 mm long; yellow flowers.
Mexico

Sedum potosinum Rose
CRASSULACEAE
Procumbent branches; erect stems 10–15 cm long; pale green leaves 15 mm long often tinged with pink; white flowers with red vein.
Mexico

Sedum pachyphyllum Rose
CRASSULACEAE
Low shrub to 25 cm tall; grey-green, cylindrical leaves (red-tipped when grown in strong sun) 4 cm long and 6 mm thick and loosely crowded towards tips of stems; yellow flowers.
Mexico

Sedum roseum (L.) Scop.
CRASSULACEAE
Small caudex from which arise several stems 20–30 cm long; fleshy green leaves 2.5–3.5 cm long, often with reddish margins; flowers yellow on male plants, greenish-yellow on female plants, deep red or pink on female plants of some North American forms.
Rhodiola rosea L.
North America to Mexico, China, central Europe

Sedum palmeri S. Watson
CRASSULACEAE
Low shrub 15–25 cm high with arching and branching stems; blue-green leaves 2–3 cm long borne in loose rosettes at ends of branches; orange-yellow flowers.
Mexico

Sedum rubrotinctum R.T. Clausen
CRASSULACEAE
Small shrub 25 cm high; numerous stems branching from base; light green leaves with red tips 1–2 cm long and round in section crowded along stems; pale yellow flowers.
Known in cultivation in Mexico

Sedum sartorianum Boiss.
CRASSULACEAE

Erect to prostrate stems 8–15 cm long; green to grey-green leaves triangular towards tips and 4 cm long; yellow flowers.

Sedum urvillei DC.

Greece, former Yugoslavia (Serbia)

Sedum sexangulare Linn.
CRASSULACEAE

Stems with many creeping stolons; green leaves arranged in spirals crowded along branches; inflorescence consists of 3 branches with yellow flowers.

Sedum boloniense Loisel.; *S. hillebrandtii* Fenzl; *S. mite* Gilib.; *S. spirale* Haw.

Central Europe to Finland and Lithuania

Sedum sieboldii 'Foliis Medio-variegatis'
CRASSULACEAE

Prostrate stems 15–25 cm long; blue-green leaves, sometimes red-margined, 1.5 cm long and to 2 cm wide; pink flowers. Two-thirds of leaf surface of this variegated form are yellow.

Japan

Sedum spathulifolium var. purpureum Praeger
CRASSULACEAE

Erect, freely branching stems to 2 cm high; green leaves in dense rosettes; leaves increase in size towards stem base and turn pink or bright red in adverse conditions; inflorescence 6–15 cm long with yellow flowers. There are several subspecies and varieties.

Sedum californicum Britton; *S. woodii* Britton

North America (California to British Columbia)

Sedum spectabile Boreau
CRASSULACEAE

Stems 30–50 cm high; light green, oval leaves 7–8 cm long and 5 cm wide; pink flowers.

China, Japan, Korea

Sedum spurium M. Bieb.
CRASSULACEAE

Many stems arising from rooting branches; dark green leaves crowded along upper part of branches; inflorescence with 4 forked branches; pink flowers.

Sedum ciliare Sweet; *S. congestum* Kock; *S. crenatum* Boiss.; *S. denticulatum* Donn; *S. lazicum* Boiss.

CIS (Armenia, Azerbaidzhan, Georgia)

Sedum stahlii Solms
CRASSULACEAE
Spreading, prostrate stems; brownish-red leaves 1.2 cm long and 6 mm wide crowded along stems; yellow flowers with greenish vein.
Mexico

Sedum stoloniferum S.G. Gmel.
CRASSULACEAE
Plants with red-striped stems growing in clumps; bright green leaves 2.5 cm long and 1.2 cm wide, lighter dorsally and scattered along stems and branches; light pink flowers.
Sedum ibericum Steven
CIS (Caucasus)

Sedum treleasei Rose
CRASSULACEAE
Small shrub with several branches arising from lower parts of stems; bluish-green, pruinose leaves 3 cm long; yellow flowers.
Mexico

Sempervivella alba (Edgew.) Stapf
CRASSULACEAE
Clump-forming rosettes 2–3 cm in diameter; hairy, light green leaves 1–2 cm long; red or white flowers.
Sempervivum album Edgew.
Western Himalayas

Sempervivum arachnoideum L.
CRASSULACEAE
Rosettes 5–25 mm in diameter forming dense mats; green leaves flushed with red and with white hairs connected at tips; pink flowers. Plant photographed in habitat.
France/Italy/Spain (Alps, Apennines, Pyrenees)

Sempervivum atlanticum O.M. Ball
CRASSULACEAE
Freely offsetting rosettes 4–8 cm in diameter; pale green leaves flushed red when exposed to sun; flower-stems 15–25 cm high; pale pink flowers with darker median band.
Morocco

Sempervivum borissovae Wale
CRASSULACEAE
Rosettes 3 cm in diameter; strongly ciliate leaves, green below, tinged red-brown above; pink to red flowers.
CIS (Caucasus)

Sempervivum caucasicum Rupr. ex Boiss.
CRASSULACEAE
Rosettes 3–5 cm in diameter; leaves with dark brown apex, short cilia and sparse hairs on lower surface; red flowers.
CIS (Caucasus)

Sempervivum calcareum (Jord.) Praeger
CRASSULACEAE
Rosettes 6 cm in diameter; glabrous grey-green leaves tipped with purple; pale pink flowers.
Sempervivum tectorum var. *calcareum* Jord.
France/Italy (Alpes Maritimes)

Sempervivum ciliosum var. borisii Degen & Urum.
CRASSULACEAE
Globose rosettes 2–4 cm in diameter; densely hairy leaves; yellow flowers.
Bulgaria

Sempervivum cantabricum J.A. Huber
CRASSULACEAE
Offsetting rosettes 5 cm in diameter with 30–40 hairy leaves to 4 cm long and 1 cm wide; inflorescence 16 cm high; dark pink flowers.
Spain

Sempervivum ciliosum var. galicium A.C. Sm.
CRASSULACEAE
Rosettes to 2.5 cm in diameter with long stolons; greyish-green leaves with short hairs; flower stem to 9 cm high; yellow flowers.
Europe (Galicia, Macedonia)

Sempervivum dolomiticum Facchini
CRASSULACEAE
Rosettes 2–4 cm in diameter; bright green, ciliate leaves; numerous offsets on slender stems; reddish flowers.
Italy (eastern Alps; rare)

Sempervivum kosaninii Praeger
CRASSULACEAE
Rosettes 4–8 cm in diameter; light to dark green leaves with red apices; offsets produced on leafy stems to 12 cm long; reddish-pink flowers.
Former Yugoslavia (Montenegro)

Sempervivum grandiflorum Haw.
CRASSULACEAE
Rosettes 2–10 cm in diameter; dull green leaves, some with brown apices, hairy and sticky to the touch, leaving resinous odour; yellow flowers tinged with purple at base. Plant photographed in habitat.
Sempervivum gaudini Christ.
Italy (Piedmont, Valle d'Aosta); southern Switzerland

Sempervivum montanum L.
CRASSULACEAE
Rosettes 2 cm in diameter with numerous offsets borne on slender stems; bright to dull green, leaves densely hairy on both surfaces; violet-purple flowers. Plant photographed in habitat.
Corsica, France/Italy/Spain (Pyrenees, Alps, northern Apennines)

Sempervivum kindingeri Adamovic
CRASSULACEAE
Rosettes 4–6 cm in diameter; pale green, purple-flushed, glandular, hairy leaves with marginal cilia; yellow flowers with pink base.
Europe (Macedonia)

Sempervivum montanum var. burnatii Wettst. ex Hayek
CRASSULACEAE
Rosettes to 8 cm in diameter; light green, hairy leaves with dark tips; violet-purple flowers. Plant photographed in habitat.
France/Italy/Spain (southwest Alps, Pyrenees)

Sempervivum nevadense Wale
CRASSULACEAE

Rosettes 2–3 cm in diameter; green, red-tinged leaves with marginal cilia; offsets on short stolons; reddish-pink flowers.

Spain (Sierra Nevada)

Sempervivum sp.
CRASSULACEAE

An unidentified taxon growing on porphyric rocks. Rosettes 2.5–3 cm in diameter; bright green, densely hairy and glandular leaves tinged with purple and with long, thin, white bristles on outer surface of older leaves; flower stems 5–6 cm; delicately scented, red to deep purple flowers.

Italy (Catena dei Lagorai)

Sempervivum pittonii Schott, Nyman & Kotschy
CRASSULACEAE

Rosettes 1.5–3 cm in diameter; green, glandular, hairy leaves with purple tips; yellow flowers.

Austria (Styria)

Sempervivum tectorum L.
CRASSULACEAE

Extremely variable species; rosettes 3–15 cm or more in diameter; glabrous or hairy, yellow-green to dark green or red-brown leaves with or without brown tip and purple base; pink flowers. Plant photographed in habitat.

Sempervivum arvernense Lecoq & Lamotte; *S. tectorum* var. *alpinum* Griseb. & Schenk; *S. tectorum* var. *glaucum* Ten.

France/Italy/Spain (Pyrenees, Alps, Apennines), northern Balkans

Sempervivum pumilum M. Bieb.
CRASSULACEAE

Freely offsetting rosettes 1–2 cm in diameter; green, glandular, hairy leaves with ciliate margins; purple flowers with pale margins. A variable species.

CIS (Caucasus)

Sempervivum tectorum var. italicum (Ricci) Zonn.
CRASSULACEAE

Rosettes 3–8 cm in diameter; numerous hairy green leaves with or without brown tips and with ciliate margins; pink flowers with narrow white margins. Plant photographed in habitat.

Sempervivum italicum Ricci

Italy (Abruzzo, Lazio)

Sempervivum thompsonianum Wale

CRASSULACEAE

Rosettes 1.5–5 cm in diameter with several offsets from base; green, hairy leaves 1.5 cm long and 4 mm wide with dark brown tips; yellow flowers with white margins and median pink band.

Former Yugoslavia (southwest Macedonia)

Sempervivum x barbulatum Schott

CRASSULACEAE

A natural hybrid of *S. arachnoideum* L. x *S. montanum* L. Small rosettes of variable size but generally 1–1.5 cm in diameter and tipped with woolly hairs; pink or violet-purple flowers. Plant photographed in habitat.

France/Italy/Spain (Pyrenees, Alps)

Sempervivum wulfenii Hoppe

CRASSULACEAE

Slow-growing plant, producing 2–3 offsets on stolons to 10 cm long during growing season; grey-green leaves purple at base; yellow flowers with purple base. Plant photographed in habitat.

Austria/Italy/Switzerland (eastern Alps)

Sempervivum x roseum Huter

CRASSULACEAE

Rosettes of grey-green leaves tipped with tuft of hairs; the flower colour is intermediate between the parents, *S. arachnoideum* x *S. wulfenii*, varying from pink to yellow. Plant photographed in habitat.

Austria/Italy/Switzerland (eastern Alps)

Sempervivum wulfenii Hoppe

CRASSULACEAE

A close-up of the flowers.

Sempervivum tectorum 'Bianco di Daniele' Zonn.

CRASSULACEAE

Rosettes 5–6 cm in diameter; grey-green, hairy leaves; flowers white.

Italy (Valtellina; limited distribution)

Sempervivum tectorum var. italicum x arachnoideum
CRASSULACEAE

Rosettes 3–7 cm in diameter; reddish, glandular, ciliate leaves with tuft of white hairs at tips. Plant photographed in habitat.

Italy (Abruzzo, Lazio)

Senecio archeri (Compton) Jacobs
COMPOSITAE

Aromatic shrub; cylindrical stems; dark green leaves 2–4 cm long with acute apex, upper surface with translucent lines; white flowers.

Kleinia archeri Compton

South Africa (Cape Province)

Senecio articulatus (L.f.) Sch. Bip.
COMPOSITAE

Jointed, branched stems to 60 cm long and 1.5–2 cm thick with grey markings; 3- to 5-lobed, light green leaves 5 cm long; yellowish flowers.

Kleinia articulata L.f.

South Africa (Cape Province)

Senecio citriformis G.D. Rowley
COMPOSITAE

Dwarf shrub; erect to creeping stems arising from thick rootstock; blue-green leaves 1.5–2 cm long with translucent dots; cream to yellow flowers.

South Africa (Cape Province)

Senecio crassissimus Humb.
COMPOSITAE

Shrub 50–80 cm high; branched stems with rough surface caused by old leaf scars; green leaves 5.5 cm long and 2–3 cm wide, rounded at apex; yellow flowers.

Madagascar

Senecio desflersii Schwartz
COMPOSITAE

Bright green stems to 40 cm high and 3–6 cm in diameter, branching at apices; triangular, green leaves 2 mm long, persistent, rigid and spine-like when dry; inflorescence 20 cm long; green flowers.

Kleinia desflersii P. Halliday

South Yemen

0516

Senecio fulgens (Hook.f.) G. Nicholson
COMPOSITAE

Shrub 40–60 cm high; tuberous root; green stems with evident leaf scars; light green, pruinose leaves 7–9 cm long and 2–3 cm wide with prominent mid-vein on lower surface; red flowers.
Kleinia fulgens Hook.f.
South Africa (Natal)

0536

Senecio grantii (Hook.f.) Sch. Bip.
COMPOSITAE

Densely leaved stems 20–40 cm high developing from tuberous root; blue-green leaves 5–6 cm long with distinct mid-vein on lower surface; red flowers.
Kleinia grantii Hook.f.
Ethiopia, Kenya, Somalia, Tanzania

0129

Senecio haworthii (Sw.) Steud.
COMPOSITAE

Shrub to 30 cm high; silvery green leaves 5 cm long arranged in spirals; orange to yellow flowers.
Senecio tomentosus Hort.
South Africa (Cape Province)

0307

Senecio herreianus Dinter
COMPOSITAE

Prostrate stems to 60 cm long rooting at nodes; green leaves 1 cm long with translucent lines; white flowers.
Namibia

0186

Senecio jacobsenii G.D. Rowley
COMPOSITAE

Prostrate stems spreading by stolons and 50 cm long; fleshy, milky green leaves 5–8 cm long with roundish apex narrowing towards base and often purple beneath; orange-red flowers.
Kenya, Tanzania

0241

Senecio kleinia (L.) Less.
COMPOSITAE

Dichotomously branching, segmented shrub to 3 m tall; grey-green leaves 10–20 cm long and 1–2 cm wide crowded at stem apices; white flowers.
Kleinia neriifolia Haw.
Canary Islands

Senecio macroglossus DC.

COMPOSITAE

Twining stems to 2 m long; green, 3-lobed leaves 8 cm long and 4 cm wide; cream or pale yellow flowers. A form with variegated leaves is found in Kenya.

Mozambique, Zimbabwe

Senecio medley-woodii Hutch.

COMPOSITAE

Shrub to 1.5 m high; thick, branched stems; grey-green leaves 6 cm long; yellow flowers.

South Africa (Natal)

Senecio pendulus (Forssk.) Sch. Bip.

COMPOSITAE

Prostrate, mat-forming stems 20 cm long; stems rising to 10 cm then descending to root level; cylindrical leaves 2–4 mm long; red flowers.

Kleinia pendula (Forssk.) DC.

Ethiopia, Kenya (northeast), Somalia, Yemen

Senecio picticaulis
P.R.O. Bally

COMPOSITAE

Rhizomatous green stems 30–40 cm long with lines decurrent from each leaf; shiny green leaves 1–1.5 cm long; red flowers.

Kleinia picticaulis (P.R.O. Bally) C. Jeffrey

Ethiopia, Kenya, Sudan, Tanzania

Senecio radicans (L.f.) Sch. Bip

COMPOSITAE

Filiform, mat-forming stems 15–30 cm long; light green, cylindrical leaves 2–3 cm long, tapering at ends of both sides and with translucent lines; white flowers.

South Africa (Cape Province)

Senecio rowleyanus
Jacobs

COMPOSITAE

Prostrate stems 20–60 cm long, rooting at nodes; globose, light green leaves 8 mm in diameter with longitudinal, translucent band; white flowers.

Namibia

Senecio saginata (*Kleinia saginata* P. Halliday)

COMPOSITAE

Tuberous root; segmented stems 20 cm high and 4 cm in diameter with dark lines; green leaves 3 cm long and 1 cm wide borne on growing apices; red flowers. (In this dictionary we have used *Senecio* in a broad sense, including the genus *Kleinia*. We have included this species, even though it has not been validly published, to avoid a non-homogeneous treatment.)

Kleinia saginata P. Halliday.

Oman

Senecio spiculosus (Sheph.) G.D. Rowley

COMPOSITAE

Erect stems to 60 cm long and 1.5 cm thick; grey-green branches with white dots; cylindrical, light green leaves 6–8 cm long; white flowers.

Kleinia spiculosa Sheph.

Namibia

Senecio scaposus DC.

COMPOSITAE

Short stems with cylindrical, glabrous green leaves 7–8 cm long, crowded at stem and branch apices; yellow flowers.

South Africa (Cape Province)

Senecio stapeliaeformis Phillips

COMPOSITAE

Erect, green stems to 35 cm high and 1–2 cm thick with purple staining; young shoots at first growing subterranean; dark green leaves 5 mm long; red flowers.

Kleinia stapeliaeformis (Phillips.) Stapf

South Africa (Transvaal)

Senecio stapeliaeformis subsp. minor G.D. Rowley

COMPOSITAE

A subspecies with less fleshy stems.

South Africa (Transvaal)

Senecio sempervivus (DC.) Sch. Bip

COMPOSITAE

Tuberous root from which several grey-green, pruinose stems 10–15 cm long develop; leaves 6–7 cm long and 2.5 cm wide with prominent green mid-vein, lower surface reddish; red flowers.

Kleinia semperviva DC.

Saudi Arabia

Sesamothamnus lugardii N.E. Br.
PEDALIACEAE

Caudex to 2 m in diameter; succulent branches with grey-white, peeling bark; oval, dark green leaves at axils of thorns; white flowers.

Namibia

Sinningia canescens (Mart.) Wiehler
GESNERIACEAE

Tuberous root with densely hairy stems 25 cm long; white leaves 15 cm long and 10 cm wide covered with short white hairs; flowers orange to red.

Brazil

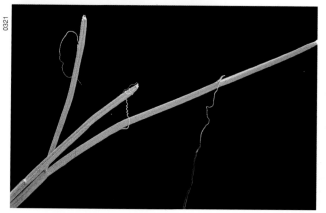

Seyrigia gracilis Keraudren
CUCURBITACEAE

Tuberous root with climbing stems 2–3 m long and long, purplish-grey tendrils; insignificant, greenish-yellow flowers.

Madagascar

Sinocrassula densirosulata (Praeger) A. Berger
CRASSULACEAE

Rosettes with numerous grey-green leaves 2–3 cm long, usually with red or red-brown lines; whitish flowers.

China

Seyrigia humbertii Keraudren
CUCURBITACEAE

Cylindrical, ribbed, climbing stems to 3 m long; small, caducous 3-lobed, green leaves with white hairs; tendrils 5–20 cm long; insignificant pale green flowers. Leaves persistent in cultivation.

Madagascar

Sinocrassula yunnanensis (Franch.) A. Berger
CRASSULACEAE

Numerous (to 70), blue-green leaves forming dense rosettes; leaves covered with short white hairs; whitish flowers with red tips.

China (Yunnan)

Smicrostigma viride (Haw.) N.E. Br.
MESEMBRYANTHEMACEAE

Shrub to 40 cm high; branched, erect stems; green leaves with fine translucent dots, 1.5–2 cm long and united at base, with recurved tip and ending in short terminal spine; pink flowers.

South Africa (Cape Province)

Stapelia asterias Masson
ASCLEPIADACEAE

Stem to 25 cm long with compressed angles; rudimentary, caducous leaves; 1–5 large, dark red-brown flowers with long purple hairs borne from base of stems.

Stapelia stellaris Haw.; *S. stellata* St.-Lag.

South Africa (Cape Province)

Stapelia cedrimontana Frandsen
ASCLEPIADACEAE

Stems 4-angled and to 25 cm tall; angles toothed; rudimentary, caducous leaves 2–2.5 mm long with short hairs; flowers dark purple with ochreous markings.

South Africa (Cape Province)

Stapelia gettleffii R. Pott
ASCLEPIADACEAE

Erect stems 20–25 cm high with dentate, hairy angles; rudimentary, caducous leaves; purple flowers 14–16 cm in diameter with yellowish lines and covered with light purple hairs.

South Africa (Transvaal)

Stapelia glanduliflora Masson
ASCLEPIADACEAE

Erect, 4- to 6-angled stems 15–20 cm high with small teeth and rudimentary, caducous leaves; flowers yellow with brown spots and lines, densely covered with transparent hairs.

South Africa (Cape Province, Transkei)

Stapelia grandiflora Masson
ASCLEPIADACEAE

Green, 4-angled stems to 30 cm with small teeth and densely covered with soft hairs; rudimentary, caducous leaves; purple to black-purple flowers with ciliate margins borne from base of young stems.

Stapelia ambigua Masson; *S. flavirostris* N.E. Br.

Lesotho, South Africa (Cape Province)

Stapelia hirsuta L.
ASCLEPIADACEAE

Dull green, 4-angled stems 20 cm high, depressed between the angles and armed with small teeth; rudimentary, caducous leaves; red-yellow flowers with numerous soft purple hairs.

Stapelia margarita B. Sloane

South Africa (Cape Province)

Stapelia montana L.C. Leach
ASCLEPIADACEAE

Plant branching from base; 4-angled stems 7–8 cm high; rudimentary, caducous leaves 2 mm long; red-brown flowers.

South Africa (Cape Province)

Stapelia incomparabilis N.E. Br.
ASCLEPIADACEAE

Stems 4- to 5-angled, 10–20 cm high branching from base and with teeth 2–3 mm long; rudimentary, caducous leaves; purple-red flowers. It may be a hybrid of *Stapelia* sp. x *Tromotriche* sp.

Southern Africa

Stapelia mutabilis Jacq.
ASCLEPIADACEAE

Green stems 10–20 cm high with purple spots; stems 4-angled with concave sides and small teeth; rudimentary, caducous leaves; yellowish flowers with red dots and lines. A hybrid of *Stapelia* sp. x *Tromotriche* sp.

Orbea mutabilis Sweet

Garden origin

Stapelia leendertziae N.E. Br.
ASCLEPIADACEAE

Hairy, 4-angled stems 8–10 cm high with several small teeth; rudimentary, caducous leaves; purple-black or dark brown flowers.

South Africa (Transvaal)

Stapelia olivacea N.E. Br.
ASCLEPIADACEAE

Green stems 10–15 cm high with red spots and 4 rounded angles with small teeth; rudimentary, caducous leaves; dark green to red flowers.

Namibia, South Africa (Cape Province)

Stapelia pulvinata
Masson
ASCLEPIADACEAE

Dark green to red-brown, actuely angled stems 10–20 cm high densely covered with small hairs and erect teeth along angles; rudimentary, caducous leaves; purple-brown flowers with yellow transverse bands.

South Africa (Cape Province)

Stapelianthus madagascariensis (Choux) Choux
ASCLEPIADACEAE

Erect or creeping, grey-green, 6- to 8-angled stems 10 cm long with dark red spots; tubercles with thin leaves; pale yellow flowers with red spots.

Madagascar

Stapelia similis N.E. Br.
ASCLEPIADACEAE

Grey-green to purple, 4- to 6-angled stems 10–15 cm high covered with minute hairs; rudimentary, caducous leaves; black-purple flowers.

South Africa (Cape Province)

Stomatium alboroseum L. Bol.
MESEMBRYANTHEMACEAE

Clump-forming plant with grey-green leaves 2–3 cm long with numerous dots; leaves keeled towards apex and with dentate margins; white flowers.

South Africa (Cape Province)

Stapelianthus decaryi Choux
ASCLEPIADACEAE

Erect, 6- to 8-angled stems 10 cm high; angles with alternating teeth tipped with spines to 4 mm long; dark purple, tubular flowers 2–2.5 cm long.

Madagascar

Stomatium ermininum (Haw.) Schwantes
MESEMBRYANTHEMACEAE

Clump-forming plant with light grey-green, obtuse leaves 2–3 cm long with convex lower surface, keeled towards apex; 3–4 marginal teeth near tips; yellow flowers.

South Africa (Cape Province)

Stomatium niveum L. Bol.

MESEMBRYANTHEMACEAE

Grey-green leaves 2 cm long with white dots and dentate margins; nocturnal, white flowers.

South Africa (Cape Province)

Synadenium cupulare (Boiss.) L.C. Wheeler

EUPHORBIACEAE

Shrub 1–2 m high; green stems branching from base; green leaves 10 cm long and 4 cm wide with acute apex; greenish-yellow flowers.

South Africa (Natal, Transvaal), Swaziland

Synadenium grantii
Hook.

EUPHORBIACEAE

Shrub to 3 m tall; lanceolate, green leaves 20 cm long and 6–7 cm wide often with red mid-vein; brownish-red flowers.

Mozambique, Uganda, Zimbabwe

Synadenium grantii
'Rubra'

EUPHORBIACEAE

A variety with red to purple-red leaves; otherwise the same as the type species.

Mozambique, Uganda, Zimbabwe

Talinum caffrum
(Thunb.) Eckl. & Zeyh.

PORTULACACEAE

Tuberous root; erect or spreading stems to 50 cm long; fleshy, green leaves 8 cm long; yellow flowers.

Southern and tropical Africa

Talinum paniculatum (Jacq.) Gaertn.

PORTULACACEAE

Tuberous root with erect, pink stems to 1 m high; green leaves 10 cm long; red to yellow flowers.

Central and North America (southern States)

Talinum sp.
PORTULACACEAE
Tuberous caudex with erect or prostrate green stems; numerous, small, green leaves; yellow flowers.
North America

Tavaresia angolense Welw.
ASCLEPIADACEAE
Glabrous plant; 6- to 8-angled, leafless stems to 15 cm long with conical tubercles bearing 3 whitish bristles; pale yellow flowers with red dots borne from base of young stems.
Decabelone elegans Decne; *Huernia tavaresii* Welw.
Angola

Tanquana archeri (L. Bol.) H.E.K. Hartmann & Liede
MESEMBRYANTHEMACEAE
Plant consisting of 1 pair of green or reddish leaves 2.5 cm long and 2 cm wide at base with roundish tips and small translucent dots; yellow flowers.
Pleiospilos archeri L. Bol.
South Africa (Cape Province)

Tavaresia barklyi (Dyer) N.E. Br.
ASCLEPIADACEAE
Bluish-green, 10- to 12-angled stems to 7 cm high; white tubercles with 3 purple bristles; 1–4 pale yellow flowers with red spots and stripes borne from base of young stems.
Decabelone barklyii Dyer
South Africa (Cape Province)

Tanquana prismatica (Schwantes) H.E.K. Hartmann & Liede
MESEMBRYANTHEMACEAE
Triangular, green to grey leaves 3–4 cm long with dark spots and convex lower surface borne in small clumps, 5–10 cm in diameter; 1–2 pairs of leaves from each shoot; yellow flowers.
Pleiospilos prismaticus (Marloth) Schwantes
South Africa (Cape Province)

Tavaresia meintjiesii R.A. Dyer
ASCLEPIADACEAE
Dark green to brown, 6- to 8-angled stems 8–10 cm high covered with small hairs; teeth with 3 white spines; cream to yellow flowers with numerous red-brown dots and lines. A hybrid of *T. barklyi* x *Stapelia gettlifei*.
South Africa (Transvaal)

Titanopsis calcarea (Marloth) Schwantes
MESEMBRYANTHEMACEAE
Rosettes to 10 cm wide; leaves to 2.5 cm long with truncate tip densely covered with grey tubercles; yellow flowers.
South Africa (Cape Province)

Titanopsis 'Primosii'
MESEMBRYANTHEMACEAE
Hemispherical clumps to 10 cm in diameter; light grey leaves 3 cm long, expanded above with triangular tip, tinged red with yellow-brown tubercles; canary yellow flowers with reddish tips.
Garden origin

Titanopsis fulleri Tisch.
MESEMBRYANTHEMACEAE
Clump-forming rosettes of 5–6 pairs of leaves; green (green-red when grown in full sun) leaves 2 cm long with flat upper surface, rounded keel to lower surface and tuberculate tip; yellow flowers.
South Africa (Cape Province)

Tradescantia navicularis Ortgies
COMMELINACEAE
Creeping stems rooting at nodes; grey-green, distichous, boat-shaped leaves 2–3 cm long covered with fine hairs; purplish-pink flowers.
Peru

Titanopsis hugo-schlechteri (Tisch) Dinter & Schwantes
MESEMBRYANTHEMACEAE
Clump-forming rosettes; grey-green leaves 1–1.5 cm long and reddish above tip; leaf apex triangular with numerous grey-brown to red tubercles; orange or yellow flowers.
Namibia

Tradescantia sillamontana Matuda
COMMELINACEAE
Stems about 6 cm long with green leaves, 2 cm long and covered with white hairs, forming small clumps; pinkish flowers.
Belize, Guatemala, Mexico

Trichocaulon cactiforme (Hook.) N.E. Br.
ASCLEPIADACEAE

Grey-green, globose to cylindrical stems branching from base; tubercles in dense spirals; yellow flowers spotted with red.

Namibia, South Africa (Cape Province)

Trichocaulon dinteri A. Berger
ASCLEPIADACEAE

Grey-green stems 5–10 cm long branching from base; 4- to 6-angled tubercles arranged in irregular spirals; creamy-white flowers with red spots and stripes.

Namibia

Trichocaulon flavum N.E. Br.
ASCLEPIADACEAE

Cylindrical dull green, somewhat glaucous stems to 15 cm high and 5 cm thick, branching at base with 20–30 series of tubercles arranged vertically and ending in brown bristly spine; dull yellow flowers.

South Africa (Cape Province)

Trichocaulon triebneri Nel
ASCLEPIADACEAE

Bluish- to grey-green, 15- to 16-angled stems to 30 cm high; tubercles with white spine 5 mm long; black-purple to red-purple flowers.

Namibia

Trichodiadema barbatum (L.) Schwantes
MESEMBRYANTHEMACEAE

Napiform (turnip-shaped) root with several prostrate stems; grey-green leaves 1 cm long and 3–4 mm wide with 8–10 black bristles at tips; red to purple flowers.

South Africa (Cape Province)

Trichodiadema bulbosum (Haw.) Schwantes
MESEMBRYANTHEMACEAE

Tuberous root with stems to 20 cm high; grey-green leaves 8 mm long and 3 mm thick with several white bristles at tips; red flowers.

South Africa (Cape Province)

Trichodiadema densum (Haw.) Schwantes
MESEMBRYANTHEMACEAE
Tuberous roots with short stems; green leaves 1.5–2 cm long and 4 mm thick with 20–25 white bristles at tips; carmine flowers.
South Africa (Cape Province)

Trichodiadema mirabile (N.E. Br.) Schwantes
MESEMBRYANTHEMACEAE
Small bushes with stems to 10 cm high and covered with white hairs; greenish leaves to 2.5 cm long with several brown bristles; white flowers.
South Africa (Cape Province)

Trichodiadema peersii L. Bol.
MESEMBRYANTHEMACEAE
Small shrub to 10 cm high; green leaves 1 cm long with several brown bristles; white flowers.
South Africa (Cape Province)

Trichodiadema stelligerum (Haw.) Schwantes
MESEMBRYANTHEMACEAE
Shrub to 20 cm high with curved branches; bright green leaves 1–1.5 cm long with 5–10 white bristles; purple flowers.
South Africa (Cape Province)

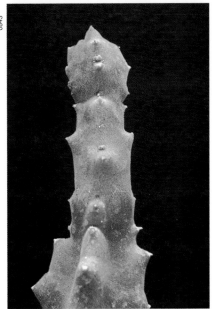

Tromotriche engleriana (Schltr.) L.C. Leach
ASCLEPIADACEAE
Grey-green, velvety, leafless stems 15–25 cm high with wide tubercles; brown flowers with yellow grooves.
South Africa (Cape Province)

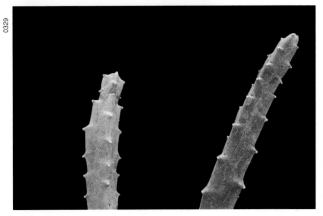

Tromotriche revoluta (Masson) Haw.
ASCLEPIADACEAE
Pale grey, 4-angled, leafless stems 30 cm long; purple flowers with recurved lobes borne near apex.
Stapelia revoluta Masson
South Africa (Cape Province)

Tylecodon buchholzianus (Schuldt & Steph.) Toelken
CRASSULACEAE
Swollen base with several pale grey to brown branches 30 cm long; yellowish-green, upwardly curving leaves 1–2 cm long with brown lines.
Cotyledon buchholziana Schuldt & Steph.
Namibia

Tylecodon paniculatus
(L.f.) Toelken
CRASSULACEAE
Thick stems to 1.5 m high and 60 cm in diameter with many branches and yellow, peeling bark; numerous, green to green-yellow leaves to 15 cm long arising at branch apices; inflorescence to 60 cm high; red flowers.
Cotyledon fascicularis Aiton; *C. mollis* Dinter; *C. paniculata* L.f.; *C. tardiflora* Bonpl.
Namibia, South Africa (Cape Province)

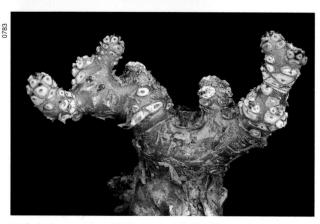

Tylecodon pearsonii (Schönland) Toelken
CRASSULACEAE
Stem covered with greyish peeling bark; grey-green to greyish-brown leaves; pale brown flowers.
Cotyledon luteosquamata Poelln.; *C. pearsonii* Schönland
Namibia, South Africa (Cape Province)

Tylecodon pygmaeus
(W.F. Barker) Toelken
CRASSULACEAE
Stems to 20 cm high and 5–10 mm in diameter covered with pale yellow bark; green leaves 2–3 cm long, with several hairs; yellowish-green flowers.
Cotyledon pygmaea W.F. Barker
South Africa (Cape Province)

Tylecodon reticulatus (L.f.) Toelken
CRASSULACEAE
Plant 20–30 cm tall; stem covered with yellow-brown, peeling bark; yellow-green leaves to 50 cm long; yellowish-green flowers.
Cotyledon reticulata L.f.
Namibia, South Africa (Cape Province)

Tylecodon schaeferianus (Dinter) Toelken
CRASSULACEAE
Tuberous root; branched stems to 25 cm; green-brown leaves 5–20 cm long; yellow-green flowers.
Cotyledon schaeferiana Dinter
Namibia

Tylecodon torulosum
Toelken

CRASSULACEAE

Stems to 25 cm high and 2 cm in diameter, covered with dark brown to white bark; grey-green to blue-green leaves 2–3 cm long with rounded apices; yellowish-green flowers.

South Africa (Cape Province)

Tylecodon wallichii
(Harv.) Toelken

CRASSULACEAE

Much-branched stem to 1.5 m high covered with the remains of old leaves; bark peeling from stem base; grey-green leaves 5–12 cm long; yellow flowers.

Cotyledon wallichii Harv.

South Africa (Cape Province)

Uncarina decaryi
Humbert

PEDALIACEAE

Large shrub or small tree; stems 2–3 m tall covered with greyish-ochre bark; triangular leaves 5–6 cm long, green upper surface covered with small hairs, lower surface grey; yellow flowers.

Madagascar

Vanheerdea roodiae (N.E. Br.) L. Bol.

MESEMBRYANTHEMACEAE

Bodies 2–3 cm long; green leaves united for two-thirds of their length and covered with microscopic hairs and transparent dots; orange-yellow flowers.

South Africa (Cape Province)

Villadia batesii (Hemsl.) Baehni & J. Macbr.

CRASSULACEAE

Stems 10–25 cm; pale green leaves 1 cm long and 3 mm wide arranged in rosettes and covered with minute tubercles; red to white flowers.

Mexico

Villadia imbricata Rose

CRASSULACEAE

Little-branched stems forming mats; closely overlapping, pale green leaves 5–6 mm long, keeled on lower surface; white flowers.

Mexico

Welwitschia mirabilis Hook.f.
WELWITSCHIACEAE
Shallow taproot with many lateral roots just below the soil's surface; short, nearly circular, dark grey, fissured trunk; 2 opposite, dark green leaves produced from marginal grooves on crown, each splitting into many parallel sections and continuing to grow throughout life of plant, possibly reaching 4 m or more. Male and female brownish cones borne on different plants. Plant photographed in habitat.
Welwitschia bainesii (Hook.f.) Carr.   Angola, Namibia

Welwitschia mirabilis Hook.f.
WELWITSCHIACEAE
View of the Namib Desert with *Welwitschia* and the author's family.

Welwitschia mirabilis Hook.f.
WELWITSCHIACEAE
The photograph shows what is probably the largest living specimen of *W. mirabilis*. It is said to be more than 1,500 years old and grows in a fenced area of the Namib Naukluft Park.

Xerosicyos danguyi Humbert
CUCURBITACEAE
Shrub with erect or procumbent stems to 50 cm long branching from base; fleshy, glaucous leaves 4 cm long and 3.5 cm wide with concave upper surface; whitish flowers.
Madagascar

Xerosicyos decaryi Guill. & Keraudren
CUCURBITACEAE
Similar to *X. danguyi* but leaves oblong and to 2.5 cm long and 1 cm wide, rounded at apex.
Madagascar

Xerosicyos perrieri Humbert
CUCURBITACEAE
Climbing stems, woody at base; thick, light green leaves 2 cm long and 18 mm wide; whitish flowers.
Madagascar

Yucca baccata Torr.
AGAVACEAE

Stemless or procumbent stems to 1.5 m long; dark green leaves 75 cm long with filiferous margins and pungent apex; inflorescence to 1 m tall; creamy-white flowers.

Mexico, USA (southwest)

Yucca carnerosana (Trel.) McKelvey
AGAVACEAE

Solitary stems 1.5–10 m high; green leaves to 1 m long and 5–8 cm wide; inflorescence branched; white flowers. Plant photographed in habitat.

Mexico

Yucca elephantipes A. Regel
AGAVACEAE

Arborescent plants to 10 m high with several densely branched stems; stiff, green leaves 50–100 cm long; inflorescence to 1 m tall; numerous white flowers. This specimen, which has grown to a remarkable size, was photographed in the Botanical Garden of the University of Palermo.

Yucca guatemalensis Baker

Guatemala, Mexico

Yucca endlincheriana Trel.
AGAVACEAE

Stemless, rhizomatous plants; bluish-green leaves to 50 cm long with short terminal spine; inflorescence 40–60 cm tall; whitish flowers.

Mexico

Yucca filamentosa L.
AGAVACEAE

Stemless, clump-forming, stoloniferous plants; erect or spreading leaves 75 cm long with filiferous margins; inflorescence 3–4 m tall; whitish flowers.

USA (south)

Zygosicyos tripartitus Humbert
CUCURBITACEAE

Caudex to 10 cm in diameter; slightly woody stems; leaves 2–3 cm long and 1 cm wide with 2–3 lobes and minute hairs; yellow-green flowers.

Madagascar

CONVENTION ON INTERNATIONAL TRADE IN ENDANGERED SPECIES

CITES Secretariat, PO Box 456, 1219 Châtelaine, Geneva, Switzerland

Habitat destruction is the major cause of the decline in wildlife populations, but the second most important threat is the exploitation of plants and animals (and their products) of wild origin. It is when this exploitation leads to international trade that CITES, the Convention on International Trade in Endangered Species of Wild Fauna and Flora, plays an important role.

CITES contributes to nature conservation by regulating the international trade through a system of permits and controls, which are issued and implemented by the exporting and importing countries. In July 1993 120 countries were party to CITES. The word 'trade' refers to all international movements of specimens of species listed in its Appendices, and it includes plants carried by tourists, large commercial consignments and material for scientific purposes. However, there are certain exemptions for registered scientific institutions. Through this control system, all Parties assist in keeping rare and threatened wildlife where it belongs – in nature reserves and in its natural habitat.

The CITES control system also permits trade in specimens from the wild up to a level that is not detrimental to the survival of the species in the wild. The international trade in animals and plants of wild origin involves a large number of specimens and has great value. The number of wild plants traded internationally increased greatly after the Second World War when people travelled more freely and to more distant countries. In addition, the increased use of central heating allowed more and more people to keep specimens from tropical regions.

HOW DOES CITES WORK?

The purpose of CITES can perhaps best be illustrated by quoting from the preamble to the Convention.

- Recognizing that wild fauna and flora in their many beautiful and varied forms are an irreplaceable part of the natural systems of the earth, which must be protected for this and for the generations to come;
- Conscious of the ever-growing value of wild fauna and flora from aesthetic, scientific, cultural, recreational and economic points of view;
- Recognizing that peoples and states are, and should be, the best protectors of their own wild fauna and flora.

Through CITES, sustainable trade in specimens of certain species is regulated, recognizing at the same time that countries have a right to exploit their natural resources or not to permit such exploitation should they so decide. The degree of protection afforded to a species by the Convention depends on the Appendix in which it is listed.

- Appendix I includes all those species of which trade in specimens of wild origin is permitted only in exceptional circumstances.

- Appendix II contains those species of which commercial or private trade in wild specimens is permitted as long as it is regulated to ensure that it is sustainable.

- Appendix III contains the species for which one country has asked other CITES signatories for assistance in their protection.

The inclusion of species in Appendices I and II requires a two-thirds majority decision of the countries that are party to CITES. The listing in Appendix III can be done by an individual country. No cacti or other succulents are listed in Appendix III; all cacti are included in Appendix I or II.

WILD-GROWN SPECIMENS

The regulation of trade in the species concerned is provided by a system of permits. Importation for commercial purposes of specimens of species listed in Appendix I of wild origin is not allowed. Trade that is not commercial – for scientific purposes, for example – requires that the country of importation issues an import permit before an export permit may be issued by the exporting country.

Commercial trade in specimens of species listed in Appendix II of wild origin is allowed on the condition that an export permit is issued by the country of export. In the case of re-export of specimens that have been imported from another country, a re-export certificate may be issued once it has been proved that the specimens were legally imported.

These are the basic requirements as included in the text of the Convention. However, each country may take stricter measures if it wishes. For example, some countries – Peru, Brazil and Mexico – have decided not to allow the export of any wild plants from their territories. This means that they do not issue export permits for wild-collected plants. By taking this measure they ensure that, if plants are taken illegally, they may not be imported legally into another country. The European Community requires that an import permit or certificate be issued for any importation of CITES specimens into the territory of its member states.

ARTIFICIALLY PROPAGATED PLANTS

A less strict regime applies to artificially propagated plants. If these plants are of species listed in Appendix I they are treated as if they were in Appendix II, so that only an export licence is required. Although an import licence is not required under CITES, some countries may still demand it as a consequence of stricter measures.

Artificially propagated plants of species listed in Appendix II are subject to a number of exemptions from CITES controls. Flasked seedlings, cut flowers, seeds and pollen are not covered by the Convention. They may also be traded with a certificate of artificial propagation. A number of European countries use the phytosanitary certificate for this purpose.

* * *

The above is a brief summary of the work of CITES. The Convention is implemented in many other ways, and interested readers are directed to *The Evolution of CITES* by W. Wijnstekers (see Further Reading).

INTERNATIONAL ORGANIZATION FOR SUCCULENT PLANTS STUDY

CODE OF CONDUCT

Sara Oldfield

This Code was first published in 1990 in volume 10 (supplement to no. 4) of *Piante Grasse*, the journal of the Italian Cactus and Succulent Society, and it has since been printed in several specialist journals. It is reprinted with kind permission of the author, Sara Oldfield. The original edition of the Code contains much useful information that, for reasons of space, cannot be included here. Copies of the full Code may be obtained from Sara Oldfield or from the IOS or the AIAS.

TO THE COLLECTOR IN THE FIELD

Before you collect anything:

- DO acquaint yourself with CITES and national and state controls, and find out which species are protected.

- DO obtain all necessary permits, both for collecting and for export and import to other countries.

- DO notify interested local organizations of your intentions.

Then:

- DO strictly observe restrictions on what may be collected (which species, how many specimens, what kind of material). Where possible, collect seeds, offsets or cuttings, not the whole plant.

- DO leave mature plants for seed production. They are needed to perpetuate the wild population, and are unlikely to transplant successfully.

- DO collect discreetly; do not lead local people to believe that the plants are valuable or encourage or pay them (or their children) to collect for you.

- DO make careful field notes, including precise locality, altitude, type of vegetation and soil, date of collection and your own field number. Try to assess the number of individuals and extent of the population, the amount of seed setting and the frequency of seedlings.

- DO note possible threats to the habitat – e.g., through grazing, drainage or cultivation, urban spread or road widening.

- DO take photographs and/or preserve representative herbarium material. Submit this material, with a copy of your notes, to an appropriate institution or organization.

- DO NOT underrate the value of your field observations: carefully recorded they will be a useful contribution to science and to conservation.

If:

- you plan to collect in commercial quantities, don't.
- you plan to sell any of the plants you collect to defray the cost of your trip, don't.
- you plan to collect for research or study, obtain the agreement (and preferably the collaboration) of competent scientific authorities, such as a government agency or university department, in the host country.
- you think 'two or three plants won't be missed', remember someone else may be thinking the same tomorrow, and the next day, and the next...

TO THE IMPORTER, PRIVATE OR COMMERCIAL

- DON'T import wild plants, even if legally permitted, except as a nucleus for propagation and seed-production.

Then:

- DO check the credentials of suppliers offering wild plants and satisfy yourself that they are 'legal'.
- DO observe international and national export/import regulations.

TO THE NURSERYMAN

- DO sell nursery-raised or propagated material only; do not advertise or sell un-propagated wild plants under any circumstances, even when legally permitted to do so.
- DO try to propagate all rare or documented material and distribute it to recognized IOS Reference Collections.
- DO keep more than one clone of rare species, even self-fertile ones, for seed production.
- DO keep careful records of the origin of all stock, especially any wild collectors' number or locality data, and pass on the information to interested purchasers.

TO THE GROWER OR COLLECTOR AT HOME

- DO make successful cultivation your prime objective, not the size of your collection or the rarity of the plants.
- DO NOT buy **any** plant unless you are sure it was nursery grown; remember that your choice will influence the seller's market.
- DO not buy wild-collected plants, even if with the aim of saving the 'individual'. We want to save the species, not the specimen. Only when importers see their wild-collected plants rotting because nobody buys them will they stop the importation of wild-collected plants.
- DO enjoy the satisfaction of raising from seed. Some of the rare or 'difficult' species will test your skill and patience, but reward your success accordingly!
- DO record when and from whom you got your plants or seeds and ask your source for any data: collectors' numbers, locality, and so on. All these are just as vital to the serious enthusiast as the name of the label.

- DO try to propagate rare and documented material and distribute it to other enthusiasts. Remember the proverb: To keep a plant, give it away!

TO THE SOCIETY AND CLUB

- DO endorse the precepts of this Code as a guide for responsible and conscientious behaviour.
- DO NOT permit wild plants to be advertised for sale in your publications, either openly or by hints.
- DO publicize national and international regulations on the export, importation and sale of wild plants.
- DO sponsor or support national and international measures to protect the habitats of rare and threatened species.
- DO inform the competent authorities of any suspect sale of collected plants. If you know of people travelling to countries where succulents grow wild with the intention to collecting, inform the competent authorities; the best way to stop habitat exploitation by collectors is to catch them at the port of entry with the plants in their hands.

TO THE SHOW COMMITTEE AND JUDGES

- DO include in the schedule some classes for plants raised from seed by the exhibitor.
- DO NOT permit species protected by CITES Appendix I to be shown in competitive classes, except as seedlings or other artifically raised propagations.
- DO make a policy of giving preference to well-grown seedlings over field-collected plants. Check that obvious or suspected 'imports' are properly rooted and established.

CHECKLIST OF ALTERNATIVE NAMES

The following list contains some of the synonyms in common use.
This is a partial listing, and several obsolete names that are seldom used have been omitted.

Genus	Species	... See
Abromeitiella	pulvinata	Abromeitiella chlorantha
Adenia	angustisecta	Adenia digitata
	buchannannii	Adenia digitata
	multiflora	Adenia digitata
Adromischus	cuneatus	Adromischus cooperi
	festivus	Adromischus cooperi
	halesowensis	Adromischus cooperi
	procurvus	Adromischus triflorus
	subcompressus	Adromischus triflorus
	subpetiolaris	Adromischus triflorus
Aeonium	bertoletianum	Aeonium tabulaeforme
	macrolepum	Aeonium tabulaeforme
	meyerheimii	Aeonium glandulosum
Agave	angustissima	Agave geminiflora
	bakeri	Agave karwinskii
	carchariodontha	Agave xylonacantha
	chihuahuana	Agave parryi
	coelum	Agave ferox
	consideranti	Agave victoriae-reginae
	coredoray	Agave karwinskii
	disceptata	Agave schidigera
	filamentosa	Agave filifera
	glaucescens	Agave attenuata
	mitis	Agave celsii var. albicans
	nickelsii	Agave victoriae-reginae
	nigra	Agave colimana
	nigrans	Agave colimana
	patoni	Agave parryi
	saundersii	Agave potatorum
	scolymus	Agave potatorum
	todaroi	Agave marmorata
	vestita	Agave schidigera
	wislizeni	Agave parrasana

Genus	Species	... See
Aloe	abyssinica	Aloe eru
	albo-cincta	Aloe striata
	barbadensis	Aloe vera
	echinata	Aloe humilis var. echinata
	ellenbergeri	Aloe aristata
	gariusana	Aloe gariepensis
	hanburyana	Aloe striata
	humilis var. candollei	Aloe humilis
	indica	Aloe vera
	lanzae	Aloe vera
	lingua	Aloe plicatilis
	linguaeformis	Aloe plicatilis
	longiaristata	Aloe aristata
	maculosa	Aloe obscura
	paniculata	Aloe striata
	perfoliata var. humilis	Aloe humilis
	picta	Aloe obscura
	prolifera	Aloe brevifolia
	punctata	Aloe variegata
	rhodocincta	Aloe striata
	schmidtiana	Aloe cooperi
	sempervivoides	Aloe parvula
	tripetala	Aloe plicatilis
	tuberculata	Aloe humilis var. echinata
	vulgaris	Aloe vera
Amaryllis	coranica	Ammocharis coranica
Anacampseros	arachnoides	Anacampseros rufescens
	intermedia	Anacampseros filamentosa
	poelnitziana	Anacampseros tomentosa
Anredera	cordifolia	Boussingaultia cordifolia
Antegibbaeum	fissoides	Gibbaeum fissoides

Genus	Species	...See
Argyroderma	*margarethae*	*Lapidaria margarethae*
Beaucarnea	*recurvata*	*Nolina recurvata*
Bryophyllum	*verticillatum*	*Kalanchoe tubiflora*
Bursera	*odorata*	*Bursera fagaroides var. elongata*
Calibanus	*caespitosum*	*Calibanus hookerii*
Caralluma	*caudata*	*Orbeopsis caudata*
	codonoides	*Caralluma speciosa*
	commutata subsp. *hesperidum*	*Caralluma hersperidum*
	corrugata	*Caralluma socotrana*
	dicapuae subsp. *turneri*	*Caralluma turneri*
	elata	*Caralluma priogonium*
	mamillaris	*Quaqua mamillaris*
	praegracilis	*Orbeopsis caudata*
	rivae	*Caralluma socotrana*
	tessellata	*Notechidnopsis tessellata*
Cephalophyllum	*clavifolium*	*Jordaniella clavifolia*
Ceropegia	*debilis*	*Ceropegia linearis subsp. debilis*
	hians	*Ceropegia dichotoma*
Cheiridopsis	*hilmari*	*Aloinopsis hilmari*
Cnidoscolus	*urens*	*Jatropha urens*
Conophytum	*praesectum*	*Ophthalmophyllum praesectum*
Cotyledon	*buchholziana*	*Tylecodon buchholzianus*
	elata	*Cotyledon orbiculata*
	fascicularis	*Tylecodon paniculatus*
	leuteosquamata	*Tylecodon pearsonii*
	mollis	*Tylecodon paniculatus*
	oblonga	*Cotyledon orbiculata*
	paniculata	*Tylecodon paniculatus*
	pearsonii	*Tylecodon pearsonii*
	pygmea	*Tylecodon pygmaeus*
	ramosa	*Cotyledon orbiculata*
	reticulata	*Tylecodon reticulatus*
	schaeferiana	*Tylecodon schaeferianus*
	tardiflora	*Tylecodon paniculatus*
	wallichii	*Tylecodon wallichii*

Genus	Species	...See
Crassula	*alooides*	*Crassula hemisphaerica*
	anthurus	*Crassula perforata*
	archeri	*Crassula pyramidalis*
	conjuncta	*Crassula perforata*
	cotyledon	*Crassula arborescens*
	cylindrica	*Crassula pyramidalis*
	flavovirens	*Crassula brevifolia*
	glabrifolia	*Crassula tomentosa*
	lycopodioides	*Crassula muscosa*
	nealeana	*Crassula perforata*
	pearsonii	*Crassula brevifolia*
	perfilata	*Crassula perforata*
	petersoniae	*Crassula perforata*
	teres	*Crassula barklyi*
Decabelone	*barklyi*	*Tavaresia barklyi*
	elegans	*Tavaresia angolense*
Didierea	*adscendens*	*Alluaudia adscendens*
Dudleya	*maranii*	*Dudleya albiflora*
Echeveria	*discolor*	*Echeveria nodulosa*
	glauca	*Echeveria pumila var. glauca*
	obscura	*Echeveria agavoides*
	sangusta	*Echeveria subrigida*
Echidnopsis	*chrysantha*	*Echidnopsis scutellata subsp. planiflora*
	somalensis	*Echidnopsis dammaniana*
Echinothamnus	*pechuelii*	*Adenia pechuelii*
Euphorbia	*antankara*	*Euphorbia pachypodioides*
	caespitosa	*Euphorbia ferox*
	calderensis	*Euphorbia copiapina*
	fructus-pinii	*Euphorbia caput-medusae*
	glomerata	*Euphorbia globosa*
	gynophora	*Euphorbia espinosa*
	hermetiana	*Euphorbia trigona*
	huttonae	*Euphorbia inermis var. huttonae*
	mammillosa	*Euphorbia squarrosa*
	medusae	*Euphorbia caput-medusae*
	moquadarensis	*Euphorbia resinifera*
	morinii	*Euphorbia heptagona*
	rhipsaloides	*Euphorbia tirucalli*
	san-salvador	*Euphorbia resinifera*
	splendens	*Euphorbia milii*
	subumbellata	*Euphorbia copiapina*

Genus	Species	...See
	tessellata	*Euphorbia caput-medusae*
	viminalis	*Euphorbia tirucalli*
Gasteria	*excelsa*	*Gasteria fuscopunctata*
Gibbaeum	*perviride*	*Gibbaeum gibbosum*
	shandii	*Gibbaeum pubescens* var. *shandii*
Haworthia	*aegrota*	*Haworthia herbacea*
	chalwinii	*Haworthia coarctata*
	fallax	*Haworthia coarctata*
	fulva	*Haworthia coarctata*
	gigas	*Haworthia arachnoidea*
	lepida	*Haworthia cymbiformis*
	luteorosea	*Haworthia herbace*
	margaritifera	*Haworthia pumila*
	musculina	*Haworthia coarctata*
	paynei	*Haworthia herbacea*
	pentagona	*Astroloba pentagona*
	picta	*Haworthia emelyae*
	pilifera	*Haworthia cooperi*
	planifolia	*Haworthia cymbiformis*
	setata	*Haworthia arachnoidea*
Hoya	*paxtonii*	*Hoya bella*
Huernia	*tavaresii*	*Tavaresia angolense*
Idria	*columnaris*	*Fouquieria columnaris*
Imitaria	*muririi*	*Gibbaeum nebrownii*
Juttadinteria	*proxima*	*Dracophilus proximus*
Kalanchoe	*farinacea*	*Kalanchoe scapigera*
	grandiflora	*Kalanchoe marmorata*
	lacinata	*Kalanchoe integra*
Kleinia	*archeri*	*Senecio archeri*
	articulata	*Senecio articulatus*
	desflersii	*Senecio desflersii*
	fulgens	*Senecio fulgens*
	grantii	*Senecio grantii*
	neriifolia	*Senecio kleinia*
	pendula	*Senecio pendulus*
	picticaulis	*Senecio picticaulis*
	saginata	*Senecio saginata*
	semperviva	*Senecio sempervivus*
	spiculosa	*Senecio spiculosus*
	stapeliaeformis	*Senecio stapeliaeformis*

Genus	Species	...See
Ledebouria	*socialis*	*Scilla socialis*
Lithops	*bella*	*Lithops karasmontana* subsp. *bella*
	dabneri	*Lithops hookeri* var. *dabneri*
	dendritica	*Lithops pseudotruncatella* subsp. *dendritica*
	elisabethiae	*Lithops pseudotruncatella* var. *elisabethiae*
	fulleri	*Lithops julii* subsp. *fulleri*
	insularis	*Lithops bromfieldii* var. *insularis*
	lericheana	*Lithops karasmontana* var. *lericheana*
	localis	*Lithops terricolor*
	marginata	*Lithops hookeri* var. *marginata*
	marthae	*Lithops schwantesii* var. *marthae*
	mennelli	*Lithops bromfieldii* var. *mennelli*
	rugosa	*Lithops schwantesii* var. *rugosa*
	susannae	*Lithops hookeri* var. *susannae*
	translucens	*Lithops herrei*
	vanzjlii	*Dinteranthus vanzjlii*
	venteri	*Lithops lesliei* var. *venteri*
Mitrophyllum	*dissitum*	*Conophyllum dissitum*
	framesii	*Conophyllum framesii*
	pisiforme	*Monilaria pisiforme*
	proximus	*Conophyllum proximus*
Nananthus	*luckhoffii*	*Aloinopsis luckhoffii*
	malherbei	*Aloinopsis malherbei*
	orpenii	*Aloinopsis orpenii*
	schooneesii	*Aloinopsis schooneesii*
Nolina	*tuberculata*	*Nolina recurvata*
Orbea	*mutabilis*	*Stapelia mutabilis*
Orostachys	*kanboensis*	*Orostachys minutus*
Pachyphytum	*roseum*	*Pachyphytum hookeri*
Pachyveria	*scheideckeri*	*Echeveria* x *scheideckeri*
Pleiospilos	*archeri*	*Tanquana archeri*
	canus	*Pleiospilos compactus* subsp. *canus*

Genus	Species	...See
	minor	*Pleiospilos compactus* subsp. *minor*
	pedunculatus	*Pleiospilos nelii*
	prismaticus	*Tanquana prismatica*
	tricolor	*Pleiospilos nelii*
Pseudolithops	*sphaericus*	*Pseudolithops migiurtinus*
Rhodiola	*rosea*	*Sedum roseum*
Rochea	*falcata*	*Crassula falcata*
Ruschia	*albiflora*	*Polymita albiflora*
	disarticulata	*Eberlanzia disarticulata*
Sarcocaulon	*burmannii*	*Sarcocaulon crassicaule*
	lorrei	*Sarcocaulon herrei*
Schizobasopsis	*volubilis*	*Bowiea volubilis*
Sedum	*aizoides*	*Sedum aizoon*
	athoum	*Sedum album*
	balticum	*Sedum album*
	boloniense	*Sedum sexangulare*
	burnatii	*Sedum dasyphyllum*
	californicum	*Sedum spathulifolium* var. *purpureum*
	ciliare	*Sedum spurium*
	congestum	*Sedum spurium*
	crenatum	*Sedum spurium*
	denticulatum	*Sedum spurium*
	glanuliferum	*Sedum dasyphyllum*
	glaucum	*Sedum dasyphyllum*
	glaucum	*Sedum hispanicum*
	hillebrandtii	*Sedum sexangulare*
	ibericum	*Sedum stoloniferum*
	lazicum	*Sedum spurium*
	maximowiczii	*Sedum aizoon*
	mite	*Sedum sexangulare*
	rotundifolium	*Sedum anacampseros*
	rufescens	*Sedum nicaeense*
	sediforme	*Sedum nicaeense*
	sexfidum	*Sedum hispanicum*
	shastense	*Sedum lanceolatum*
	spirale	*Sedum sexangulare*
	stenopetalum var. *subalpinum*	*Sedum lanceolatum*
	subalpinum	*Sedum lanceolatum*
	subtile	*Sedum lineare*
	turgidum	*Sedum album*

Genus	Species	...See
	urvillei	*Sedum sartorianum*
	verlotii	*Sedum anopetalum*
	woodi	*Sedum spathulifolium* var. *purpureum*
	woodwardii	*Sedum aizoon*
	zentaro-tashiroi	*Sedum lineare*
Sempervivum	*album*	*Sempervivella alba*
	arvernense	*Sempervivum tectorum*
	gaudini	*Sempervivum grandiflorum*
	italicum	*Sempervivum tectorum* var. *italicum*
	tectorum var. *alpinum*	*Sempervivum tectorum*
	tectorum var. *calcareum*	*Sempervivum calcareum*
	tectorum var. *glaucum*	*Sempervivum tectorum*
Senecio	*tomentosus*	*Senecio haworthii*
Sphalmanthus	*viridiflorus*	*Nycteranthus viridiflorus*
Stapelia	*ambigua*	*Stapelia grandiflora*
	dummeri	*Caralluma dummeri*
	europaea	*Caralluma europaea*
	flavirostris	*Stapelia grandiflora*
	margarita	*Stapelia hirsuta*
	revoluta	*Tromotriche revoluta*
	stellaris	*Stapelia asterias*
	stellata	*Stapelia asterias*
	variegata	*Orbea variegata*
	verrucosa	*Orbea verrucosa*
Stultitia	*hardyi*	*Orbeanthus hardyi*
Tacitus	*bellus*	*Graptopetalum bellum*
Testudinaria	*elephantipes*	*Dioscorea elephantipes*
	paniculata	*Dioscorea sylvatica* var. *paniculata*
Titanopsis	*luckhoffii*	*Aloinopsis luckhoffii*
	setifera	*Aloinopsis setifera*
Urbinia	*agavoides*	*Echeveria agavoides*
Welwitschia	*bainesii*	*Welwitschia mirabilis*
Yucca	*guatemalensis*	*Yucca elephantipes*

FURTHER READING

GENERAL

Jacobsen, H., *A Handbook of Succulent Plants* (3 volumes), Blandford Press, Poole, UK, 1960 (reprinted 1978)

Rauh, Werner, *The Wonderful World of Succulents*, Smithsonian Press, Washington D.C., USA, 1984

Wijnstekers, W., *The Evolution of CITES*, Secretariat of the Convention on International Trade in Endangered Species of Wild Flora and Fauna, Lausanne, Switzerland, 1992 (3rd edition)

Willert, D.J. von, Eller, B.M., Werger, M.J.A., Brinckmann, E. and Ihlenfeldt, H.D., *Life Strategies of Succulents in Deserts*, Cambridge University Press, Cambridge, UK, 1992

AGAVACEAE

Chahinian B.J., *The Sansevieria trifasciata Varieties*, Trans Terra Publications, Reseda, California, USA, 1986

Gentry H.S., *Agaves of Continental Northern America*, The Arizona University Press, Tucson, Arizona, USA, 1982

Matuda E. and Pina Lujan I., *Las Pantas Mexicanas del Genero Yucca*, Coleccion Miscelanea Estado de Mexico, Toluca, Mexico, 1980

Ulrich B., 'On the discovery of *Agave schidigera* Lemaire and status of certain taxa of the section *Xysmagave* Berger', *British Cactus & Succulent Journal*, vol. 10, pp. 61-70, 1992

ASCLEPIADACEAE

Bruyns P.V., 'Notes on Ceropegias of the Cape Province', *Bradleya* , vol. 3, pp. 1-47, 1985

Bruyns P.V., 'A revision of the genus *Echidnopsis* Hook. f. (Asclepiadaceae)', *Bradleya* , vol. 6, pp. 1-48, 1988

Dyer R.A., *Ceropegia, Brachystelma and Riocreuxia in Southern Africa*. A.A. Balkema, Rotterdam, The Netherlands, 1983

Gilbert M.G., 'A review of *Caralluma* R.Br. and its segregates', *Bradleya* , vol. 8, pp. 1-32., 1990

White A. and Sloane B.L., *The Stapeliae*, Abbey San Encino Press, Pasadena, California, USA, 1937

BROMELIACEAE

Rauh W., *Bromeliads for Home, Garden and Greenhouse*, Blandford Press, Poole, UK, 1979

COMPOSITAE

Halliday P., 'Noteworthy Species of *Kleinia*', *Hooker's Icones Plantarum* (Bentham-Moxon Trustees, Royal Botanic Gardens, Kew, UK), vol. 39, part IV, 1988

CRASSULACEAE

Evans R.L., *Handbook of Cultivated Sedums*, Science Reviews Ltd, Northwood, Middlesex, UK, 1983

Toelken H.R., 'Crassulaceae', *Flora of Southern Africa*, vol. 14 (ed. O.A. Leistner), Botanic Research Institute, Pretoria, South Africa, 1985

Walther E., *Echeveria*, California Academy of Sciences, San Francisco, California, USA, 1972

DIDIEREACEAE

Choux P., 'Les Didiereacées, Xerophytes de Madagascar', *Mémoires de l'Académie Malgache*, vol. 17, 1934

Rowley, G.D., 'Didiereaceae', *Cacti of the Old World*, British Cactus & Succulent Society, 1992

EUPHORBIACEAE

Bally P.R.O., *The Genus Monadenium*, Benteli Publications, Berne, Switzerland, 1961

Carter S., 'New Succulent Spiny Euphorbias from Eastern Africa', *Hooker's Icones Plantarum* (Bentham-Moxon Trustees, Royal Botanic Gardens, Kew, UK), vol. 39, part III, 1982

Carter S. and Smith, A.R., 'Euphorbiaceae' (part 2), *Flora of Tropical East Africa* (ed. R.M. Polhill), A.A. Balkema, Rotterdam, The Netherlands, 1989

Euphorbia Journal, vols. 1-8, published by Strawberry Press, Mill Valley, California, USA, 1983-92

White A., Dyer R.A. and Sloane B.L., *The Succulent Euphorbiae (Southern Africa)*, Abbey Garden Press, Pasadena, California, USA, 1941

FOUQUIERIACEAE

Humphrey R.R., *The Boojum and Its Home*, The University of Arizona Press, Tucson, Arizona, USA, 1974

GERANIACEAE

Van der Walt, J.J.A., *Pelargoniums of Southern Africa*, Purnell, Cape Town, South Africa, 1977

Van der Walt, J.J.A. and Vorster, P.J., *Pelargoniums of Southern Africa* (vol. 2), Juta & Co. Ltd, Kenwyn, South Africa, 1981

Van der Walt, J.J.A. and Vorster P.J., *Pelargoniums of Southern Africa* (vol. 3), National Botanic Gardens, Kirstenbosch, South Africa, 1988

LILIACEAE

Bayer M.B., *The New Haworthia Handbook*, National Botanic Gardens of South Africa, Kirstenbosch, South Africa, 1982

Jeppe B., *South African Aloes*, Purnell, Cape Town, South Africa, 1969

Pilbeam J., *Haworthia and Astroloba: A Collector's Guide*, Batsford, London, UK, 1983

Reynolds G.W., *The Aloes of Tropical Africa and Madagascar*, The Aloes Book Fund, Mbabane, Swaziland, 1966

Reynolds G.W., *The Aloes of South Africa*, A.A. Balkema, Rotterdam, The Netherlands, 1982

Van Jaarsveld, E. 'The genus *Gasteria*: a synoptic review', *Aloe* (Journal of the Succulents Society of South Africa), vol. 29, pp. 1-32 (special issue), 1992

MESEMBRYANTHEMACEAE

Cole D., *Lithops: Flowering Stones*, Acorn Press, Randburg, South Africa, 1988

Hammer S., '*Conophytum*, an annotated checklist', *Bradleya*, A-C, vol. 6, pp. 101-20; D-K, vol. 7, pp. 41-62; L-R, vol. 8, pp. 53-84; S-Z, vol. 9, pp. 105-28, 1988-91

Herre H., *The Genera of the Mesembryanthemaceae*, A.A. Balkema, Rotterdam, The Netherlands, 1973

PORTULACACEAE

Mathew B., *The Genus Lewisia*, Timber Press, Portland, USA, 1989

CREDITS

Key: t top, c centre, b bottom, l left, r right.

All the photographs were taken by Pierfranco and Daniele Costanzo, with the exception of: Enzo Bisso 33cr; Andrea Cattabriga 120bl; Carlo Doni 106bl; Luca Magagnoli 26bl, 26tl, 33tl, 45bl, 90br, 96tl, 97cl, 194tr, 196cl, 202tl, 203bl, 205tl and 227tr; Roberto Mangani 94br, 121cr, 138tr, 140cl and 143tl; Annarosa Nicola 51cl, 55bl, 67cr, 70cr, 70br, 71tl, 71bl, 71tr, 71cr, 71br, 72tr, 72cr, 72br, 73tl, 73cl, 73bl, 73cr, 73br, 74tl, 74bl, 74tr, 74br, 75cl, 75bl, 75cr, 76tl, 76cl, 76bl, 76tr, 76cr, 77tl, 77cl, 77bl, 77tr, 77br, 78tl, 78bl, 78tr, 78cr, 78br, 79cl, 90tl, 91tr, 91cr, 132bl, 137tr, 137cr, 138bl, 139cl, 173cr, 176br, 177bl and 177cr; Pasquale Ruocco 72bl, 80cr, 85cr, 97cr, 119tr, 138cl, 145cl, 165tr, 174cr, 182tr, 190tr and 221tr; Maurizio Sajeva 43cr, 45tl, 46bl, 46tr, 47cl, 49br, 52br, 56tl, 58br, 59tl, 89tl, 89cr, 94tl, 103bl, 106tl, 107bl, 107tr, 116cl, 124cl, 126br, 129cl, 129bl, 135tl, 143cl, 144bl, 196bl, 197cr, 199cr, 226tl, 226cl, 226bl, 227cl and 227bl.

The following photographs were taken at the Succulent Collection of the Municipal of Zurich: 31cr, 36br, 41cl, 41bl, 49bl, 89br, 90cl, 90bl, 91cl, 95br, 131bl, 134bl, 136cr, 155cr, 173tl, 173cl, 175tr, 179tr, 185tl, 189bl, 189cr, 194bl, 200tr, 201tl, 202cl, 202tr, 203tr, 204cr, 227tl and 227cr; the following photographs were taken at the Garden of the National Herbarium of Namibia, Windhoek: 46bl, 46tr, 49br and 196bl; and the following photographs were taken at the Botanical Garden of the University of Palermo: 33cr, 48tr, 59tl, 89cr, 94tl, 135tl, 143cl and 227bl.